JOSHUA STEELE · PROSODIA RATIONALIS

Anglistica & Americana

A Series of Reprints Selected by
Bernhard Fabian, Edgar Mertner,
Karl Schneider and Marvin Spevack

125

1971
GEORG OLMS VERLAG
HILDESHEIM · NEW YORK

JOSHUA STEELE

Prosodia Rationalis
(1779)

1971
GEORG OLMS VERLAG
HILDESHEIM · NEW YORK

Note

The present facsimile is reproduced from a copy in the possession of the British Museum, London.
Shelfmark: 73 g 16

K. S.

Reprografischer Nachdruck der Ausgabe London 1779
Printed in Germany
Herstellung: fotokop wilhelm weihert, Darmstadt
ISBN 3 487 04156 1

PROSODIA RATIONALIS:
OR,
AN ESSAY TOWARDS ESTABLISHING
THE MELODY AND MEASURE OF
SPEECH,
TO BE EXPRESSED AND PERPETUATED
BY PECULIAR SYMBOLS.

THE SECOND EDITION AMENDED AND ENLARGED.

LONDON,
PRINTED BY J. NICHOLS:
AND SOLD BY T. PAYNE AND SON, MEWS-GATE;
B. WHITE, AT HORACE'S-HEAD, FLEET-STREET;
AND H. PAYNE, PALL-MALL.

MDCCLXXIX.

The Reader is requested to correct the following Errors with the Pen.

Page. Line.
- xv. 4. from the bottom, *for* Epamininondas *read* Epaminondas
- — 16. *for* Summan, *read* Summam
- 9. 6. from the bottom, *for* but *read* for
- 10. 11. from the top, *for* Thrax. *read* Thrax,—In the note, *for* επι πολης, *read* ἐπ' ἐπιπολῆς.
- 22. 17. *read*, 3 in the numerators
- 29. 11. *for* |3/4| *read* |2/4|
- 40. 1. *for* the marks, *read* the other marks
- 43. 1. *for* deſ- *read* deſ-
- 3. *for* he him *read* he him
- 6. *for* | but that the | dread of | *read* | but that the | dread of |
- 54. *for* amphyctions *read* amphictyons.
- 70. laſt but one, *for* rhythmus *read* metres
- 72. 2d line from the bottom, *for* quantity, *read* quantities
- 75. 4. *for* or *read* and
- 88. 4. *for* viz. *heavy* and *light* which govern *read* viz. the POIZE of *heavy* and *light* which governs
- 109. 11. *for* (the ſame as § 7. ‖.) *read* § 15. (the ſame as § 7. ‖.)
- 114. 9. *for* parts; *read* parts,
- 16. *for* odd number three *read* odd number three,
- 17. *for* (or MEASURE) *read* (or MEASURE);
- 126. 4. from the bottom, *for* ra ta pa ta *read* ra ta pa ta
- 134. 10. *for* | ſay going to | *read* | ſay going to |
- 141. 6. *for* ſpe ci fic, dactyl. *read* ſpe ci fic, cretic.
- 147. 6. from the bottom, *for* (p. 23. 29. 30.) *read* (23. 29. 32.)
- 160. 2. *for* | the | love | tale | *read* | the | love | tale |

163.

Page. Line.

163. 18. *for* |given.| *read* |given.|

175. 2. *for* undeſtand *read* underſtand
184. 3. *for* intermiſſions, *read* remiſſions
 2 from the bottom, *read* force of loudneſs
202. 2 from the bottom, *for* long *read* ſong
206. laſt, *for* making *read* marking
213. 3 from the bottom, *for* |temples| *read* |temples|

ibid. and *for* |maid con| *read* |maid con|

220. 10. in the muſical example the 5th bar or cadence of the firſt clauſe,

222. 14. *for* look upon a *read* look upon a

TO THE RIGHT HONOURABLE AND HONOURABLE

THE PRESIDENT AND FELLOWS OF

THE ROYAL SOCIETY,

INSTITUTED FOR THE IMPROVEMENT OF

NATURAL KNOWLEDGE;

AND

TO THE RIGHT HONOURABLE AND HONOURABLE

THE PRESIDENT AND MEMBERS OF

THE SOCIETY

FOR THE ENCOURAGEMENT OF ARTS,

THIS TREATISE

ON THE

MELODY AND MEASURE OF SPEECH

IS RESPECTFULLY INSCRIBED,

BY THEIR MOST HUMBLE SERVANT,

THE AUTHOR.

TO

SIR JOHN PRINGLE, BART.

PRESIDENT OF THE ROYAL SOCIETY.

SIR,

FINDING that, of this Child, which I have so long nourished in private, some imperfect rumours are spread abroad; and, exciting curiosity, have moved my friends and others to discourse variously about it; I have thought proper to let it go into the world, and speak for itself. And though it may appear aukward or deficient, for want of that farther education which I intended to have procured for it, under the advice of those learned persons, to whom I made it known last year; yet reflecting on the many advantages of a more public schooling, I am resolved to keep it at home no longer: however, as I cannot think of letting it set out under my name alone, without some other of better authority to recommend it, I hope I may be indulged with the liberty of prefixing yours as its sponsor. I might say, as something more; for, as my love of science owes very much to the happiness I had of an early acquaintance with you, so if I had not been lately prompted by your spirit of investigation, I think, this offspring of mine had never seen the light at all.

I am, SIR, with great regard,

Your most obedient humble servant,

Margaret Street, Cavendish Square,
September 25, 1775.

JOSHUA STEELE.

PREFACE.

THE following sheets, so far as the two first parts, were written as remarks on a few chapters of a late philosophical treatise, called *The Origin and Progress of Language*; and being communicated to the Author of that ingenious work, he was candid enough to give up many of the musical opinions which he had published in his first edition: opinions which he was led into by authors of great fame, as well as by practical musicians, whom he had consulted.

As, I believe, it seldom, or perhaps never, has happened, that the first knowledge or renovation of any art or science, came into the world compleatly systematized, I am more desirous of submitting my imperfect endeavours to the corrections of abler hands, than ambitious of praise for having produced a finished piece. And therefore, I have thought it best, on this occasion, to give the following matter nearly in its original form; selecting from the first edition of *The Origin and Progress*, those opinions, as a text, to which the remarks and conclusions, that made the subject of my two first letters, more immediately relate; the substance of which letters are contained in the two first parts. And next in order, the queries and doubts afterwards proposed by the ingenious author of *The Origin and Progress*, with my answers to them, make out the third and fourth parts and the postscript.

And

viii   P R E F A C E.

And probably, thefe altogether, though in this fcattered manner (and incumbered with fome repetitions) may be more clear and fatisfactory to an inquiring reader, than if they were polifhed into a more formal fyftem.

The puzzling obfcurity relative to the *melody and meafure* of fpeech, which has hitherto exifted between modern critics and ancient grammarians, has been chiefly owing to a want of terms and characters, fufficient to diftinguifh clearly the feveral properties or accidents belonging to language; fuch as, *accent, emphafis, quantity, paufe,* and *force*; inftead of wihch *five terms*, they have generally made ufe of *two* only, *accent* and *quantity*, with fome loofe hints concerning *paufes*, but without any clear and fufficient rules for their ufe and admeafurement; fo that the definitions required for diftinguifhing between the expreffion of *force* (or loudnefs) and *emphafis*, with their feveral degrees, were worfe than loft; their difference being tacitly felt, though not explained or reduced to rule, was the caufe of confounding all the reft.

In like manner, there ftill exifts another defect in literal language of a fimilar kind; that is, there are in nature, neither more, nor lefs, than feven *vowel founds*, befides diphthongs; for which feven founds, the principal nations in Europe ufe only five characters (for the *y* has, with us, no found diftinct from the *i*), and this defect throws the orthography and pronunciation of the whole into uncertainty and confufion.

In order to diftinguifh what are VOWELS and what are not, let this be the definition of a *vowel found*; *videlicet*, a fimple found capable of being continued invariably the fame for a long time

(for

(for example, as long as the breath lasts), without any change of the organs; that is, without any movement of the throat, tongue, lips, or jaws.

But a *diphthong sound* is made by blending two *vowel sounds*, by a very quick pronunciation, into *one*.

So that to try, according to the foregoing definition, to continue a diphthong sound, the voice most commonly changes immediately from the first vowel sound, of which the diphthong is composed, by a small movement in some of the organs, to the sound of the vowel which makes the latter part of the said diphthong, the sound of the first vowel being heard only for one instant. For example, to make this experiment on the English sound of U, as in the word USE, which is really a *diphthong* composed of these two English sounds EE and OO; the voice begins on the sound EE, but instantly dwindles into, and ends in, OO.

The other English sound of U, as in the words UGLY, UNDONE, BUT, and GUT, is composed of the English sounds AU and OO; but they require to be pronounced so extremely short and close together, that, in the endeavour to prolong the sound for this experiment, the voice will be in a continual confused struggle between the two component sounds, without making either of them, or any other sound, distinct; so that the true English sound of this diphthong can never be expressed but by the aid of a short energic aspiration, something like a short cough, which makes it very difficult to our Southern neighbours in Europe.

To try the like experiment on the English sound of I or Y, as I in the first person, and in the words MY, BY, IDLE, and FINE,

PREFACE.

FINE, (both which letters are the marks of one and the same *diphthong sound* composed of the English sounds AU and EE,) the voice begins on the sound AU, and immediately changes to EE on which it continues and ends.

The English sound of E, in the words *met, let, men, get*, is a diphthong composed of the vocal sounds A and E (being the second and third vowels in the following arrangement) and pronounced very short.

In order the better to ascertain the tones of the seven vocal sounds, I have ventured to add a few French words in the exemplification; in the pronunciation of which, I hope, I am not mistaken. If I had not thought it absolutely necessary, I would not have presumed to meddle with any living language but my own; the candid reader will therefore forgive and correct my errors, if I have made any in this place, by substituting such other French syllables as will answer the end proposed.

The *seven natural vowel sounds* may be thus marked and explained to sound,

in English as the words,	in French as the words,
α = all, small, or, for, knock, lock, occur.	en, grande.
a = man, can, cat, rat.	Paris, *ha*bit, *par*don.
e = may, day, take, nation,	ses, et.
i = *e*vil, keen, it, be, *i*niquity.	Par*is*, hab*it*, ris, dit, il.
o = *o*pen, only, broke, hole.	so*l*dat, côtes, offrir.
ω = fool, two, rule, tool, do.	ou, vous, jour, jal*ou*x.
u = { s*u*perfluous, tune, su- preme, cred*u*lity, } very rare in English.	du, plus, une.

Diphthong

PREFACE.

Diphthong sounds in English.

αi = I, *fi*ne, h*i*re, l*i*fe, r*i*de, *spy*, *fly*, (a long sound).
ae = met, let, get, men, (a short sound).
iw = you, use, new, due, few, (a long sound).
αw = { makes the English sound of *un* or *ug*, and is pronounced extremely short, } *un*kind, *un*done, beg*un*, *u*gly, b*u*t, sh*u*t, g*u*t.
oω = how, bough, sow, hour, gown, town, (this diphthong is sounded long, dwelling chiefly on the latter vowel).

The letters and sounds, which in modern languages pass under the names of diphthongs, are of such different kinds, that they cannot properly be known by any definition I have seen: for, according to my sense, the greatest part of them are not diphthongs. Therefore, that I may not be misunderstood, I will define a *proper diphthong* to be made in speech, by the blending of *two vowel sounds* so intimately into *one*, that the ear shall hardly be able to distinguish more than one uniform sound; though, if produced for a longer time than usual, it will be found to continue in a sound different from that on which it began, or from its *diphthong sound*.

And therefore the vowels, which are joined to make diphthongs in English, are pronounced much shorter, when so joined, than as single vowels; for if the vowel sounds, of which they are composed, especially the initials, are pronounced so as to be easily and distinctly heard separately, they cease to be diphthongs, and become distinct syllables.

Though the grammarians have divided the vowels into three claſſes; long, ſhort, and doubtful; I am of opinion, that every one of the ſeven has both a longer and ſhorter ſound: as,

α is long in α*ll,* and ſhort in *lock* and *oc* (lαck and αc)

A is long in *arm,* and ſhort in *cat.*

E is long in *may* and *make,* and ſhort in *nation.*

ɪ is long in *be,* and ſhort in *it.*

o is longer in *hole* than in *open;* long in *corrode,* ſhort in *corroſive.*

ω is long in *fool,* ſhort (by compariſon) in *fooliſh.*

ᴜ is long in *tune* and *plus,* and ſhort in *super* and *du.*

But the ſhorteſt ſounds of o, ω, and ᴜ, are long in compariſon with the ſhort ſounds of the four firſt vowels.

The French, the Scotch, and the Welſh, uſe all theſe vowel ſounds in their common pronunciation; but the Engliſh ſeldom or never ſound the ᴜ in the French tone (which I have ſet down as the laſt in the foregoing liſt, and which, I believe, was the ſound of the Greek ὐπσιλὸν) except in the more refined tone of the court, where it begins to obtain in a few words.

I have been told, the moſt correct Italians uſe only five vowel ſounds, omitting the firſt and ſeventh, or the α and the *u.* Perhaps the Romans did the ſame: for it appears by the words which they borrowed from the Greeks in latter times, that they were at a loſs how to write the η and the υ in Latin letters.

As the Greeks had all the ſeven marks, it is to be preſumed that at ſome period they muſt have uſed them to expreſs ſo many different ſounds. But having had the opportunity of converſing with a learned modern Greek, I find, though they ſtill uſe all

the

the seven marks, they are very far from making the distinction among their sounds which nature admits of, and which a perfect language requires: but all nations are continually changing both their language and their pronunciation; though that people, who have marks for seven vowels, which are according to nature the competent number, are the least excusable in suffering any change, whereby the proper distinction is lost.

Some very useful alterations and additions might be made among the consonants, towards attaining a rational orthography. But I forbear to go any farther here, on this head, than just to throw out these hints; from which it may be judged, what very great advantages might arise to the lingual and literary commerce of the world, by a set of learned men sitting down, under some respectable authority, to reform the alphabet, so as to make it contain distinct elementary marks for expressing all the lingual sounds of the European languages at least; in doing which, the difficulty would be infinitely over-balanced by the great and general utility.

So much it was necessary for me to say on the incongruity between our present letters and our natural elementary sounds; because having, for many years past, considered *that* and the *melody* and *measure* of *speech* together, as parts of the same subject, it is probable, I may have used, in the following sheets, expressions with a latent reference to these elementary sounds, which, without this slight explanation, might be unintelligible.

But to return to the immediate subject of the following essay. I set out with supposing the reader to have some practical knowledge of modern music;—I say *practical*, for without that in some

degree,

degree, it is next to impossible by *theory* alone, to comprehend clearly and distinctly, either the *rhythmical* or *metrical* divisions of time; the difference between *emphasis* and *force of loudness*; and still less the differences of ACCENT, *acute*, *grave*, and the *circumflexes*. To musicians, these will be no difficulties at all; and a very few lessons of a master, either on a bass viol, or a great * *pitch-pipe*, or the voice, will be sufficient to enable any person, with a tolerable ear, to overcome them.

Music among moderns, though much cultivated for pleasure, has been considered by men of letters, at best, only as a feminine ornament, or an amusement for an hour of relaxation; but, if this system be adopted, the grammarian must either associate with, or submit himself to, the musician, until such time as he himself becomes a musician: for, to make the best use of this knowledge, it should be blended with the first doctrinal elements of speech. And now, in support of this opinion, because I know ancient, or classical, authorities are oftentimes more convincing than modern reason, I will call a few to my assistance. Ælian in his Various-Histories, b. VII. ch. 15. tells us (Ἡνίκα τῆς θαλάσσης, &c.), "When the Mitylenians had the chief command "at sea, they inflicted this punishment on their deserting allies, "*That their children should not learn letters, nor be instructed in* "*music*; being, in their opinion, the heaviest of all punish- "ments, *to live* (ἐν ἀμαθίᾳ ᾗ ἀμουσίᾳ) UNLETTERED and UNMU- "SICAL." When *Parmeno*, in Terence's *Eunuch* (act iii. sc. 2.), is extolling the accomplishments of the slave presented to *Thais*,

* I mean by a *great pitch-pipe*, any large *flute-pipe*, or *diapason-pipe* of an *organ*, fitted with a long sliding stopper, by means of which, may be made, sliding tones, like those of the voice.

he

he says: "Examine him in literature, prove him in gymnastics,
"try him in *music*; I will vouch him skilled in every thing
"becoming a gentleman." *Socrates*, in *Plato's* dialogue called
Theages, asks the young man, "Whether his father had not
"taught him all those things in which noble youths were com-
"monly instructed; γράμματά τε, ἢ κιθαρίζειν, ἢ παλαίειν, ἢ τὴν
"ἄλλην ἀγωνίαν; that is, literature, MUSIC, wrestling, and the
"other exercises." *Xenophon*, treating of the manners of the
Lacedæmonians, says: "But other Greeks, and especially those
"who wish to have their children educated in the most elegant
"manner, as soon as they are able to understand what is said,
"put them under the care of (παιδαγωγὲς θεραπεύοντας) servants
"capable of conducting their education; and immediately also
"send them to masters to teach them (ἢ γράμματα, ἢ μυσικὴν, ἢ
"τὰ ἐν παλαίςρᾳ,) letters, *music*, and corporal exercises." Cicero
(in his first book of Tusculan Questions) tells us, "Summan
"eruditionem Græci sitam censebant in nervorum vocumque
"cantibus. Igitur et Epaminondas .... fidibus præclarè
"cecinisse dicitur. Themistocles ..... cum in epulis recu-
"sasset lyram, habitus est indoctior: ergo in Græciâ musici
"floruerunt, discebantque id omnes, nec, qui nesciebat, satis
"excultus doctrinâ putabatur." "To sing, and play on mu-
"sical instruments, was by the Greeks held to be a chief part
"of polite education. Epaminondas .... was said to have
"been a fine performer. Themistocles, ... for having
"refused the lyre at an entertainment, was accounted an igno-
"rant fellow. Therefore, in Greece musicians flourished; every
"one

" one learned that art; and whofoever knew it not, was looked
" upon as under-bred."

We have fome *foundations* in England for bringing up fcholars both to mufic and letters, at the fame time; but hitherto thefe ftudies have not been joined together, fo as to afford mutual fupport to each other. In the education of a modern gentleman, mufic has only been confidered on the fide of entertainment, not on that of ufeful erudition: and thofe who have made this art their profeffion (with the exception of very few) have feen it in the fame light. For to excel in the practical part has been fo lucrative, that they have generally given all their time and application to attain that end, to the neglect both of literature and fcience; and hence, I fuppofe, it is, that, being looked upon only as the minifters of our pleafures, we do not give them the fame rank in public eftimation, as we do to the profeffors of other fciences. Moreover, having never yet blended the ftudy of mufic and language together, fo as to treat the modulation of *fpeech* as a *genus* of *mufic* under the rules of *Melopœia*, it is not to be wondered at, that the Greek writers in this learning have been overlooked or mifunderftood. However, I fhould think it is in the power of our univerfities to bring this fcience (and the arts under it) into fome better degree of note than it has been hitherto; and as it lies properly within their province, I hope, they will think it not beneath their attention: for it is too much to expect from the accidental labours of private volunteers, that the overwhelmed ruins of a Herculaneum fhould be retrieved from rubbifh, and reftored to their former fplendour.

But if the *amousoi** should have inclination and power sufficient to disappoint such an expectation for some time, may we not still hope, that the system proposed in this Essay may be patronized by the ladies. The study of music being almost universally thought a necessary part of their education, they will find no difficulty in understanding the subject of this treatise; and if they should make the care of their nursery their principal amusement, as all the best of them do, may we not expect to see the rising generation instructed by their fair mothers in the joint knowledge of letters and music, and our typical marks of ACCENT, QUANTITY, EMPHASIS, PAUSE, and FORCE, added to their spelling book (which will then be a compleat *Gradus ad Parnassum*), and as familiarly known as the alphabet.

Then if the Attic plant of literature should thus spring from the labours of those lovely pædagogues, its branches may in time spread abroad, and its fruit at length be propagated and cultivated to the utmost perfection in those renowned seminaries of the Muses, on the banks of the Isis and Cam.

* Unskilled in music.—I have met with no one to whom this system has been communicated, that was not immediately convinced of its truth and utility; but some of the *amousoi* (though otherwise persons of genius), upon reflection, have seemed not well pleased with the discovery, by endeavouring to prove its inutility. However inconsistent this conduct may appear, we know, by other instances in mankind, it is not unnatural: for we find many, who are less ashamed to expose their vices, than to acknowledge their poverty.

EXPLANATION OF SOME MARKS OF ABBREVIATION AND MUSICAL TERMS, USED IN THIS TREATISE.

=	⎫⎬⎭ signifies ⎨	equal, or equivalent to; as, 2 and 3 = 5; that is, 2 and 3 are equal to 5.
+		plus, more, or to be added; as 2 + 3 = 5; and $\frac{1}{2}+\frac{1}{2}=1=\frac{1}{3}+\frac{1}{3}+\frac{1}{3}$; that is, two halves are equal to one whole; and one whole, being equal to three-thirds; of consequence two halves are equal to three-thirds, as $\frac{1}{2}+\frac{1}{2}=\frac{1}{3}+\frac{1}{3}+\frac{1}{3}$. So ♩ ♩ = ♩· = ♪♪♪; see page 8, 25, &c.
SUB-DUPLE,		half, ⎫ being proportionally as much below
SUB-TRIPLE,		a third, ⎭ unity, as double and triple are above it.
FORTE,		loud.
PIANO,		soft.
ALLEGRO,		quick, or fast.
ADAGIO,		slow.
LARGO,		a middle degree between fast and slow.
STACCATO,		successive tones with a short pointed expression, and so distinctly sounded, that they seem as if separated by small interruptions.
SOSTENUTO,		the contrary to *staccato*; that is, successive tones so blended and so evenly supported, that no interruption of sound can be perceived between them.

All other marks and terms are explained as they occur.

THE

THE MELODY AND MEASURE OF SPEECH.

I HAD long entertained opinions concerning the melody and rhythmus of modern languages, and particularly of the English, which made me think our theatrical recitals were capable of being accompanied with a bass, as those of the antient Greeks and Romans were, provided a method of notation were contrived to mark the varying sounds in common speech, which I perceived to run through a large extent between *acute* and *grave*; though they seldom or never coincided, in their periods, with any of the tones or semitones of our ordinary music, which is an imperfect mixture of those two genera, called by the Greeks *diatonic* and *chromatic*.

I was of opinion that, in pronunciation, the voice moved up and down by such small gradations as that, whether the degrees were by quarters of a diatonic tone, or by smaller divisions, they seemed, in comparison with those of our *chromatico-diatonic*, to be by imperceptible slides.

But though I had often communicated these notions to many gentlemen of genius and learning, as well as capital artists, hoping some of them would turn their minds to the revival of the antient *chromatic* and *enharmonic* genera of music, and of a proper bass accompaniment for the declamation of the stage, so long lost; yet I never digested my own thoughts on paper, till my learned and honoured friend Sir John Pringle, President of the Royal Society, desired me to give him, in writing, my opinion on the *musical part* of a very curious and ingenious work lately published at Edinburgh, on *The Origin and Progress of Language*, which I should find principally in part II. book ii. chap. 4. and 5. wherein several propositions, denying that our language has either the *melody of modulation*, or the *rhythmus of quantity*, gave occasion to the following systematic attempt to prove the contrary. And as the substance of it was originally communicated to that gentleman in two letters, so I have continued the same form of division here, by giving it in two parts.

THE PROPOSITIONS CONTROVERTED.

See Origin and Progress, vol. II. p. 276, &c. " That there is
" no accent, such as the Greek and Latin accents, in any modern
" language.—And lastly, the impossibility for us, that are not
" accustomed to it, to sound those antient accents, has perswaded
" many people that it was as impossible for the antients to do it."
P. 298.

P. 298. " Mr. Foster would fain persuade us, that in English there are accents, such as in Greek or Latin; but to me, it is evident that there are none such: by which I mean, that we have *no accents upon syllables*, which are musical tones, *differing in acuteness and gravity.* — For though there are changes of voice in our speaking, from *acute to grave*, and *vice versâ*, these changes are *not upon syllables*, but *upon words* or *sentences.*" P. 299. " Our accents—neither are nor can by their nature be subjected to any rule; whereas the antient,— are governed by rules, &c.—We have accents in English, and syllabic accents too; but there is *no change of the tone in them*; the voice is only raised more, so as to be *louder* upon one syllable than another.—That there is no other difference is a matter of fact, that must be determined by musicians. Now I appeal to them, whether they can perceive any difference of tone betwixt the *accented* and *unaccented* syllable of any word? And if there be none, then is the *music of our language*, in this respect, *nothing better* than the *music of a drum*, in which we perceive no difference except that of *louder* or *softer.*"

PART I.

WE suppose the reader to have some knowledge of the modern scale and notation of music, namely the *chromatico-diatonic*; which may be defined practically, as,

A series of sounds *moving distinctly* from grave to acute, or *vice versâ* (either gradually or *saltim*) by intervals, of which the semitone (commonly so called) may be the common measure or divisor, without a fraction*, and always dwelling, for a perceptible space of time, on one certain tone.

Whereas the *melody of speech moves* rapidly up or down by *slides*, wherein no graduated distinction of tones or semitones can be measured by the ear; nor does the voice (in our language) ever dwell distinctly, for any perceptible space of time, on any certain level or uniform tone, except the last tone on which the speaker ends or makes a pause. For proof of which definition we refer to experiment, as hereafter directed.

Whilst almost every one perceives and admits singing to be performed by the ascent and descent of the voice through a variety of notes, as palpably and formally different from each other as the steps of a ladder; it seems, at first sight, somewhat extraordinary, that even men of science should not perceive the

---

* I omit the critical distinction of major and minor tones and the diesis, because the modern chromatico-diatonic octave is practically divided into 12 semitones, supposed equal to the ear.

rapid

rapid slides of the voice, upwards and downwards, in common speech. But the knowledge of the various distinct notes of ordinary music is not only laid open to those multitudes who learn that art; but also, being rendered visible and palpable to the unlearned, by the keys of organs and such like instruments, it happens that almost every one knows, the variety of music to arise, in part, from the difference of acute and grave tones.

In traveling through a country, apparently level, how few people perceive the ascents and descents that would astonish them, if the man of art were to demonstrate them by his instrument, and to bring the sluggish stream to form a cascade! In like manner, when the modulation of the melody of speech shall be ripened into method by art, even the vulgar may be taught to know what the learned can now scarce comprehend.

A METHOD OF DELINEATING NOTES OR CHARACTERS TO REPRESENT THE MELODY AND QUANTITY OF THE SLIDES MADE BY THE VOICE IN COMMON SPEECH.

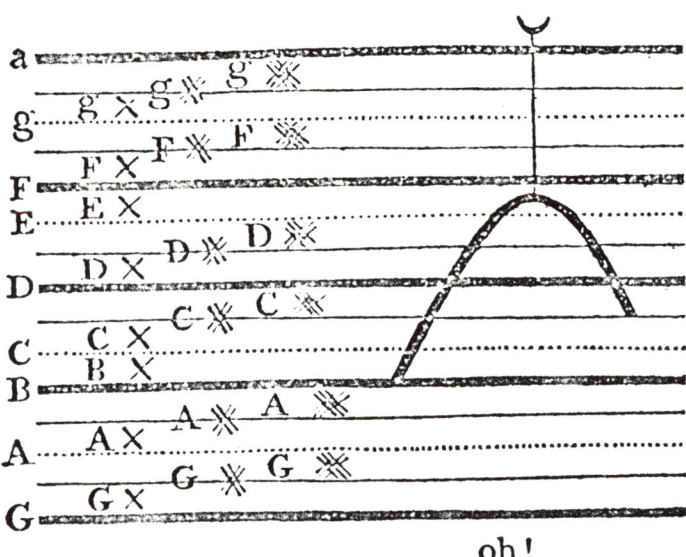

Let the 5 black lines, such as are made use of in noting music, according to the ordinary modern method, be drawn, as in the margin, strong; and let them be interlined with red or faint black; *videlicet*, with two continued lines and one dotted line between them, except in the interval between B and C, and in the interval between E and F, as hereafter explained. So that, supposing the strong black line at bottom to be that whereon the note G is to be marked, then the space between that and the red or faint line next above it, will be the space for G+¼ tone, or G× (with a single crofs); and the said red or faint line itself, being the first red or faint line from the bottom, will be the line for G+½ a tone, or G⁎ (with a double crofs); and the space between this red or faint line, and the dotted line next above it, will be for G+¾ tones, or G※ (with a triple crofs); the dotted line will be

for

[7]

for A, the same tone that would have been marked on the whole space, if there had been no red or faint lines at all. The additional quarter tones of A×, A⚹, and A※, will proceed in like manner; and the second strong black line will be for the note B, the next space for B+¼ tone or B×; and here, omitting the continued red or faint line, we come immediately to the dotted one, which is for C; because the interval between B and C contains only two quarters, or a semitone; the interval also between E and F, being of the same dimension, is provided for in a similar manner: and these lines, so drawn, I call the *Scale*.

Then, instead of using round or square heads for the notes to be marked on this scale (as in the ordinary music) let us substitute *sloping* or *curving lines*, such as the expression may require; as ╱, or ╲, or ⌢, or ⌣; which lines, when drawn on the foregoing scale, will easily shew through how many quarter tones the voice is to slide; and these I call the *accents* or *notes of melody*.

In the next place, the quantity or proportion of time allowed to each note, may be distinguished by adding tails of different forms, always drawn upwards, to prevent confusion, by mistaking the head for the tail, or *vice versâ*; because our heads have some resemblance to the tails and tyes of quavers in the ordinary music, and our tails have some resemblance to their heads of minims and briefs; as thus,

Various forms of tails to express the difference of quantity,

The heads which mark the *accent* or difference of melody,

Tails

[8]

Tails and heads joined together, the heads being at the bottom and the tails drawn upwards, which, being thus joined, form, as it were, one note, expressing both *accent* and *quantity*.

Though we differ somewhat in form, let us however (since the measures of time in music and in speech are both the same) adopt the names by which the different quantities or proportions of time, are distinguished in common music.

Such as a semi-brief = 2 minims = 4 crotchets = 8 quavers.

For which let our marks be,

And let the rests or pauses be represented thus,

a semi-brief rest = 2 minim rests = 4 crotchet rests = 8 quaver rests.

We also adopt the method used in common music, of lengthening a note, by the addition of a point, as,

Then the note, on the foregoing scale, over the interjection *Oh!* whose duration in time is only that of a crotchet, represents the melody of the voice to have made a slide from B to E×, and thence down again to C×; a flight, up and down, through nineteen quarter tones; and this I apprehend may very properly be called a *circumflex*.

In devising a scheme for expressing on paper the musical slides of the voice, in the melody of speech, I chose one which might come as near as possible to the modern notation of music, in order to make it the easier to be comprehended by those whose ideas of sounds and measure of time are already formed on that plan.

plan. I had no intention of imitating the figures of the *Greek accents*; and yet, by meer accident, in purfuing my own fcheme, I found my new invented notes were exactly in the Greek form. From this fortuitous coincidence, may we not fufpect, that we have hit on the true meaning of the Greeks (who wrote, as we do, from the left to the right) by their marks, of *acute* for the flide upwards, and of *grave* for the fliding return downwards: for (omitting the tails, which are only for the purpofe of meafuring the time,) to mark a flide progreffively upwards by our fyftem, it muft go thus ▭, and progreffively downwards, thus, ▭. Why did the Greeks mark their accents by exactly fuch floping lines, if they did not mean them as we do, for the expreffion of a flide upwards ╱, or of a flide downwards ╲?

I muft allow, however, that this coincidence between the marks which I have adopted and thofe ufed by the Greeks is fomewhat extraordinary, confidering that they called their moft acute found, low; and their moft grave found, high; and alfo that their diftinctions of notes in writing, were not made by pofition as ours are (that is, the higher notes occupying the higher parts of the fcale, and *vice verfâ*); but their notation ran in one ftrait line, each different note being diftinguifhed by a particular character, like a line of common writing. But to folve this difficulty to myfelf, I have fuppofed their calling the graveft note, high; and the moft acute, low; was in relation to the pofition of their notes on their inftruments: for I think their expreffions of

ἐπίτασις

ἐπίτασις and ἀνάτασις * as applied to the *acute*, and of ἄνεσις to the *grave*, seem to imply that they considered the voice as ascending to the first, and descending to the last; for unless they had been led by this sentiment, they should have made their marks for the acute and grave quite contrary to what they really did, and to what I have done, by making them conformable to our modern notation of music.

If the learned author of the *Origin and Progress of Language*, had conceived that the melody of our speech was formed by slides, he would have found his quotation (page 278.) from Dion. Thrax. (φωνῆς ἀπήχησις ἐναρμονίε, ἢ κατ᾽ ἀνάτασιν ἐν τῇ ὀξείᾳ ἢ καθ᾽ ὁμαλισμὸν ἐν τῇ βαρείᾳ, ἢ κατὰ περίπλασιν ἐν τῇ περισπωμένῃ) to have been perfectly agreeable to our system; and his difficulty to comprehend why the grave, marked on a last syllable, should (by some commentators be said to) denote the acute would vanish, if he had considered that a grave accent must begin comparatively acute, in order to end grave, by sliding downwards.

The true sense of these words of Dionysius is probably this: "That accent is the change of the enharmonic voice, by an "extent or stretch up to the acute, or by levelling it to the grave, "or by making a circuit in the circumflex." In other words, sliding up to the acute, sliding down to the grave, and sliding up and down, without change of articulation in the circumflex.

Suppose the word οὐρανος to be noted in our manner: ὀυ, with the acute, rose or slid up about a fifth; ρὰ, with a grave, fell or slid

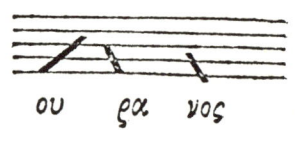

* Aristid. Quint. says expressly (in Meibom. vol. II. p. 8. and 9.) γίνεται δὲ, ἡ μὲν βαρύτης, κάτωθεν ἀναφερομένε τῶ πνεύματος· ἡ δ᾽ ὀξύτης, ἐπὶ πολῆς προϊεμένε; that is, a grave sound is produced from the bottom or lowest part of the breath; and an acute sound, from the top or upper part.

down to the common level; consequently, to let νὸς slide to the *grave,* in like manner, the voice must be allowed to get to the top, or acute part of the grave, in order to slide down again; otherwise, if the identical tone that ρα ended on should be continued uniformly to the whole of the syllable νὸς, it would fall under the description or definition of common song, by dwelling for a perceptible space of time on one tone. Wherefore I think it must be understood, that *acute* and *grave* were not single fixed tones, like the notes of diatonic music, but were the marks of vocal slides; *viz.* that the *acute* began grave and ended acute; and on the contrary, the *grave* began acute and ended grave.

As all speech, prose as well as poetry, falls naturally under emphatical divisions, which I will call cadences: Let the thesis or pulsation, which points out those divisions, be marked by *bars,* as in ordinary music. Modern musicians, very improperly, use the words *accented* and *unaccented* in the place of thesis and arsis; but the proper sense of *accent* refers only to the melody of *acute* and *grave,* or diversity of tone; whereas the *thesis* and *arsis* should relate solely to *pulsation* and *remission.* By which diversity of expression, *emphatic* and *remiss,* the modes of time are pointed out, and the measure governed.

Of modes of time there are only two genera; the one, where the whole time of a *bar,* or *cadence,* is divided by 2, and its sub-duples or sub-triples; the other, where the whole time of a *bar* or *cadence* is divided by three, and its sub-duples or sub-triples. More shall be said of this and of emphasis hereafter, under the head of Measure or Rhythmus.

Almoſt every ſyllable in our language (monoſyllables excepted) is affected poſitively either to the *arſis* or *theſis*, though ſome are of a common nature, and may be uſed with either.

Our heroic, or ten ſyllable lines, moſt commonly begin with a ſyllable under arſis: and ſuppoſing the line to conſiſt of 5 feet, or rather according to our ſyſtem, of 5 *bars* or *cadences* of muſical time (excluſive of reſts or pauſes), there will be half a bar at the beginning, and half a bar at the end; that is, it will begin with *arſis* and end with *theſis:* but ſometimes the affection of the firſt ſyllable is ſo poſitive to *theſis*, as to oblige the meaſure of the line to begin with a whole bar (for the beat, or *theſis*, conſtantly falls on the firſt note or ſyllable of the bar); but always ſome *reſts* or *pauſes* are neceſſary, as being more agreeable both to the ſenſe and to the meaſure; ſo that, including the *reſts*, a line of nominal 5 feet, or ten ſyllables in words, occupies at leaſt the time of 6 *bars* or *cadences*, as in the example following; in which the ſyllable, *oh!* is poſitively *emphatical* and under *theſis*, and the ſyllable *our* (agreeable to the ſenſe in this expreſſion) is, as poſitively, *remiſs*, and under *arſis*.

But here let it be obſerved, that this *emphaſis of cadence* and the *expreſſion of loudneſs*, are not to be conſidered as equivalent terms or affections of the ſame kind; for the *arſis*, or *remiſs*, may be *loud*, or *forte*; and the *theſis*, or *emphatic*, *piano* or *ſoft*, occaſionally. The *theſis and arſis* being periodically alternate, whether expreſſed or ſuppoſed; whereas the applications of the *forte* and *piano* are *ad libitum*, or *apropos*.

Therefore, beſide the characters which diſtinguiſh the variety of ſounds and of meaſure of time, there are others required to

mark

[13]

mark where the *forte* and *piano* should be expressed. The modern musicians have no other characters for these than the words themselves. However, they will be better supplied in our scheme by the asper ☩, and lenis ꝯ, of the Greeks*; the *crescendo, rinforzando*, or *swell*, by ᴧᴧᴧᴧ; and the *smorzando*, or *dying away*, by ᴧᴧᴧᴧ; all which will be more conveniently written under than over the words, to prevent their interfering with apostrophes or tittles of the letter *i*.

THE FOREGOING CHARACTERS APPLIED IN THE FOLLOWING EXAMPLE.

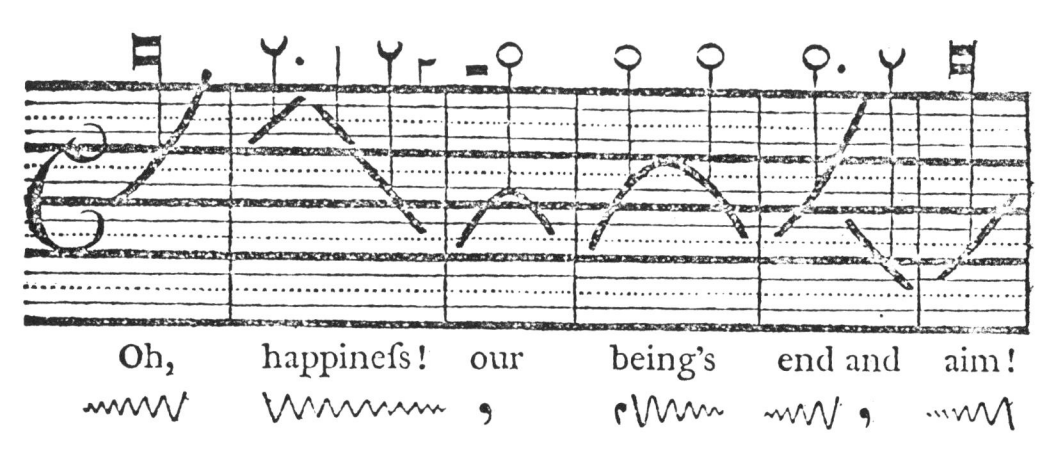

Oh, happiness! our being's end and aim!

In an attempt so new in our age, as the reducing common speech to regular notes, it will not be expected that this first

* I mean, by adopting these marks, to insinuate a conjecture; and, if I am right, will not the necessity of *two spirits*, as well as two *accents*, be apparent?—Though very learned men have thought otherwise. In the ancient guttural languages, the forte was probably aspirated; that is, the sound of the letter H was frequently thrown in: for a frequent energic aspiration is a principal cause of the Irish vicious tone in pronouncing English; and that aspirated tone is derived from the original Irish language, which, like all the other antient languages, is extremely guttural.

essay

essay should be extremely accurate; for there is a great latitude in the slides not only of different speakers, but also of the same speaker at different times.

People who play by ear on instruments of music, as well as those who play by notes, can seldom play their voluntaries a second time without great variation. Now all people, orators of pulpit, bar, and stage, in respect of the melody and rhythmus of language, are but as players of voluntaries exhibiting by ear, having no notes as a test or standard to prove their correctness, and to measure the degrees of their excellence.

We have heard of Betterton, Booth, and Wilks, and some of us have seen Quin; the portraits of their persons are probably preserved, but no models of their elocution remain; nor any proofs, except vague assertions and arbitrary opinions, to decide on the comparative merits in the way of their profession, between them and the moderns. Had some of the celebrated speeches from Shakespeare been noted and accented as they spoke them, we should be able now to judge, whether the oratory of our stage is improved or debased. If the method, here essayed, can be brought into familiar use, the types of modern elocution may be transmitted to posterity as accurately as we have received the musical compositions of Corelli.

But perfection and accuracy in this art can only be attained by experience and a close attention, in estimating the pitch and extent of vocal slides by the ear, with the assistance of a proper instrument.

I hope, however, this example will shew, that the *melody of speech* is formed by *slides*; and that by these, or some other apt characters,

characters, the mufical expreffion of fpeech may be defcribed and communicated in writing.

But if this effay be not fufficient to prove what the *melody of fpeech* is, let us, in the next place, endeavour to fhew *what it is not.*

It is not like the proclamation of a parifh-clerk announcing the pfalm,

Let us fing to the praife and glory of God!

where the whole fentence is in one tone, without any change of acute or grave.

Oh, happinefs!—our being's end and aim!

Neither is it like the intonation of the choroftates, or precentor in our cathedrals, where the change of tone is made between one fentence and another, or between one word and another; that is, where the change is made, *not upon fyllables*, but *upon words* or *fentences.*

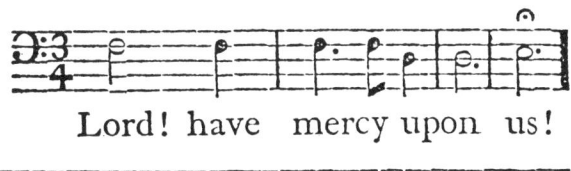

Lord! have mercy upon us!

Oh, happinefs!—our being's end and aim!

Now to fubmit thefe feveral examples to the judgement of common ears, let a bafs viol have a paper pafted on the whole length of the finger-board near the 4th ftring, marking all the chromatico-

[16]

chromatico-diatonic stops or frets, suitable to that bass, from the bottom to the top, as in the figure represented below.

For the experiment of the slides, let the 4th string (though actually tuned to CC) be called G for the sake of keeping our slides within the compass of the five black lines, or nearly so; and also to keep the hand, making the slides, so high on the shift, as never to fall down to the open string.

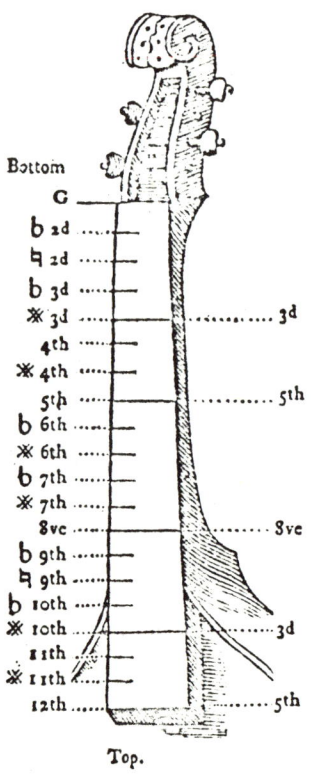

Then while the player draws the bow over the 4th string, let him try, by sliding his left hand on the same string up or down the finger-board, to imitate the rapid turns or flections of the voice in common speech, and he will soon find, that they will have either their beginnings or endings, for the most part, in the intervals between the frets; which intermediate stops, we may call quarter tones: for it will be accurate enough for our purpose, to call every degree of tone a quarter, that does not coincide with any tone or semitone of the chromatico-diatonic. And then, if he can pronounce, being thus assisted by the instrument, all the foregoing examples, as they are written or noted, the auditors will most probably agree in the following conclusions.

1st, That

1st, That the sound or *melody of speech* is *not monotonous*, or confined like the *sound of a drum,* to exhibit no other changes than those of *loud* or *soft.*

2dly, That the changes of voice from *acute* to *grave,* and *vice versâ,* do not proceed by pointed degrees coinciding with the divisions of the chromatico-diatonic scale; but by gradations that seem infinitely smaller (which we call *slides*); and though altogether of a great extent, are yet too rapid (for inexperienced ears) to be distinctly sub-divided; consequently they must be submitted to some other *genus of music* than either the diatonic or chromatic.

3dly, That these *changes are made,* not only *upon words* and *upon sentences,* but *upon syllables and monosyllables.* Also,

4thly, and lastly, That in our changes on syllables or monosyllables, the voice slides, at least, through as great an extent as the Greeks allowed to their accents; that is, through a fifth, more or less.

PART II.

THE art of music, whether applied to speaking, singing, or dancing, is divided into two great branches, *sound* and *measure*, more familiarly called *tune* and *time*. Instead of which words, I use (for the most part) the Greek terms of *melody* and *rhythmus*, being more significant, as generals, than our vulgar terms.

Whether the notes or characters used by the Greeks for writing their music, were as good or better than ours, is a matter worth the labour of the curious to enquire into: but the modern scale and notes (which may be called the accidence of our musical grammar) are now so thoroughly known all over Europe, that, with a little alteration and addition, they will serve better for the exponents of what I have to offer concerning rhythmus, than if I was to attempt to follow the obscure track of another system, now totally unknown to the majority, and only very imperfectly to the few.

When the *cadences* of our language, either poetry or prose, are properly marked in our way, every person initiated in the practical knowledge of music, will be able to comprehend our meaning, and to read the words according to the *melody* and *rhythmus* we shall mark to them. Neither would the Greek feet, under all their various names, answer in any suitable degree to the rhythmus of our language; for the commentators have told us, their long and short syllables were in proportion to each other, only as 2 to 1; whereas in our rhythmus we have the several proportions of 2. 1. $\frac{1}{2}$. $\frac{1}{4}$. and 3. 1. $\frac{1}{3}$. $\frac{1}{6}$, all which will appear in the examples which we shall set down. Besides, I apprehend, whoever takes up the consideration of this subject in our way, will find it much easier to examine it in the Greek system afterwards, when he may perhaps be able to detect the errors of commentators, some of whom, not being musicians, misunderstood the subject they undertook to expound.

The fifth chapter of part II. book ii. of *The Origin and Progress of Language*, treats, according to the plan of the contents placed at the head of the chapter, " Of rhythm in general, and the " division of it into the rhythm of motion without sound.— " Sub-division of the rhythm of sound into five different spe- " cies.—Of that species of it which is called quantity or metre.— " Verse in English not made by quantity, but by what we call " *accent*." The ingenious author resolves the different perceptions, of *sound*, as acute and grave; of *cadence*, as arsis and thesis; of *quantity*, as long and short; and of *quality*, as loud and soft; into one original cause, *motion*. Which, however true, seems not so necessary in this place, as it would have been to have described, in apt terms, how these several effects of motion differed from each other. He has very justly explained the true sense of the term *accent*; and yet, from too much complaisance to a vulgar error, uses it in a sense contrary to his own definition, and contrary to his own very sensible remark at the end of this chapter. " In matters of science, the ideas of different things " should be kept, and expressed by different names: for, as I

" observed

" obferved before, I am perfuaded that it was fome fuch confu-
" fion in the ufe of the word *profody*, that contributed to lead
" men into the error concerning the ancient *accents*." p. 328.
Therefore, in order to avoid the confufion made by moderns in
the mifufe of the word *accent*, let us call the note or fyllable on
which the cadence falls, *heavy*, and, where neceffary, denote it
by this mark (△); and the note, or fyllable, erroneoufly called
unaccented, we will call *light*, and mark it thus (∴); and as we
fhall find, there are two forts of light notes, let the lighteft be
reprefented thus (..).

Our breathing, the beating of our pulfe, and our movement
in walking, make the divifion of time by pointed and regular
cadences, familiar and natural to us. Each of thefe movements,
or *cadences*, is divided into two alternate motions, fignificantly
expreffed by the Greek words *arfis* and *thefis*, *raifing* and *pofing*,
or fetting down; the latter of which, coming down as it were
with weight, is what we mean to call *heavy*, being the moft
energic or emphatic of the two; the other, being more remifs,
and with lefs emphafis, we call *light*.

So when we lift our foot, in order to walk, that motion is
arfis, or *light*; and when we put it on the ground, in order to
proceed, that act of pofing is *thefis*, or *heavy*.

If we count on our fingers every ftep or *cadence* we make in
walking, we fhall find each of them confifting of, and fub-
divided by, thefe two motions, *arfis* and *thefis*, or the *light* and the
heavy; and if we count only on every fecond *cadence* or ftep
(which makes a pace), we fhall find each pace fub-divided by

four

[21]

four motions; two of which will be *theses* or *heavy*, and the other two *arses* or *light*.

This division of the step by the even number 2, and of the pace by the even number 4, naturally arises from the walk of a sound or perfect man.

The halting of a lame man makes a pace divisible into six, instead of four; that is, the *thesis* or *posing* of one of his feet rests twice as long on the ground as that of the other foot; consequently, in each pace of this lame walk, there will be one *thesis* of so much greater weight or emphasis than the other, that the second thesis appears, in comparison with it, to be light. Wherefore this whole pace is considered only as one cadence, divided unequally into heavy (∆), lightest (..), light (∴), and lightest (..).

Here then are two general modes or MEASURES of time. The *first*, wherein each step makes a *cadence*, and is divided equally by the even number 2, and the pace, or *double cadence*, by 4; and is in music called *common time*, andante, or the MEASURE of a march. The *second*, where the whole pace, making only *one* cadence, may be equally divided by the number 6, as the double of 3; and is called *triple time*, or the MEASURE of the minuet and jigg. But the two steps composing the pace of triple time, are so far dissimilar, that one of them is composed by $\overset{\Delta \;..}{3+1}$, and the other by $\overset{\therefore \;..}{1+1}$; as, [musical notation]; which diversity, when

flow,

flow, makes the graceful variety of the minuet; and, when faster, the merry hobble of the jigg *.

Now all speech, as well as other music, is subject to the influence of CADENCE, by *arsis* and *thesis*, or the *light* and the *heavy*, as well as of MEASURE, which determines those cadences to the *common* or the *triple*, and likewise to the affection of QUANTITY (as an inferior division of RHYTHMUS or MEASURE) by the *long* and the *short*.

And as the *length* of syllables, as well as their particular affections to the *light* and the *heavy*, is various, according to the genius of the language; so some words and sentences must be measured by *common time*, and some by *triple time*.

Musicians mark the modes or *measures* of time, according to which their music is to be performed, by prefixing at the beginning of the movement, the marks $\frac{2}{4}$, or the letter C or ₵ for common time; and 3, or $\frac{3}{4}$, or $\frac{6}{8}$, or any of the multiples of 3 in the numerators for triple time (the denominator serving only to shew into how many parts a semibrief is supposed to be divided in that air); and at every *cadence* a perpendicular stroke or *bar* is put, or supposed; as thus,

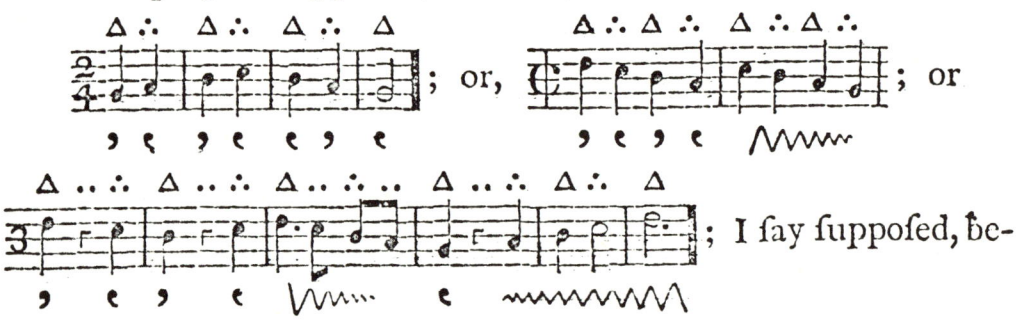

; or, ; or

; I say supposed, be-

* It is probable the Greeks derived their notions of the rhythmus in music from the action of walking, by their having made the word *foot* a principal term in the art of prosody.

cause

cause two or more cadences may be comprized within the space called a bar, as in the second example, or there may be a bar at every cadence, as in the first; the bar of itself being of no other signification than as an eye-mark to the performer, to shew where some cadences are, by which he can easily observe the others: for, at the pleasure of the composer, the space between bar and bar may contain either 1, or 2, or 3, or 4, or 6, or 8, or 9, or 12, &c. cadences; that is, any number of cadences which may be the multiples of 2, or of 3, but whereof neither 5, 7, 11, 13, or any prime number, except the foregoing, 2 or 3, shall be the divisors or factors: (I mean this more strictly as applied to the composition of music, than to the rhythmus of speech; and perhaps the number 5, as being composed of the prime numbers 2 and 3, should be also excepted.) But here I will observe again, that (in common music) no less than a whole pace must be allowed for a cadence of triple measure; because, as before mentioned, it is composed of two unequal steps. However, in the *rhythmus* of speech, where the two *genera* are continually intermixed, the *triple cadence* is only equal to one step.

In the above examples, I have written the marks of *light* and *heavy* over the notes, and of the *piano* and *forte* under them, in order to shew clearly, that there are five orders of accidents incident to melody and measure, essentially different in their nature and effects from each other, and very material to be attended to in the consideration of the melody and measure of speech.

[24]

For I conceive,

Speech to consist of
- melody by *accentual* slides { acute and grave } loud and soft.
- measure or rhythmus } of sound, or motion; and of silence, or rest; governed by *emphatic* cadences { heavy and light. } metrically subdivided by quantity { long and short. }

And here it may be proper to recapitulate and bring the several marks, which we have adopted for the expression of these five orders of accidents, into one view.

1st, ACCENT. Acute /, grave \, or both combined ∧∨, in a variety of circumflexes.

2dly, QUANTITY. Longest ⊢, long ?, short ?, shortest |.

3dly, PAUSE or *silence*. Semibrief rest ▮, minim rest ▬, crotchet rest ⌐, quaver rest ⌐.

4thly, *EMPHASIS or *cadence*. Heavy △, light ∴, lightest ..

5thly, FORCE or *quality of sound*. Loud, ℓ, louder ℓℓ, soft ℓ, softer ℓℓ. Swelling or increasing in loudness ⌒⌒⌒, decreasing in loudness or dying away ⌒⌒⌒. Loudness uniformly continued ⌒⌒⌒⌒⌒⌒⌒.

Also the sub-division of bars or *cadences* may be, at the pleasure of the composer, in any fractional parts, the sum of which will make the whole *quantity* of the bar or *cadence*, provided that the denominators of the said fractional parts are always, either sub-duples or sub-triples, of the whole number of the bar or *cadence*. And also all measured *rests* or pauses are as significant in computation of time and in value of place, respecting cadence or the

* Hereafter called *Poize*. See p. 77.

heavy

heavy and light, as express notes of sound. For example, let the time of a whole bar in a piece of music be equal to 1, then the sub-division of other bars in the same piece may be

$\frac{1}{2}+\frac{1}{2}=\frac{1}{3}+\frac{1}{3}+\frac{1}{3}=\frac{1}{4}+\frac{1}{4}+\frac{1}{4}+\frac{1}{4}=\frac{3}{6}+\frac{1}{6}+\frac{2}{6}=\frac{2}{3}+\frac{1}{3}=\frac{2}{3}+\frac{1}{6}+\frac{1}{6}=\frac{1}{2}+\frac{1}{6}+\frac{1}{6}+\frac{1}{6}=\frac{1}{2}+\frac{1}{6}=\frac{3}{12}+\frac{1}{12}+\frac{2}{12}+\frac{3}{12}+\frac{1}{12}+\frac{2}{12}$, &c. the sum of each bar making always 1. And this diversity of division within a *cadence* or bar is the subject of quantity.

That member of *rhythmus* which I call *a cadence*, has, in my system, nearly the same effect as that which by the Greeks was called *metron*.

The division of $\frac{1}{2}+\frac{1}{2}$ is naturally governed by the andante or walking cadence of a perfect man.

The division of $\frac{2}{3}+\frac{1}{3}$ is the halting of a lame man, or minuet measure.

And the $\frac{3}{12}+\frac{1}{12}+\frac{2}{12}+\frac{3}{12}+\frac{1}{12}+\frac{2}{12}$, or, as commonly marked by musicians, $\frac{6}{8}$*, equivalent to $\frac{3}{16}+\frac{1}{16}+\frac{2}{16}+\frac{3}{16}+\frac{1}{16}+\frac{2}{16}$, is the cantering of a horse, or the measure of a jigg. The example in page 15, of the parish clerk announcing the psalm, is in this measure; the natural rhythmus and metres of those words will admit of no other.

The division of all rhythmical sounds by the multiples or subduples of 2 or of 3, is so strongly affected by our nature, that either a tune or a discourse will give some uneasiness, or at least not be quite satisfactory to nice ears †, if its whole duration be

---

* $\frac{6}{8}$, the denominator 8, shews into how many parts a semibrief is supposed to be divided, and consequently, that a bar of this measure contains only three quarters of a semibrief. If a semibrief represented any positive length of time, this rule, of making it appear as a standard, would have some useful meaning; but as its length is only relative, it has little or none, and the figures 2 and 3 would be sufficient to denote all changes of measure, and be more simple and more satisfactory.

† The last movement in the celebrated overture of *La Buona Figliuola* has this defect, and every nice ear feels it.

[26]

not measured by an even number of *compleat cadences*, commensurable with, and divisible, by 2 or by 3. For this reason, the judicious composer or orator (if he does not mean to make his audience restless) will lengthen his piece with proper expletives, or with adequate rests or pauses, so as to make his periods duly commensurable *. And whoever would pronounce our heroic lines of ten syllables with propriety, must allow at least six cadences, by the assistance of proper rests, to each line, and frequently eight; as,

Oh, | happiness | our | being's | end and | aim!

in six bars or cadences; or in eight bars, as the following:

Oh, | happiness! | our | being's | end and | aim!

ANOTHER EXAMPLE OF SIX CADENCES.

3 | To | all in | ferior | animals | 'tis | given |

| To en | joy the | state al | lotted | them by | heaven |

* It were to be wished, that something more than an assertion, with an appeal to nature, and a conjecture, could be offered as an illustration of this mysterious law. But may not space of time be analogous to space in geometry? which can only be equally and uniformly divided by quadrilateral or triangular polygons, their multiples, or sub-duples; that is, by squares □, parallelograms ▱, triangles △, or hexagons ⬡; for with a series of pentagons or heptagons, or any other polygons than those first mentioned, no space can be uniformly covered, without leaving void interstices of heterogeneous forms; whereas any quadrilateral or triangular space can be compleatly covered with homogeneous quadrilateral or triangular figures.

No

| No | vain re | searches | e'er dif | turb their | rest |

| No | fears of | dark fu | turity | mo | left. |

Or the second line thus,

| To en | joy the | state al | lotted them | by | heaven |

Which division of the line into six bars or cadences of time, is as little as can be allowed for the reader or speaker to fetch his breath; and this in the plain narrative stile, for if there be required any very pointed expression, more rests or pauses must be thrown in, which must necessarily either increase the number of bars, or, by using shorter notes in some parts, throw the syllables of two bars into the time of one, or partly one, partly the other. Wherefore our heroic lines are truly *hexameters*.

The *thesis* or *heavy* note or syllable, on which the hand or foot beats time, is always the first in the bar; and if in that place, instead of an express note of sound, there should be marked a rest, then the thesis or heavy part of the cadence falls on that rest: the last note in a bar (or in that extent which we allow to a cadence) is always *light*. If there be only one note or syllable which fills the whole extent of a cadence, of course, that one note is at first heavy, and then the latter continuance supposed light. For these affections are always alternate, except cut off by rests, or long-holding tones, without change of articulation. If a cadence be sub-divided into many notes or syllables, they

shall

shall be nearly divided under the several degrees of emphasis of heavy (△), light (∴), and lightest (..); as thus,

[musical notation examples]

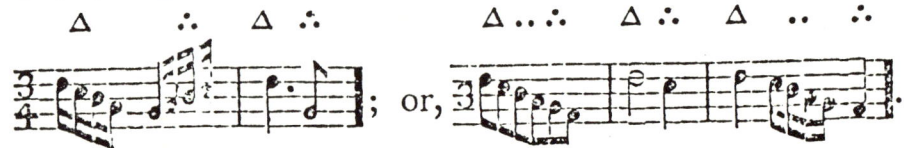

Having premised so much, I will now give a general precept and example in the following sentence:

[musical notation] Every | sentence | in our | language, | whether | prose or | verse,

[musical notation] has a | rhythmus | | pe | culiar | to it | self;

[musical notation] That is, in the | language of | modern mu | sicians, | | it is

[musical notation] either in | common time | | or | triple time; | | vi | delicet,

[musical notation] minuet time, | | or | jigg time, | | or | mixed.

To the first member of the above sentence (which I have written in common time, as marked by ²⁄₄), I have noted the *accents*, the *quantity* and *cadence*; to the latter member, which is in triple measure, I have only marked *quantity* and *cadence*, together with the proper *rests* or *pauses* throughout the whole. I have

have omitted the marks of piano and forte, becaufe in calm unempaffioned fentences the addition of thofe expreffions, to any fenfible degree, would convert plain difcourfe into bombaft.

Where this mark ⌢ (minu) or ⌢ (in the) is ufed, it is to fhew, that as many fyllables or refts as are written over that line or embrace, are all to pafs as one in refpect of the △, or the ∴.

I will now fhew fome fmall alterations that may be made in the meafure of the foregoing example, and fill up the refts, between *rhythmus* and *peculiar*, by expletives.

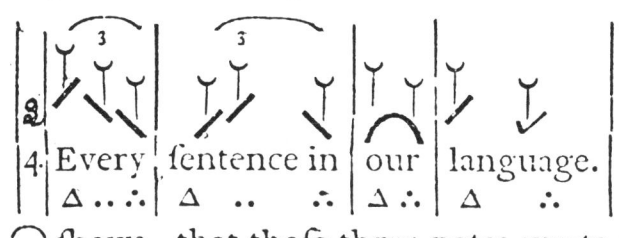

4| Every | fentence in | our | language.

The mark ⌢₃ fhews, that thofe three notes wrote under that arch pafs off in the time of two; by which means, the two modes, *common* and *triple*, are eafily intermixed.

In this alteration, the monofyllable *in* (one of our pliant fyllables) which before was *heavy* and *acute*, becomes *light* and *grave:* and *our* becomes *heavy* on the diphthong *ou*, and *light* on the liquid *r*; and extending to the length of two fyllables, is accented with a circumflex, as before.

2| Has a | rhythmus | of its | own pe | culiar | to it | felf.

The foregoing example confifts in the whole of 32 *bars* or *cadences*, including the refts, which were abfolutely neceffary,

in

in order to pronounce it with propriety; and with thofe refts it divides into 8 rhythmical *claufes*, of 4 *cadences* in each.

Though I have given a fcale, in my firft part, in order to demonftrate with accuracy, the nature and extent of the flides we make in fpeech, yet with a little practice I found, that drawing my flides on the common five black lines was fufficient (at leaft for a perfon who is already a mufician and mafter of the language) to direct the voice to the proper tones; for there is a great latitude which may be ufed without any feeming blemifh; as whether the flide runs a quarter of a tone or three quarters, up and down, more or lefs, feems of little confequence, provided the proprieties of (the RHYTHMUS) *quantity and cadence*, are duly obferved. And with ftill more practice I found, that drawing the accents fimply over the fyllables, without the black lines, (but with fome regard to higher or lower, by pofition of the marks, as in the examples here given), was fo certain a guide, that I could always read the fentences, *fo marked*, nearly in the fame melody; but the other four accidents, of *quantity*, *paufing*, *emphafis*, and *fortepiano*, excepting the laft, I could no how abridge or omit. And I alfo found, that the marks of *quantity*, *paufing*, and *emphafis* alone, were fo fufficient that a native needed fcarce any farther help to read with furprizing correctnefs of expreffion; though I muft acknowledge the meaning of a fentence may often be entirely altered, by changing the accent from acute to grave, or *vice verfá*.

I will now fet down fome of the lines of Englifh poetry (quoted by the learned author of *The Origin and Progrefs of Language*, in the firft edition of his 8th chap. of book iii. part II.) which I will accompany with the marks of *refts*, *quantity*, and

cadence

[31]

cadence, in order to shew, that the method of measuring by the Greek feet, without any allowance for pauses, is inaccurate and indecisive: for, since the ingenious author admitted (what he called accent, by us called) *cadence* of *heavy* and *light* to be in our language, though he denied us to have quantity, it will appear, that his verses of five feet consist at least of six *cadences*, and commonly those of four feet consist of five. Lines which consist of five *cadences* or metres have less grace and dignity than those of six or eight.

3| Daughter of | God and | man, | | ac | complish'd | Eve. |

| Pleasures, | the | Sex, | as | children | birds pur | sue. | |

| Tho' | deep, | yet | clear; | tho' | gentle, | yet not | dull; |

| | Strong, | without | rage; | with | out o'er | flowing | full. |

Or thus, as pronounced by Mr. GARRICK:

| | Strong with | out | rage; | with | out o'er | flowing | full. |

| Thou, | Stella, | wast no | longer | young, |

| When | first, for | thee, my | lyre I | strung. |

I shall

[32]

      △ ∴   △ ∴
I shall omit the Hudi*brastic*, of rhyming upon *a stick*; because, though such doggrell may help out a laugh, the particle *a*, in English, is so absolutely *light*, that it cannot be put in the heavy part of the cadence, without violence to our pronunciation and a shock to gravity.

     △ ∴ △ ∴ △ ∴ △ ∴
     Before Porto Bello lying.

If this was the original of this song, the *vox populi*, whose ears were too nice to suffer so barbarous a misapplication of the word *before*, have long since altered it to

As near	Porto	Bello	lying,
△ ∴	△ ∴	△ ∴	△ ∴
On the	gently	swelling	flood.
△ ∴	△ ∴	△ ∴	△

      ∴ △
For *be*, in the word *before*, is so positively *light* that it cannot bear to be put out of its place; though *be*, as a monosyllable, is so pliant as to serve any where; and the latter syllable *fore*, is as positively *heavy*, and cannot without the greatest violence be put under the *light*.

3 | From the | knaves, and the | fools, and the | fops of the | time, |
    | From the | drudges in | prose, and the | triflers in | rhyme. |

My

My	time, oh, ye	Muses, was	happily	spent,
When	Phœbe went	with me, where	ever I	went.
If	e'er in thy	sight, I found	favour, A	pollo,
De	fend me from	all the dis	asters that	follow.

These three distichs are all in triple time and jigg measure; and the syllable more or less, at first or at last, makes no difference in the rhythmus. In applying my rules to these examples, I endeavour to do justice to the proper measure of our language, without the least intention of adapting them to the feet of the Greek prosody.

I shall add one more from the 9th chap. page 403.

3| Place me in | regions of e | ternal | winter,

| Where not a | blossom to the | breeze can | open; but

| Darkening | tempests | closing all a | round me,

| Chill the cre | ation.

Place me where | *sun-shine* | *evermore me* | *scorches;*

Climes where no | *mortal* | *builds his habi* | *tation;*

Yet with my | *charmer* | *fondly will I* | *wander*

Fondly con | *versing.*

Now if after all I have said, any one should still doubt or deny that our language has both melody and measure, I would refer to the following experiment:

Take three common men; one a native of Aberdeenshire, another of Tipperary, and the third of Somersetshire; and let them converse together in the English language, in the presence of any gentleman of the courtly tone of the metropolis; his ears will soon inform him, that every one of them talks in a tune very different from his own, and from each other; and that their difference of tone is not owing merely to *loud* and *soft*, but to a variety both of melody and of measure, by a different application of *accents*, acute and grave; and of *quantity*, short and long; and of *cadence*, light and heavy. Every one of the four persons will perceive the other three have very distinct tones from each other,

other, and that the tone of each is plainly diſtinguiſhed by the *alto* and *baſſo*, though each in particular may fancy his own tone to be quite uniform, and in the uniſon with itſelf.

The extreme familiarity exiſting between a man and his native language, makes him loſe all ſenſe of its features, of its deformities, and of its beauties; though under this ſtate of indifference, if the love of variety, ſo natural to man, ſhould prone him into a liking of ſome foreign tongue, ſuch a circumſtance may make him very ſharp-ſighted towards the faults of his own, and as blind to its perfections. I will not pretend to compare our language to the Greek; but as to its melody, I think it about as good as the Latin, and much better than French or German, though far inferior to the Italian, which, in that quality, exceeds the Greek; I ſay, exceeds the Greek in melody, as far as we can judge of the Greek pronunciation; for, I apprehend, the beſt Grecians in modern Europe, not excepting the inhabitants of Greece itſelf, know no more of the ancient tone of that language, as it was ſpoken in the age of Demoſthenes, than we do of the Britiſh in the age of Alfred, and much leſs than an Engliſh boarding-ſchool miſs does of the Pariſian tone of French.

Having proceeded ſo far in this ſyſtem, as to convince myſelf that our language, under the influence of the two general modes of time, common and triple, has an exact *rhythmus*, both as to *cadence,* by the *heavy* and the *light,* and as to *quantity,* by the *long* and the *ſhort*; and alſo that it has an *accented melody* of great variety and extent by *ſlides, acute* and *grave,* and *mixed* in the *circumflex*; my next endeavour was to find out, whether our

theatrical

theatrical declamation might not be agreeably and advantageoufly affifted, as well as that of the ancient Greeks and Romans, by a fuitable bafs accompaniment.

I confidered, that as the profodical changes of the voice by *flides*, acute and grave, were very rapid, the bafs accompaniment ought, by the rules of harmony, to be very fedate, with little or no motion by the acute or grave: for, in the *diatonic genus*, whenever the cantus takes a rapid flight, either up or down, through all the notes of the octave, the moft proper and agreeable bafs is one continued found, either of the *fundamental key-note*, or of the 4th to the key-note, or of the 5th to the key, or of two of them founded together, in difcord or harmony, as the occafion and the tafte of the compofer may require. Neither could it be proper for the accompaniment of the flides, to exhibit the found of the bafs otherwife than by *tafto folo foftenuto*, or one holding note; becaufe to continue it *ftaccato*, or by feveral repeated ftrokes, might interfere with, and confound, the articulation of the fpeaker. Experience muft teach us when this note may be intermitted, and when changed for another.

I therefore concluded, that there could be no occafion, in the accompaniment of fpeech, for the bafs to found any other tone than the fundamental of the key, its fourth, or its fifth; or the key-note with its fifth, in concord; or perhaps with its *fourth reverfed*, alfo in concord: becaufe, while any of thefe are continued founding, the voice, by fliding through the whole extent of the octave, muft, in its progrefs, exhibit every concord of harmony that is poffible between two founds. And therefore I made trial of the fundamental (or deepeft note on the inftrument) that feemed to be key-note to the common level of my

voice

voice in speaking, which I suppose to be [♪] C of consort pitch, and made use of the open tone of the fourth string of a violincello, [♪] CC which was the octave below * my common level.

I found my slides in common discourse went about a fifth (of the diatonic scale) above the level or key-note, and about a seventh below it; but if empassioned, it run two whole tones higher, which made in the whole extent a compass of 13 notes, or octave and sixth.

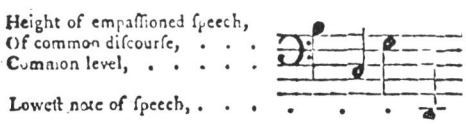

Height of empassioned speech,
Of common discourse, . . .
Common level, ...
Lowest note of speech, . . .

I sometimes added the fifth (or the open tone of the third string) in harmony with the fundamental; and perhaps if there was another string, a fifth below the fundamental (which would be the fourth of the key reversed), the harmony of that, with the fundamental, might be occasionally used with advantage; for though the fourth may be had, by letting the third string down to that tone, and the fifth also, by stopping the same string (so let down) on the second fret, yet the effect is different; because the fourth above, in conjunction with the key-note, makes a

---

* The deeper the fundamental bass is taken, the more agreeable it will sound; that is, it will be better to be two octaves below the cantus than one: for, the farther two discordant notes are removed from each other, the less harsh their discord will sound to the ear; as the ninth sounds less uncouth than the second, and the sixteenth still less so than the ninth; but especially the more grave the accompanying sound is, the less it will tend to out-voice the speaker.

Whether a stringed instrument with a bow, or wind instruments, such as very deep flutes or French horns, will have the best effect, must be proved by future experiments.

discord,

[38]

discord, or at best an imperfect concord; but being reversed, it falls a fifth below the key-note, and consequently sounds in concord with it.

I then read, and at the same time sounded continually the bass, observing the proper expressions of the forte and piano, and sometimes, where it was marked forte, adding the harmony of the fifth to the bass, as in the example annexed.

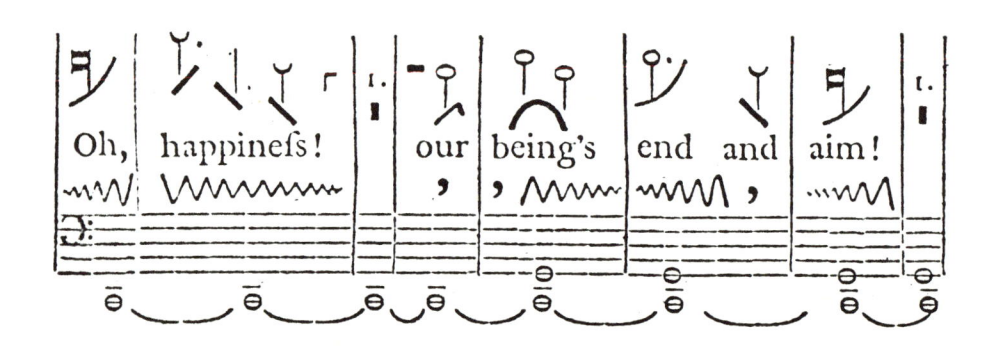

Oh, happiness! our being's end and aim!

Where the notes for the slides are drawn in this form ∕ it is to shew that the sound hangs longer on the first part of the slide than on the last, on account of the vowels.

I made several other trials on the same principles, both alone, and calling in the judgement of others; the result whereof is, that I remain confirmed in the opinion, that an accompaniment animates the reader or speaker to pronounce with more confidence, and pleasure to himself, than he could without it.

That it will be advantageous both to elocution and action on the stage, in all tragic and heroic dramas, whether mixed with other music or not; but especially in all operas, where the
species

species of song called *Recitative accompanied**, will be an agreeable medium between this and the common song.

That being generally played soft, and being a very low or grave sound, it does not seem, in the least, to out-voice the speaker, so as to interrupt the hearing.

That by the discreet use of the forte and piano, with the occasional addition of the fifth, it enlivens, or softens, the empassioned expressions, according to the proper degree; and would contribute much to keep an actor in the true pitch of expression, neither ranting above, nor sinking below, what the nature of his part required, supposing the marks of ꜀ and ꜂, VVVVVVV and WWWWWW, and the occasional addition of the fifth in harmony, to be judiciously written, and as exactly performed by the accompanying musician.

It is so many years since I saw the tragedy of Hamlet performed, that I have no remembrance of the expressions sufficient to enable me to set the following speech in the manner of any great actor: but as it was one of those which I made my expement upon with the bass accompaniment. I shall set it down as I pronounced it, the first nine lines accented and fully noted, the

---

* The ordinary Italian recitative seems to be an endeavour, under some obscure traditional hints (the memory of which is now lost), to continue the ancient manner of accompanied declamation; the basses of which being generally by a *tasto solo* on a ground, or single note, seem, according to our system, to countenance this conjecture; but for the rest, the moderns having no proper idea of the ancient chromatic or enharmonic genera, and none at all of the melody and vocal slides in speech, write the cantus of their recitative in the chromatico-diatonic, which, until our ears are debauched into a customary liking, sounds unnatural and disgusting.

[40]

remainder with all the marks of expression, but without th
accents.

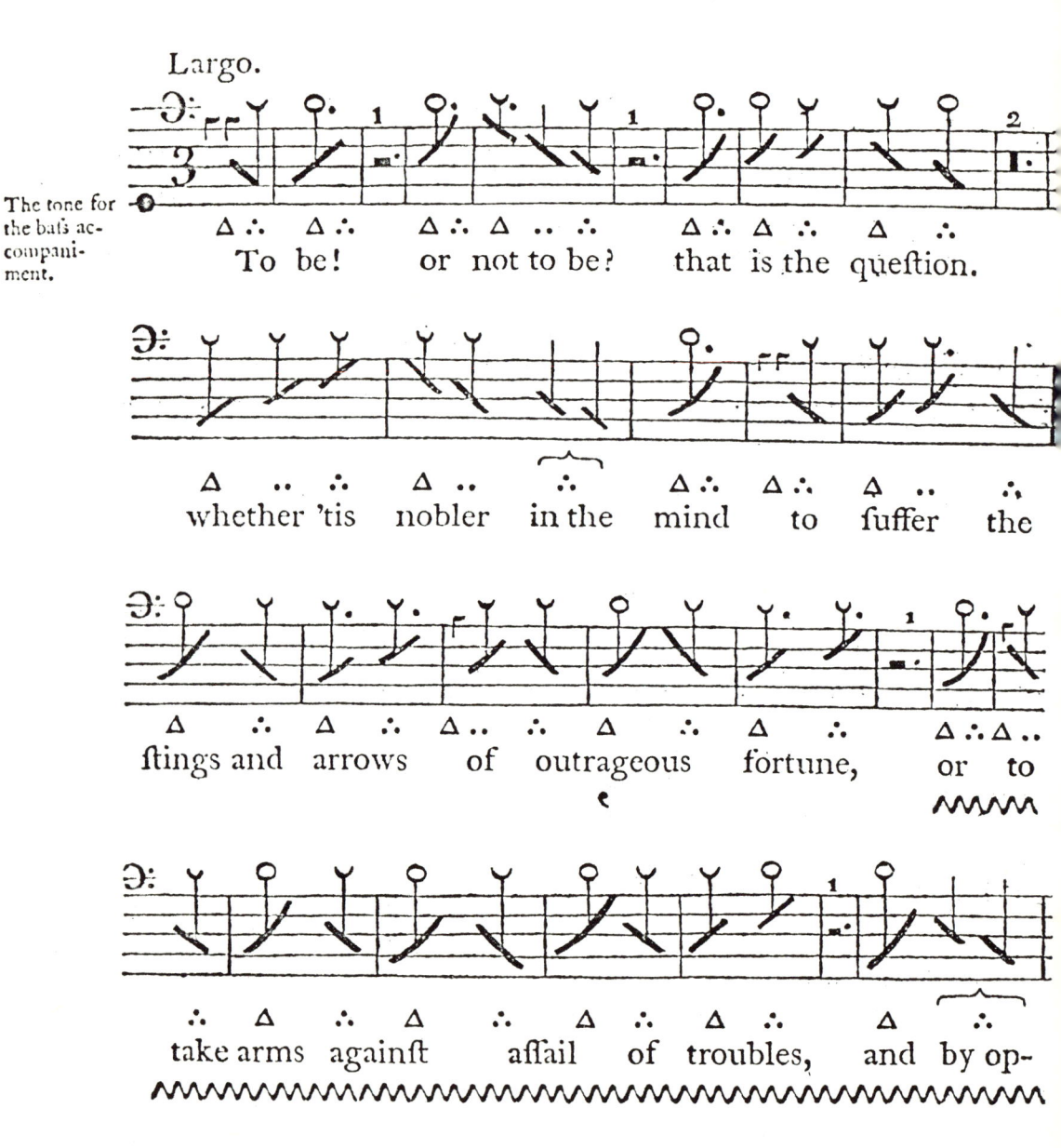

Largo.

The tone for the bass accompaniment.

To be! or not to be? that is the question.

whether 'tis nobler in the mind to suffer the

stings and arrows of outrageous fortune, or to

take arms against assail of troubles, and by op-

posing

[41]

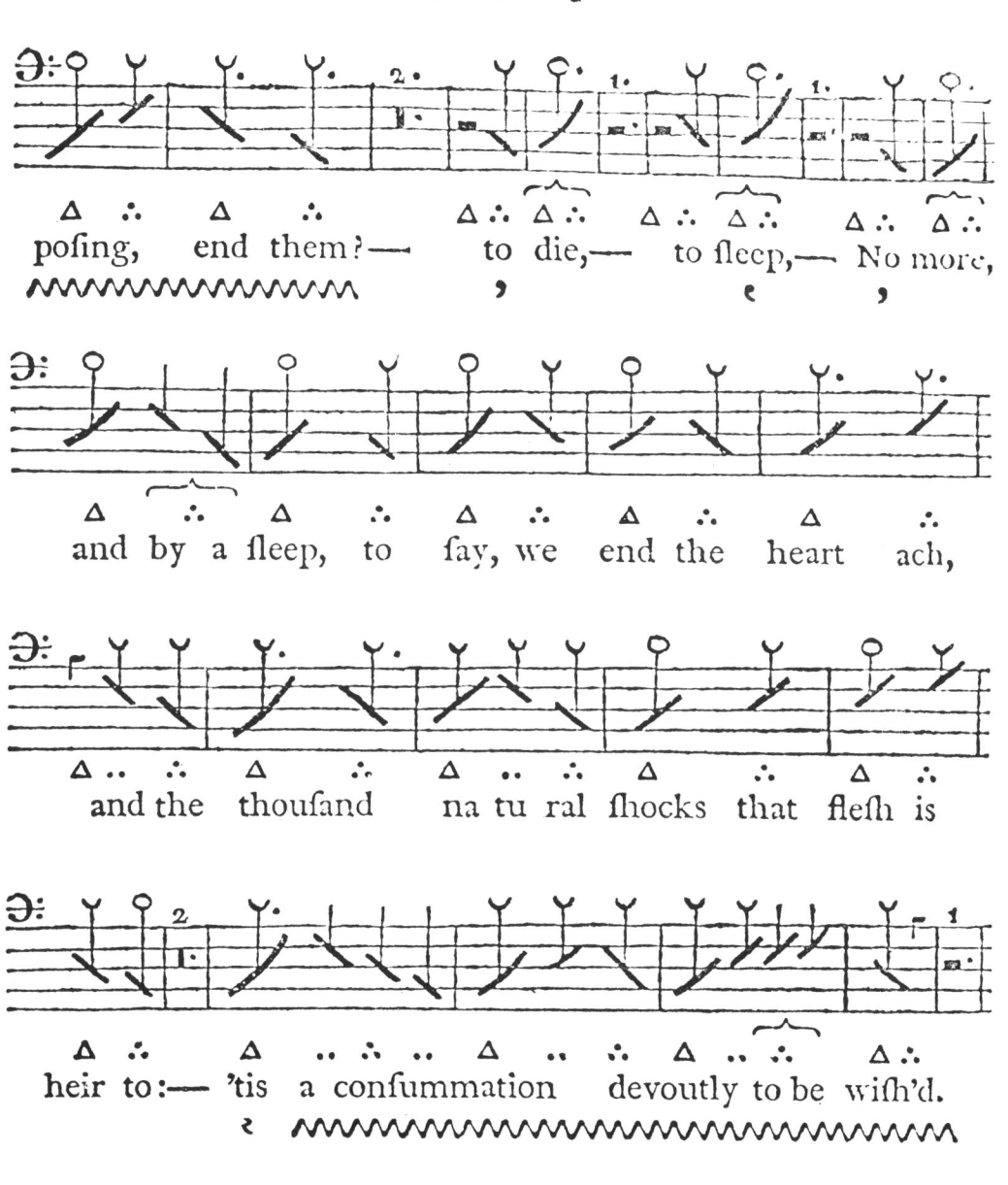

posing, end them?— to die,— to sleep,— No more,

and by a sleep, to say, we end the heart ach,

and the thousand natural shocks that flesh is

heir to:— 'tis a consummation devoutly to be wish'd.

| To | die | — to | sleep | — to | sleep! | | per | chance to | dream; |

dream;

[42]

aye, there's the rub; for in that sleep of death what dreams may come, when we have shuffled off this mortal coil, must give us pause. There's the res-

Allegretto.

pect that makes calamity of so long life: 2.) for who would bear the whips and scorns of time, th' oppressor's wrong, the proud man's contumely, the

pang

pang of | des- | pis'd | love, | the | law's de- | lay, | the

insolence of | office, | and the | spurns that | 3.) patient | merit,

of the un | worthy | takes; | when | he him | self | might

Allegretto.

his qui | etus | make, | with a | bare | bodkin? | 2.) who would

Largo.

fardles | bear, | 3.) to | groan and | sweat | under a | weary | life,

but that the | dread of | something | after | death, | (that undis-

covered | country, | from whose | bourne no | traveller re | turns)

puzzles

puzzles the will; and makes us rather bear the ills we have, than fly to others that we know not of. Thus conscience does make cowards of us all: and thus the native hue of resolution is sicklied o'er with the pale cast of thought: and enter prizes of great pith and moment, with this regard, their currents turn awry, and lose the name of action.— *Allegretto.* Soft you, now! *Largo.* the

fair

[45]

| fair Op | helia? | 1. | Nymph, | in thy or | isons, | be | all my |

| fins re | member'd. |

VARIATIONS.

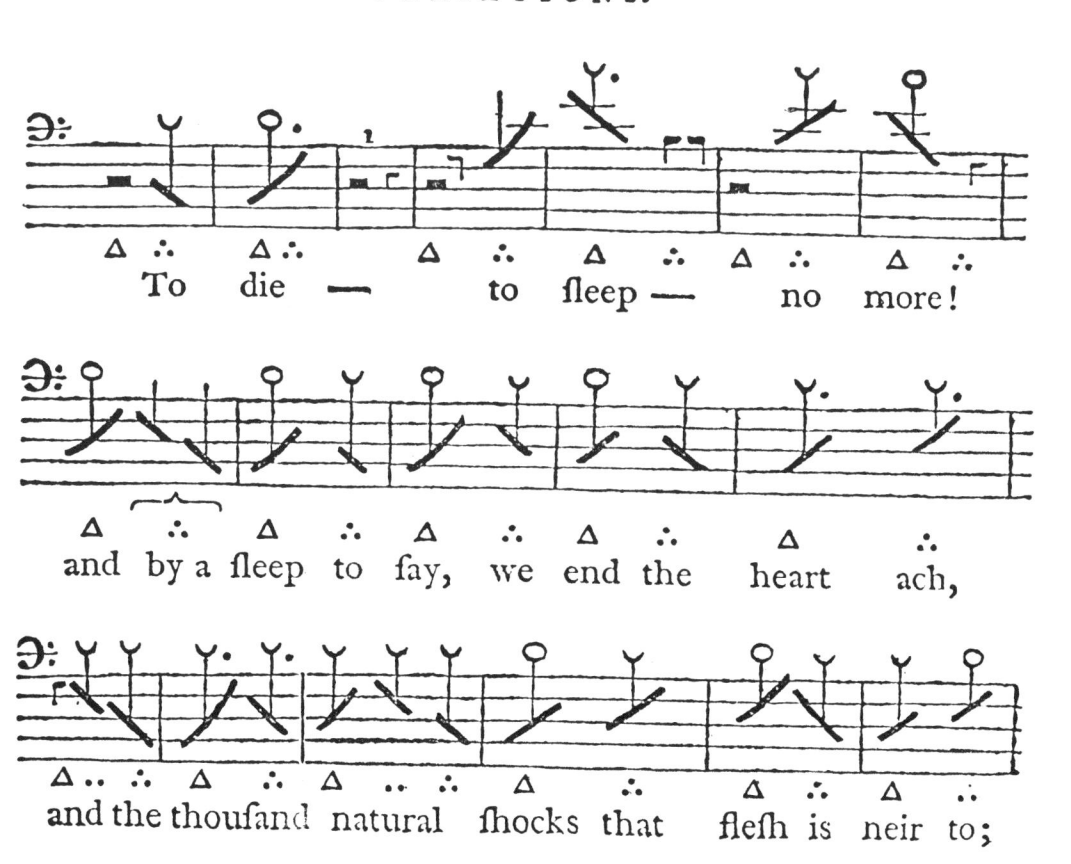

To die — to sleep — no more!

and by a sleep to say, we end the heart ach,

and the thousand natural shocks that flesh is heir to;

'tis

—'tis a confummation devoutly to be wifh'd!

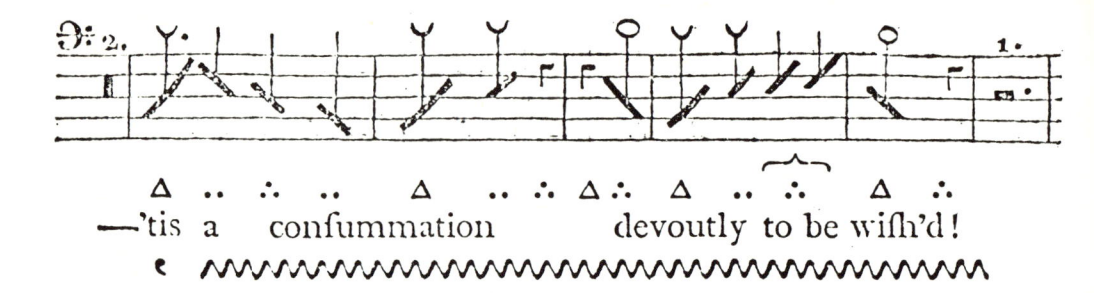

But to conclude, as the practice of the enharmonic genus of mufic, and the art of reducing the *melody* and *meafure* of fpeech to practicable and legible notes (if it was ever compleat), and of accompanying the fame by a *continual bafs**, have lain, as it were, in a *terra incognita*, for at leaft a thoufand years paft, I think, thefe fmall fpecimens produced, may be our vouchers to prove, that we have difcovered the land, and marked out the route which may be followed by others: and therefore, I hope, gallant adventurers will not be wanting, to pufh thefe difcoveries further, to explore and bring to light thofe rich curiofities that ftill lie hid in the interior parts of the country.

* In the modern practice of mufic there feems no fignificant reafon, why the common accompanying bafs, of all forts of airs, fhould be called *baffo continuo,* or *thorough bafs,* unlefs the term was taken from that bafs, which, by accompanying theatrical declamation, was *continued* all *thorough* the performance, while the other baffes, for the accompanyment of incidental chromatic or diatonic airs, as interludes, were only introduced now and then. For the fact is, the modern *baffo continuo* is no more continual than the cantus, or any other part of the fymphony. Nor do I know any thing which can properly be called a thorough bafs, in our days, except the drone of that ancient inftrument the bag-pipe, made by *tibiis imparibus,* founding exactly the two notes (key note and fifth) which I have made ufe of in thefe experiments.

SINCE

SINCE writing the foregoing treatise, I have heard Mr. Garrick in the character of Hamlet; and the principal differences that I can remember, between his manner, and what I have marked in the treatise, are as follow:

In the first place, that speech, or soliloque, which I (for want of better judgement) have noted in the stile of a ranting actor, swelled with *forte* and softened with *piano*, he delivered with little or no distinction of piano and forte, but nearly uniform; something below the ordinary force, or, as a musician would say, *sotto voce*, or *sempre poco piano*.

Secondly, as to measure, the first line thus:

musical notation: To be | or not to be | that is the | question.

Thirdly, as to accent and quantity, thus:

musical notation: To die, — to sleep, — no more.

The words, *as flesh is heir to!* he pronounced as I have marked them in my variation, page 46.; where the two syllables, *heir to*, are both acuted, and by that modulation, give the idea of the

sense

sense being suspended, for the thought which immediately follows.

Lastly, *Nymph, in thy orisons,* he pronounced in common measure, as,

|2| Nymph, |in thy| orisons,

making the word *orisons* quite different from mine; I was led to make the first syllable *o* short and light, and the second *ri* long and heavy, by supposing the word to have been originally Norman French, *oraison*; but I suppose I was wrong in this, as in every other instance where I have shewn the difference. I shall forbear to give any more specimens of that great actor's elocution, from the memory of once hearing, lest I should do him injustice, as my intention here is not to play the critic; but merely to shew, that by means of these characters, all the varieties of enunciation may be committed to paper, and read off as easily as the air of a song tune.

There is a perfection in the pronunciation of the best speakers (which was remarkable in the late Mrs. Cibber, and is the same in Mr. Garrick): they are distinctly heard even in the softest sounds of their voices; when others are scarcely intelligible, though offensively loud.

This essential quality is chiefly owing to the speaker's dwelling with nearly uniform loudness on the whole length of every syllable,

syllable, and confining the extent of the accents, acute and grave, within the compass of four or five tones; and also to adopting, in general, a deliberate instead of a rapid measure.

For if a person pronounces from six to nine syllables in a second of time, as many people do, an auditor must be extremely quick and attentive to be able to keep up with so rapid an utterance.

But good speakers do not pronounce above three syllables in a second, and generally only two and a half, taking in the necessary pauses.

There are several public speakers, whose speeches, if committed to paper, would appear to have combined all the force of logical argument, all the flowers of rhetoric, with an elegant choice of words capable of being pronounced with graceful euphony; but by an erroneous delivery in respect of *accent, rhythmus, pause,* and *force,* though they may be just in *quantity* and *emphasis,* under their mistaken measure, their speeches want much of that beauty and effect which they should derive from a proper enunciation.

Now to shew that such errors might easily be corrected, by the use of the foregoing rules, let us only suppose such speakers instructed in the practice of ordinary music; might they not then be able to sing their song according to the notes set before them, keeping the prescribed *measure* of *fast* or *slow*; and, under *quantity,* observing the just *pauses,* and the several expressions of *staccato,* or *sostenuto*; and also of *piano* or *forte?* And this being admitted, the practicability of the other (which is by much the easier of the two) cannot be denied.

The tenor of speech in private conversation may be *(allegro* or*)* rapid; for there, if the auditor misses a word, he may desire the speaker to repeat his sentence: but all discourses delivered to a large audience should be *(largo e sostenuto)* deliberate, and the sound of each syllable, as to loudness, continued uniformly audible to its just length or *quantity*.

In the various tumults of passion, the voice runs very high into the *acute*, and very low into the *grave*; but in speaking to an audience, where the first intention is to be heard, and the next to invite attention, the excesses of *acute* and *grave* should be avoided, particularly the latter; because few people fall to a very *grave accent* without dwindling into a whisper: and as long sounds are more audible than short ones, all syllables (I repeat it again) should be supported to the full extent of their proper quantity with nearly an uniform strength of voice, and not dying away, or interrupted by rests after every syllable, as if they were sighed out, nor so as to give a *staccato* or short-pointed expression, both which manners, though natural in passions, are unseemly and disadvantageous in argumentative oratory; and in general, all rapid pronunciation keeps the audience in a painful attention, which the want of proper pauses increases, by leaving them no time to assist their apprehension by recollection.

I will exemplify what I have said by setting a few lines, from Leland's Demosthenes, in three different manners.

First

First manner. *Bombastic, by an excess in the extension of acute and grave, and of the piano and forte, and the tones not sostenuto or equally supported.*

* *Ordinary walking measure.*

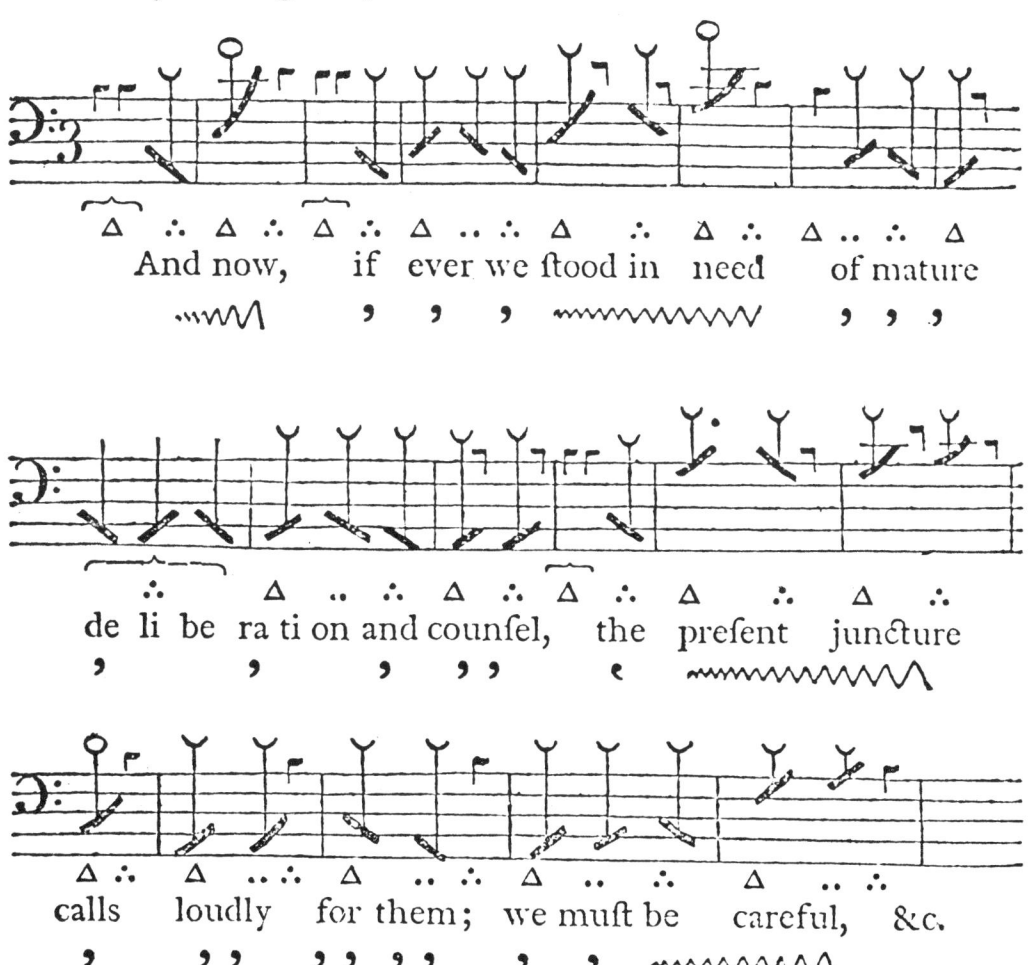

And now, if ever we stood in need of mature

de li be ra ti on and counsel, the present juncture

calls loudly for them; we must be careful, &c.

---

* *Walking-measure* means, that the duration of the whole quantity of syllables and pauses contained in *one cadence* (that is, as much as are marked between two bars), should be equal to the time of making one step of walking; which admits the varieties of *slow*, *ordinary*, and *quick walking*; the next degree above which, in velocity, is *running measure*.

[52]

Second manner. *Too rapid, though in an uniform tenor of loudness.*

Corrente, or *running measure.*

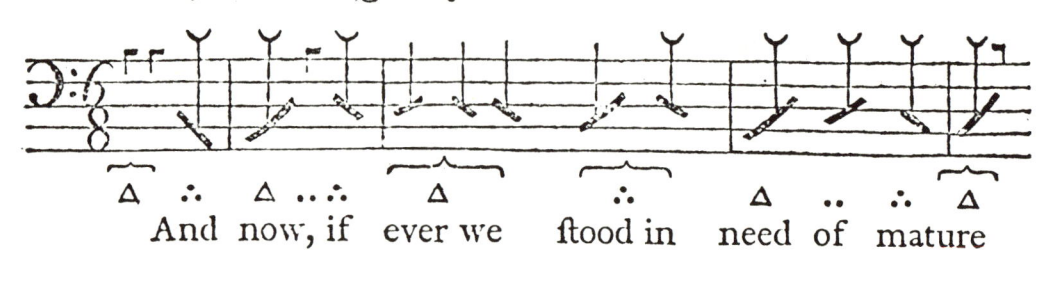

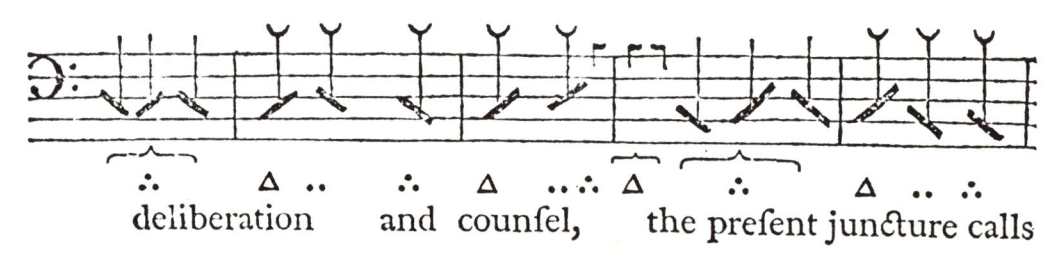

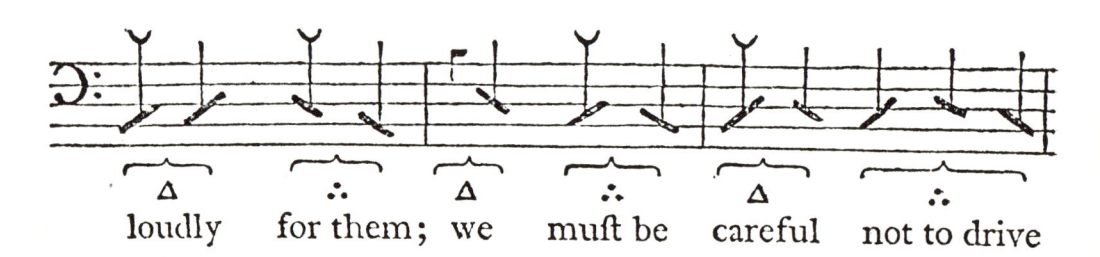

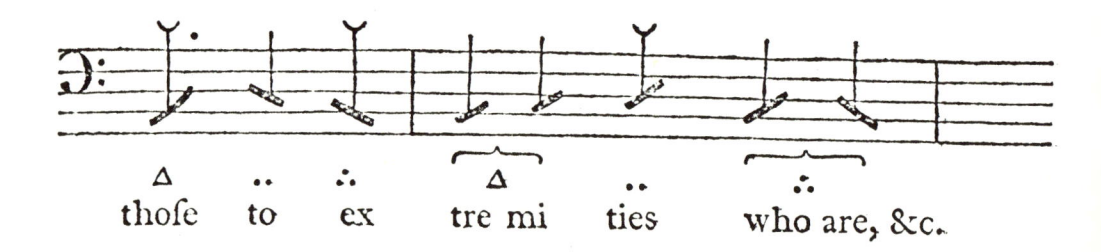

△ ∴ △ …∴ △ ∴ △ .. ∴ △
And now, if ever we stood in need of mature

∴ △ .. ∴ △ …∴ △ ∴ △ .. ∴
deliberation and counsel, the present juncture calls

△ ∴ △ ∴ △ ∴
loudly for them; we must be careful not to drive

△ .. ∴ △ .. ∴
those to ex tre mi ties who are, &c.

Third

[53]

Third manner. *Slow, firm, and uniformly loud.*

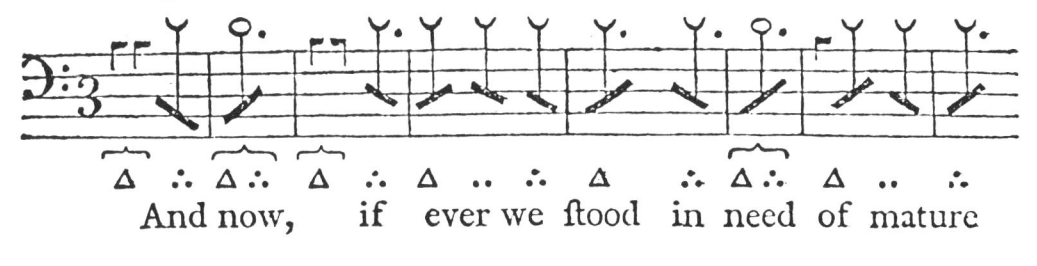

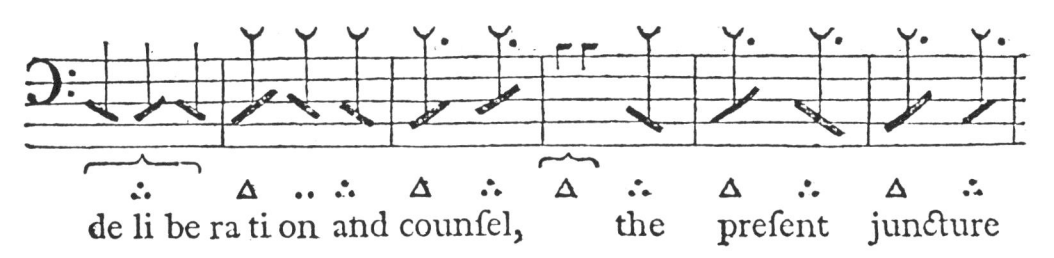

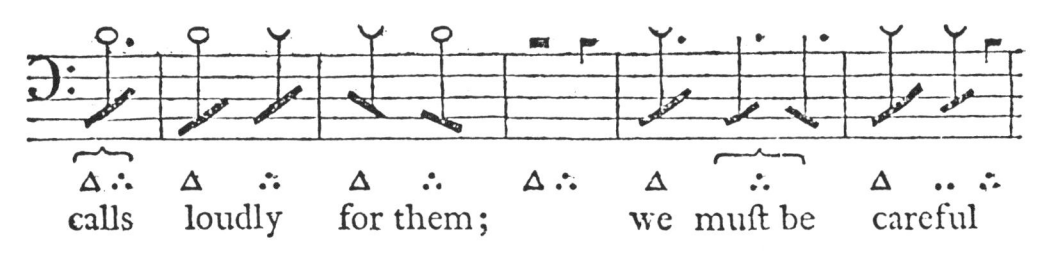

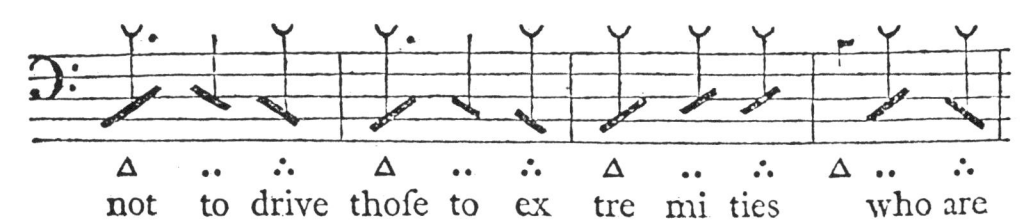

Walking measure.

And now, if ever we stood in need of mature deliberation and counsel, the present juncture calls loudly for them; we must be careful not to drive those to extremities who are

now

[54]

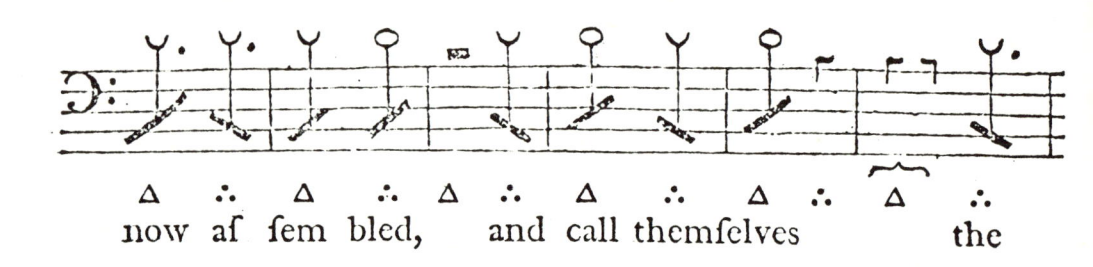

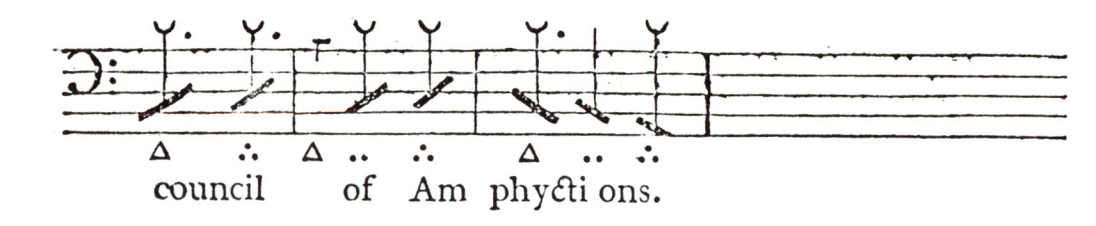

now aſ ſem bled,   and call themſelves   the

council   of Am phycti ons.

When this ſyſtem was explained to Mr. Garrick, among many judicious remarks and queries, he aſked this queſtion:

Suppoſing a ſpeech was noted, according to theſe rules, in the manner he ſpoke it, whether any other perſon, by the help of theſe notes, could pronounce his words in the ſame tone and manner exactly as he did?

To which he was anſwered thus:

Suppoſe a firſt-rate muſician had written down a piece of muſic, which he had played exquiſitely well on an exceeding fine toned violin; another performer with an ordinary fiddle might undoubtedly play every note the ſame as the great maſter, though perhaps with leſs eaſe and elegance of expreſſion; but, notwithſtanding his correctneſs in the tune and manner, nothing could prevent the audience from perceiving that the natural

tone

tone of his inftrument was execrable: fo, though thefe rules may enable a mafter to teach a juft application of accent, emphafis, and all the other proper expreffions of the voice in fpeaking, which will go a great way in the improvement of elocution, yet they cannot give a fweet voice where Nature has denied it.

OBSERVATIONS AND QUERIES, BY THE AUTHOR OF THE ORIGIN AND PROGRESS of LANGUAGE, IN HIS ANSWER TO SIR J. P. WHO HAD TRANSMITTED TO HIM THE TWO LETTERS CONTAINING THE FOREGOING SYSTEM.

§ 1. "I HAVE perused with much pleasure and instruction,
" the very ingenious dissertation you have sent me from
" your musical friend, and am now fully convinced that there
" is both a *melody* and *rhythm* even in our common speech in
" English. As to melody, I was before convinced that there
" was a different tone in the different languages of Europe.
" Secondly, that in the same language there is a variation of
" tone, arising from the passions, or even the character, of the
" speaker; but I did not know before, that in plain speech,
" without passion, humour, or any other mark of character,
" there was any variation of tone: and even after reading the
" dissertation, I was very unwilling to believe that there was any
" variation upon the same syllable. I was soon convinced that
" there was a variation in the whole tenor of the speech; so that
" before we had spoken two or more sentences, or even one
" sentence to an end, the tone of the voice is changed: but I
" thought this change proceeded from word to word, or from
" different syllables of the same word, without any change upon
" the same syllable. But upon considering the matter more
" fully, and conferring with some learned musicians of this
" place,

" place, I am convinced that Mr. S—— is in the right, and that
" the voice does not rest in the same tone, even upon the same
" syllable; but goes on continually changing, not only upon
" different words and syllables, but upon the same syllable.
" And indeed I now begin to think, that to keep the voice in the
" same tone, even for the shortest time; or, in other words,
" to speak in a perfect monotony, is a thing of art which nobody
" but a musician can perform. I am also convinced, that the
" voice does not only rise or fall upon the same syllable (I mean
" in musical modulation), but also that it sometimes does both
" rise and fall upon the same syllable, particularly upon such
" syllables as make a word by themselves, or are pronounced
" with any pathos; such as the syllable *oh!* given as an instance
" by Mr. S——, who has observed, with great accuracy, that the
" voice rises upon this monosyllable twelve enharmonic intervals
" or quarter tones, but falls only seven. Such syllables he very
" properly calls *circumflex*; and he has made a distinction of
" them, which no grammarian ever made, but which, for any
" thing I know, may be well founded in the use of the English
" language; into those circumflexes which begin with rising and
" end with falling; and those which, *vice versâ*, begin with
" falling and end with rising. And the observation he has
" made on the circumflex † of the monosyllable *oh!* that it does
" not fall so much as it rises by five quarter tones, is also an
" observation, I am persuaded, entirely new, and such as could
" have been made only by a man of so nice an ear, and so accu-
" rate an observer, as Mr. S——.

† This and the following marks refer to the answers hereafter given to these observations.

§ 2. But

§ 2. "‡ But still it remains to be considered, whether there
"be any difference with respect to tone, betwixt the accented
"and unaccented syllables of words in English; that is to say,
"whether the voice does not rise or fall in its tone, or do both,
"upon what is commonly called the accented syllable, as upon
"any other. Upon this point, I hope, Mr. S—— will take the
"trouble to inform me. If it be true, that there is no difference
"in this respect betwixt the accented and unaccented syllables in
"English, then I am in the right in saying, that it is only loud-
"ness or softness in the pronunciation which distinguishes these
"syllables from the rest;—that it is by this variety, and this
"variety only, that all the various kinds of verse are made in
"English, more various than the verse of any other language in
"Europe; because none of these languages has its syllables so
"much distinguished in that way: whereas in point of tone
"there is not, I believe, any great difference betwixt them and
"the English. This is a matter of some curiosity, and I hope
"Mr. S—— will think it worth his while to consider it atten-
"tively.

§ 3. "As to the Greek accents Mr. S—— supposes, that the
"voice rose by slides up to a fifth, which made the acute accent,
"and fell down again upon the next syllable in the same way;
"and that in the circumflex accent it slid up and down
"upon the same syllable. I was much inclined at first to
"reject this hypothesis, and to suppose, that the voice rose at
"once upon the acuted syllable, and fell at once to the grave,
"as commonly happens in music; but upon studying attentively
"the passages which I have myself quoted from the ancient
"writers,

" writers of mufic, *videlicet*, Ariftoxenus and Gaudentius (vol.
" II. p. 286.), and likewife from Dionyfius Thrax. *(ibid.* p. 278),
" which I fee is obferved by Mr. S——, I am fully convinced, that
" in founding the acute accent in Greek the voice rofe by flides
" to a fifth, and fell again upon the next fyllable in the fame
" manner; and that it both rofe and fell in that way upon the
" circumflex accent; and that this way of rifing and falling was
" the principal diftinction betwixt the melody of fpeech and of
" mufic. Upon this fuppofition, the pronunciation of the Greek
" language will not be fo like chanting, as it would be, if the
" voice had rifen at once to a fifth upon a fingle fyllable, and
" will be much liker the pronunciation of our Englifh, though I
" think it is impoffible to deny, that it was much more mufical.
" For upon every word of Greek that was not an enclitic, the
" voice rofe a fifth, which is certainly not the cafe in Englifh,
" though I do not deny, that the tone of a whole declamation,
" or perhaps of one fentence of it, may, by fmall intervals, rife
" even higher; and perhaps upon one fingle paffionate word,
" fuch as *oh!* the tone may come near a fifth. And indeed I
" think we need no other proof of the Greek language being
" more mufical than ours, than that it was a beauty in their
" compofition to arrange their acute and circumflex accents, fo
" as to make a variety in the melody of their language agreeable
" to the ear. See what I have faid upon this fubject, p. 380. *et*
" *feq.* of vol. II. Now this is a beauty of compofition unknown
" in Englifh. And fo much for the *melody* of fpeech, confifting
" of the mixture of *acute* and *grave,* to which, as Mr. S—— very
" properly obferves, the word *accent* ought to be intirely appro-

" priated,

" priated, that being its true etymological signification. I have
" indeed used it in its common meaning in English; but, I think,
" I have always distinguished it from accent, properly so called,
" by the addition of *English* to it, or some other expression,
" which, I hope, has removed all ambiguity, though I acknow-
" ledge that it were better that different things were distinguished
" by different names; and that, in treating a subject scientifically,
" so much complaisance should not be shewn to vulgar use as to
" confound different things under the same name. I will there-
" fore for the future, use Mr. S——'s terms of *light* and *heavy*,
" which correspond very well to the ancient terms of *arsis* and
" *thesis*.

§ 4. " Besides *acute* and *grave*, Mr. S—— observes in common
" speech three things; videlicet, *light* and *heavy*, *forte* and *piano*,
" or *loud* and *soft*, under which are included *swelling* and *dying*
" *away*, being modifications of loud and soft; and lastly, *long*
" and *short*. ‖ Now as I am no musician, I am not able to
" make the distinction betwixt *light* and *heavy*, and *loud* and *soft*;
" and though I have consulted more than one of the greatest
" musicians here, I cannot discover the difference; nor do they
" seem to me to understand it any more than I do, even in music.
" And as to words, I cannot conceive how the *heavy*, or accented
" syllable, as it is commonly called, should be sounded *soft*, or
" the *light* syllable *loud*. I can indeed conceive how the whole
" sentence may be pronounced in a softer or louder voice; but
" still the *heavy* syllable will be *louder* than the rest, and the *light*,
" *softer*. Now I hope Mr. S—— will take the trouble to explain this.
" As to the difference betwixt *short and long* (that is, *quantity*), and

" light

" *light and heavy*, I perfectly agree with him: and I am also
" convinced, that we have not only long and short syllables in
" English; but that some syllables are four times as long as
" others, even without the vowel or diphthong, being lengthened
" by position; that is, by the addition of consonants in the same
" syllable; and so I find Mr. S—— has marked some of them in
" the notation that he has given us of the music of some sen-
" tences. It was not so in the learned languages; for there,
" though a long syllable was made somewhat longer by the
" addition of consonants, and a short syllable shorter by the
" taking them away, a long vowel was always to a short vowel
" in the ratio of two to one; for a long vowel was just the short
" vowel twice pronounced. But we are not to expect that a
" barbarous language such as the English, not formed by rules
" of art, should be so regular in its pronunciation.

" Upon the whole, it is my opinion, and I find it is the
" opinion of all the musical men here to whom I have shewn it,
" that Mr. S——'s Dissertation is a most ingenious performance.
" It is reducing to an art what was thought incapable of all rule
" and measure; and it shews, that there is a melody and rhythm
" in our language, which I doubt not may be improved, by
" observing and noting what is most excellent of the kind in the
" best speakers. In that way I should think that both the voice
" and ear of those who do not speak so well might be mended,
" and even the declamation of our best actors may be improved,
" by observing in what respects they fall short or exceed; for as
" soon as a thing is reduced to art, faults will be found in the
" best performers, that were not before observed. If ever I publish
                                                    " another

" another edition of my second volume, I shall certainly make
" that part of it, which treats of the melody and rhythm of
" speech, more perfect from his observations, if he will allow
" me to make use of them. It is true what he observes, that I
" have, in explaining that matter, gone to very general prin-
" ciples, and made many divisions of the subject, more perhaps
" than are necessary for practice; but I profess to give the philo-
" sophical principles of every part of language, and, as I see
" that Mr. S—— is a man of a philosophical turn, as well as a
" practical musician, I must beg the favour that he would let
" me know, if he thinks I have erred in the philosophy of that
" part of language."

LETTER to the AUTHOR of the ORIGIN and PROGRESS of LANGUAGE, at EDINBURGH.

London, March 17, 1775.

I CONFESS it is a long time since my much esteemed friend Sir J. P. communicated to me the *Queries and Observations* made by your l——p on my little treatise concerning the melody and measure of speech: observations that do me great honour, and at the same time impress me with the highest opinion of your candour and condescension, in adopting a system so contrary to what your l——p and many other great men have so ably advanced.

Temporary and unavoidable business has prevented me hitherto from giving the attention that was absolutely necessary in order to give your l——p satisfactory answers to your doubts.

The method I have taken for that end is this: I have read over the 5th chap. of book ii. vol. II. of your very learned and ingenious work, and have set down my further remarks thereon, referring generally to the page; after which, I again read over and considered your l——p's remarks and queries, and thereupon added such explanations as I thought would remove all difficulties. From which, together with the re-consideration of the treatise, I hope your l——p will comprehend my meaning in full.

In the study of music, as in common arts, an artist can attain a much more apparent degree of perfection, without knowledge in the theory, than a theorist can without practice in the art.

Hence it happens, that the carpenter who works, unconscious of the science, under the rules of geometry, though he cannot demonstrate a single proposition, is, in the eyes of the vulgar, a more valuable man than a perfect geometrician.—The practising musicians are often without a tincture of the theory; for to excel to a certain degree in playing, and even to compose in taste, are both far short of that theory in which your l—p has entered very deep. The greatest part of the skill of some great masters is derived more from practice and *instinct*, than from the study of first principles; therefore I do not much wonder that your l—p had not satisfactory answers to your inquiries among them.

The desire your l—p expresses, to make use of my treatise in a re-publication of your excellent system, does me too much honour to suffer me to make the least objection.

I am about to print privately a few copies, somewhat more enlarged than that your l—p had, in order to submit it to the judgement and correction of my friends; among whom, I shall be very happy if you will permit me to count your l—p.

I am, &c.

PART

PART III.

FARTHER REMARKS ON THE ORIGIN AND PROGRESS OF LANGUAGE, VOL. II. BOOK II. CHAP. 5.

PAGE 304. " This rhythm (with found) is of two kinds; " for it is either of founds not articulated, which may be " called mufical rhythm; or it is of founds articulated; and that " is the rhythm of language."

REMARK.

Language is articulated by fyllables; and MUSIC is articulated by a divifion of any one found into many or more than one found; as fuppofe the femi-brief equal in duration of time to the fwing of a pendulum of 160 inches, to be put as the complement of a bar in mufic; it can be articulated into two minims, or four crotchets, or eight quavers, Therefore the femi-brief being a continued found of one whole bar's length; and its feveral fub-divifions into two, four, and

and

eight notes, being also each of them a whole bar's length, and unisons with the semi-brief; so are they, properly, sub-articulations of the original semi-brief.

Speech is necessarily articulated by syllables, in as much as two syllables cannot possibly be sounded or pronounced, without articulating or dividing the tone, under which they are to be sounded, into two parts, at the least; for if the word *folly* were to be sung under the tone of [♩], the singer must necessarily divide that tone into two articulated parts, as [♩♩] or [♩.♩]. I have said, into two parts at least, because when words are joined with music (in the modern stile) even syllables, by the aid thereof, are capable of being variously and minutely articulated, as [musical notation] which, independent of music, they

" *what a fol - - - - - - ly !*"

are not. A division of notes, which are unisons with each other, is a division simply by articulation. Those which are not unisons, but either ascend or descend, are divided both by articulation and modulation.

Page 305. and 306. " And first it is evident, that without
" some change of one kind or another in the sound, there could
" be no rhythm, &c. — In order, therefore, to know the nature
" of rhythm, when applied to sound, we must consider the
" several changes and modifications which sound admits. The
" first

" firft and moft fenfible variation, is when the found ceafes
" altogether, &c."

REMARK.

Our animal exiftence being regulated by our pulfe, we feem to have an inftinctive fenfe of *rhythmus*, as connected with, and governing, all founds and all motions; whence it follows, that we find all people feel the effects of *rhythmus*, as they do thofe of light and warmth derived from the Sun; fo that, without fearching for the reafon, it has generally been paffed over as a firft principle, or felf-evident truth. The fwing of the arm, and other fuch motions, made by public fpeakers, are derived from their inftinctive fenfe of *rhythmus*, and are, in effect, beating time to their orations. Alfo curfing, fwearing, and many other unmeaning words, fo frequently interwoven in common difcourfe, are merely expletives to fill the meafure, and to round each rhythmical period.

From this inftinctive fenfe of *rhythmus*, when we mean to meafure either motions or founds continued, articulated, or interrupted by fhorter or longer paufes, we muft pre-fuppofe an exact periodical pulfation, as regular as the fwings of a pendulum, the velocity of which periodical pulfation we may vary according to our pleafure, as often as we would chufe to quicken or flacken the movement; and then all continuation of founds or paufes are to be fubferviently meafured and regulated by this uniform and fteady pulfation, as long as that proportion of pulfation (or pendulum) fhall be continued.

Page 307. " The queftion then is, what changes continual " found admits of, and what are the rhythms thence arifing?

" And there is one obvious change which very strongly strikes
" the sense; namely, that from *louder* to *softer*, or *vice versâ*."

REMARK.

The variety of *loud* and *soft* should never be considered as (necessarily) a governing principle of *rhythmus*; because though it may, sometimes, be accidentally coincident with rhythmical pulsation, yet it would be offensive if it continued so for any considerable length of time: for the application of *the loud* and *the soft*, both in music and language, either for use or ornament, must not be indiscriminate or periodically alternate, but as occasion calls for it; whereas the rhythmical pulsation is regularly periodical and constant as the swings of a pendulum, but of itself implies no noise or sound at all. And agreeable to this, a band of musicians are much better governed in their measures by a *silent* waving of the hand, or of any thing that may catch the eye, than by the more ordinary *noisy* way of beating time with the foot.

The expressions, or rather the affections of *heavy* and *light* are necessarily the governing principles of *rhythmus*; for they are as constantly alternate and periodical as the pulse itself, and they must be continued, by conception in the mind, during all measured rests or pauses, as well as during the continuance of either uniform, articulated, or modulating sounds.

The affections of *heavy* and *light* were always felt in music, though erroneously called by some moderns *accented* and *unaccented*; however, the *accented*, or *heavy note*, was never understood to be *necessarily loud*, and the other *necessarily soft*; because if it were so, there could be no occasion for separate directions, where to apply the *forte* and *piano*, in as much as the affections

of

of *heavy* and *light* are continued in every *cadence* of every air, from the beginning to the end: whereas the *forte* and *piano* are often applied directly contrary to *heavy* and *light*; as in the following example, almost all the *heavy notes* are *piano*, and the *light notes*, *forte*.

Therefore the distinctions of *loud* and *soft* must not be reckoned among the governing powers of *rhythmus*, though they may sometimes accidentally, or occasionally, coincide with the *heavy* and *light*, which are the true and only governing principles of it.

Page 310. — " That sound which continues any length of
" time, we call a *long sound*; and that which continues a short
" time, we call a *short sound*. And as this quality of sound
" depends intirely upon the time of its duration, it is commonly
" known by the name of *time*."

REMARK.

This is not what is called *time* in music. *Time* is measured by *pulsation*, quicker or slower. The *pulsation* of any one sort of *time* must continue as uniform as the swinging of a pendulum of a given length; but the intervals between the *pulses* of the pendulum may be filled variously.

As,

As, for example:

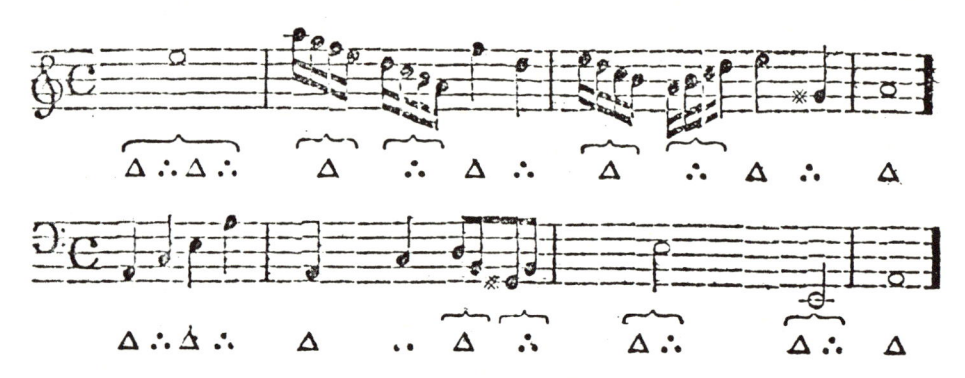

Supposing thefe four bars of mufic equal to four fwings of a pendulum, the whole is but one fort of *time*, notwithftanding the fub-divifion, or articulation, in the feveral bars, is different; and confequently, there is a great variety of *longer* and *fhorter* (that is, of *quantity*), without any difference in the *time*, *meafure*, or *rhythmus* of the tune. If this fame tune is to be played fafter, the length of the bars muft be meafured by a fhorter pendulum; and if to be played flower, by a longer pendulum.

The foregoing fpecimen is of the genus of *common time*, where the *cadences* or *pulfes* are divifible by the even number two. The following example is of the other genus, called *triple time* (or *meafure*); becaufe the *cadences*, or metres between the *pulfes*, are divifible by the odd number three. In this example the modulation and harmony fhall be the fame as in the former; but the melody will be different by the change of the *rhythmus*, or *meafure*, or *time*.

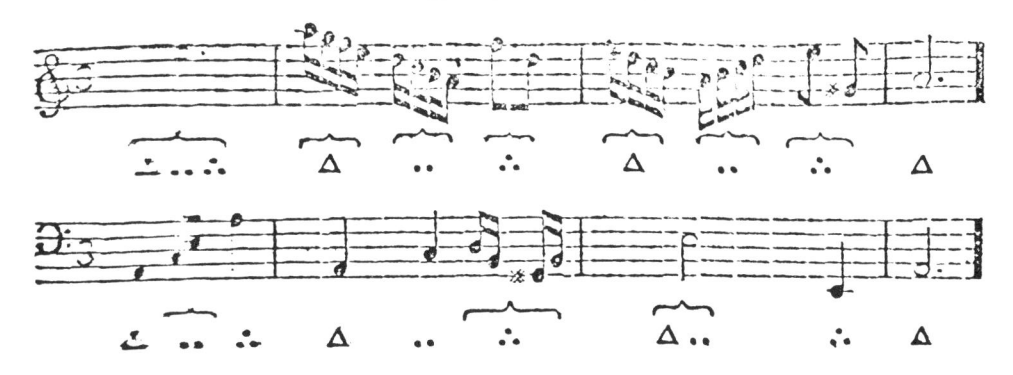

Page 312. "— In the harpsichord, the notes are all of the "same length, without the distinction of long or short;— nor "has it what is properly called *time*, but its whole music is a "jingle of sounds differing in acuteness and gravity, and diver- "sified by different pauses and stops, or different degrees of "quickness and slowness."

REMARK.

The notes of the harpsichord and of all pulsatile instruments have the same allowance made for the duration of their tones, that instruments sounded by the bow, or by inspiration, have. For though in the harpsichord, the loudness of the tone, from the first moment of percussion, diminishes very fast, nevertheless it is still sounding, and the player is, by rule, obliged to keep the finger on the key, corresponding with each note, during the length of time which that note should continue; for the instant the finger is removed, by the construction of the instrument, a damper falls on the string and stops the farther vibration. And moreover, the harpsichord being contrived for playing, at once, several different parts in harmony, is much more capable of

keeping

keeping the player in true time, than any single instrument, such as flute or violin; for, as in the two last preceding examples, whilst the treble in the first bar consists only of one continued sound, the same bar in the bass is so sub-divided as to shew exactly how long the single sound of the treble is to be continued.

Page 313. " —— Long and short —— and this is the fifth and
" last species of rhythm. For if the mind perceives any ratio
" betwixt sounds, with respect to their length and shortness,
" then it has the idea of this kind of rhythm, which, in music,
" is commonly called *time*; but in language the ancient authors
" call it by the name of the genus, *rhythm*; whereas in modern
" authors, it is commonly distinguished by the name of
" *quantity*."

REMARK.

RHYTHMUS is a general term, and is divided into *two general modes* of *time*, *common* and *triple*; each of which is sub-divided into specific differences of *faster* and *slower*; consisting of cadences whose metres may be uniform or *mixed*, *even* or *pointed*. The diversities of *uniform* or *mixed*, *even* or *pointed*, arise from the different manners of subdividing and disposing the *quantities* contained in the whole of each cadence or bar.

QUANTITY, or duration of sounds, distinguished by *longer* and *shorter*, is subservient to the cadences of rhythmus, as fractional or aliquot parts are to integers; and it is the business of *metre* to adjust the *quantity* of notes or syllables contained in each *cadence* or *bar*; *rhythmus* is to keep, by its *pulsation*, all the

cadences

cadences of an equal length. *Long* and *short* notes or syllables are the common component parts of all metres of all *cadences* under all kinds and species of *rhythmus*; that is, each *cadence* under any species of either of the general modes may be metrically sub-divided into fractional or aliquot parts.

As this *cadence of common time,*

may be sub-divided uniformly into

or thus, the two genera of common and triple measure may be mixed,

or thus, pointed,

or thus, even,

or any other way, so that the fractions, being aliquot parts, shall altogether make up the whole quantity of the *bar* or *cadence*. And in the like manner, this bar or cadence of triple measure,

may be uniformly divided into

or, by dividing it into two equal parts, the two genera are virtually mixed,

or thus, into a pointed metre,

or thus, even,

Even and uniform are the same, but are considered under these two different terms, in respect of the *metres* to which they are opposed, *mixed metre,* and *pointed metre.*

Page 313 and 314. " Now all motion is either interrupted
" by *paufes* or *intervals*, or it is without fuch interruption. If it
" be interrupted, either the *intervals* are greater or lefs, or the
" diftances between the *intervals* are greater or lefs. And hence
" arife the two firft kinds of *rhythm* I mentioned, belonging to
" the *intervals* of found."

REMARK.

The *intervals* or *paufes* between founds do not neceffarily conftitute any regular diftinction of *rhythmi*, or *modes of time*: for the *pulfes* of *cadence*, as well as its fub-divifions of *heavy* and *light*, are to be counted on in the mind, during the paufes or intervals, as well as during the continuation of found. (See the feveral examples in this treatife.)

Page 318. " —— Here, as in accents, or notes of mufic, there
" is nothing abfolute, but all is relative; for there is not, nor
" cannot be by nature, any fixed ftandard for the length or
" fhortnefs of fyllables. All therefore that art can do, is to
" afcertain the ratio that a long fyllable has to a fhort. And this
" the grammarians have fixed to be as two to one. And thus all
" fyllables in Greek and Latin, compared together, are either of
" equal length, or in the ratio of two to one. It is not, however,
" exactly true, that all fhort fyllables are of equal length, or all
" long; but fome fhort fyllables are fhorter than others likewife
" fhort, and fome long fyllables longer than others. But in the
" metrical art, this difference is not attended to, and all the
" fhort

" short syllables are held to be equal to one another, and all the
" long."

REMARK.

We have *standards* both for *accent* or *quantity*; as thus, for *accent*; bring two voices, or two instruments, or any two sounds, into *unison* with each other,—that *unison* is taken as a *standard* or *key note*; from which, either upward or downward, all relative sounds are measured by our scale, with accuracy. As a *standard* for *rhythmus* by *cadences*, and their sub-divisions in *quantities*, we have the *pendulum*, or the *human step*, instead of the pendulum.

In our treatise, we have marked out a more accurate proportion between longer and shorter syllables than that recommended by our Greek masters; and we have shewn the necessity of it in *our language*, more especially in *our poetry*. For if the rhythmical and metrical rules, as there laid down, are attended to, there will be little or no occasion for clipping off syllables in any good poetry, which our best authors have hitherto practised, though, as I think, needlessly. For example:

3 | To | all in | fer'or | animals | 'tis | giv'n,

| T' en | joy the | state al | lotted | them by | heav'n.

[76]

Why not write these two hexameters thus?

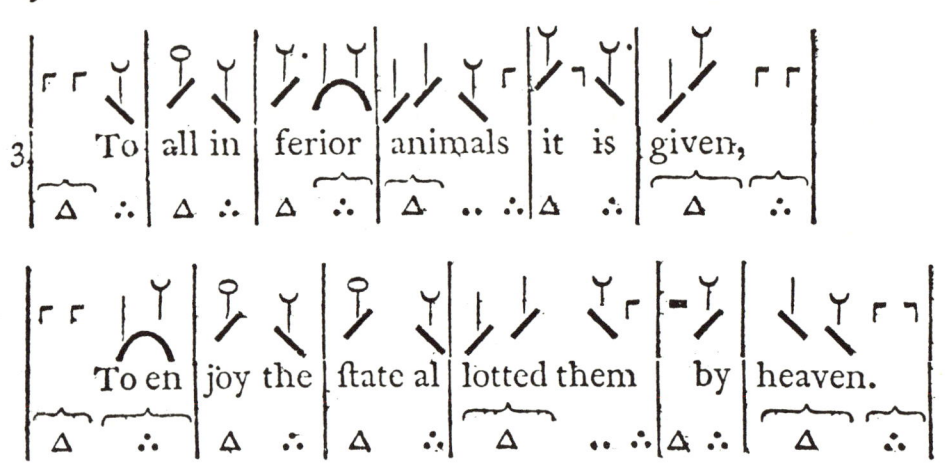

3. To | all in | ferior | animals | it is | given,

To en | joy the | state al | lotted them | by | heaven.

Each line is still measured by six bars or *rhythmical cadences,* and the syllables, now restored, are provided for, without injuring the metre of the *cadences,* by sub-dividing their *quantities* into as many aliquot parts (not exceeding the integer of each *cadence*) as are required for expressing the recovered syllables, within the time of the *bar* or *cadence* under which they fall.

Page 326. "— Our verse made by accent and not by "quantity.—— Take for example the first verse of the *Paradise* "*Lost*; *Of man's first disobedience, and the fruit.* Here the five "accented syllables are, *man's, dis, be, and, fruit.*"

REMARK.

Poetry is often read in a certain formal manner, supposing the ten syllables of *our heroics* must be cut exactly into five *cadences* of two syllables in each, or of four whole and two half *cadences*; whereas they always require the *time* of *six cadences* at least; but those

4

thofe who have only the idea of five *cadences*, feldom attend to the neceffary *refts* or *paufes*, or to a nice *metrical* fub-divifion of the *cadences* according to the natural and neceffary *emphafis* (or *poize**) and *quantity* of each fyllable; and therefore frequently mifplace the *light* and the *heavy*.

To give the proper expreffion to the firft lines of *Milton's Paradife Loft*, I humbly conceive, they fhould be noted thus.

3| Of | man's | firft difo | bedience, | and the | fruit of | that for- |

| bidden | tree, | whofe | mortal | tafte brought | death | into the |

| world | and | all our | woe; | fing, | heavenly | Mufe. |

Page 316. "I fhall fay nothing further of this mufical " rhythm, except to obferve, that the ancients were very accu- " rate in it, as in every thing elfe; for they meafured it by feet,

---

* I fhall take the liberty for the future to appropriate this word *poize* as a common term for the △ *heavy* and the ∴ *light*, as *accent* is for *acute* and *grave*, and *quantity* for *long* and *fhort*.

" as

" as they did the rhythm of their language, and had dactyls
" and spondees, and the like in their music, as well as in their
" poetry."

REMARK.

As I consider our sense of *rhythmus* to be much more *instinctive* than *rational*, I am of opinion, that the ancient Greeks might have been practically as excellent in that part of music, as the moderns; but, from any thing I have read, I cannot think they had so accurate a manner, of describing or noting it, as we have. Their distinctions, by various feet, compared with our musical rhythmus, seem, many of them, only serving to puzzle, without any real difference as to measure. Our rules, which reduce all the possible species to two genera, are obviously more excellent, because more simple; of which I have given some examples in the foregoing treatise.

I am of opinion, that no language was ever spoken under so confined a proportion of *quantities* as two and one, for the *long* and the *short*; and yet those commentators, who hint at a greater latitude, have mentioned no rule of proportion except the two and one: neither have they left us any sufficient or satisfactory rules for *rests* or *pauses*, without which neither poetry or prose can be graceful or just in its expression.

Aristides, it is true, says, κενὸς μὲν ὃν ἐςι χρόνος, lib. I. p. 40.; that is, " There is a vacant or *silent time*, which is left without any sound
" to compleat the *rhythmus*. The *shortest silent time* in *rhythmus* is
" called *leimma* or a remnant; and a *long silent time*, double to
" the short, is called *prosthesis* or an addition." And he had said just before, " That where in the *rhythmus* of mixed feet, a foot
" happened

" happened to be insufficient to fill the *metre*, the vacancy was to
" be supplied by a *silence*, either of a *leimma* or of a *prosthesis*."

This, however, is all he says of it: though, as it agrees perfectly with my system, it is sufficient to convince me, that the accidents of *rhythmus* belonging to our language, were also the same to the Greek. But as those grammarians who composed the treatises of prosody now in use, have made no rules or allowances at all for *rests* or *silences*, it is to be presumed it was not intelligible to them, or they would never have omitted so material a part, both of *rhythmus* and *metre*. And further it is plain, that determining Greek and Latin heroics, such as the Iliad and Æneid, to be hexameter lines, excludes *rhythmical pauses* altogether.

For example, to set the first four lines of the Æneid in our notes, strictly according to the Latin prosody, they will be thus, in common time:

Arma vi	rumque ca	no Tro	jæ qui	primus ab	oris
I ta li	am, fa	to profu	gus, La	vinaque	venit
Litora;	mult' il	l' et ter	ris jac	tatus et	alto
Vi supe	rûm, fæ	væ memo	rem Ju	nonis ob	iram.

[80]

Here is no room for variety of metre, nor a moment's paufe even for breathing, each line being ſtrictly confined to the ſix *metres* or *cadences*. I have ſet the lines above, according to their quantities preſcribed by the rules of profody; but it is fit I ſhould alſo ſhew them as they are generally ſcanned in our ſchools; where, by making the laſt ſyllable of the dactyl longer than the firſt (in direct contradiction to the real quantities), they turn dactyls into anapeſts.

| Ar ma vi | rumque ca | no Tro | jæ qui | primus ab | or is. |

If I could meet with a living Virgil, I ſhould aſk him, why theſe lines might not be ſet in the following manner, in triple meaſure, ſtill preſerving the *long* and the *ſhort* ſyllables, but with an extended variety of *long* and *longer, ſhort* and *ſhorter*, and alſo with the proportion of *triples* and *thirds* as well as of *doubles* and *halves?* And if he gave me a better reaſon why they ſhould not, than either the grammarians or the commentators have done, I would certainly ſubmit to him, and copy his manner of pronouncing exactly, in *accent* as well as quantity, which would moſt probably be quite new to all Europe.

3 | Arma vi | rumque ca | no, | Tro | jæ qui | primus ab | oris

I ta li | am, | fa to profu | gus, | La | vinaque | venit

Litora

[81]

Litora; | multum il | le et ter | ris jac | tatus et | alto

Vi supe | rûm, | sæ | væ memo | rem, Ju | nonis ob | iram.

In this manner, the *multum ille* and the *ille et* are pronounced without any *elision*, and without any injury either to the *rhythmus* or to the *metre*, the *cadences* being all *dactylic*, under which title *spondee* is legally included. And with the addition of necessary rests for breathing time, and for stops of *expression**, these lines are *octometres* instead of *hexameters*.

It is proper I should say something for the liberty I have taken here, in varying the proportions of the syllables in the *dactyl*.

It is notorious, that this foot is so called from *dactylus*, a *finger*; because, as Isidorus says (De Gram. lib. I. c. 16.), "It "begins from the longer joint, and ends in two short ones." It is certain the longest member of a finger is about equal in length to the two shorter; but it is also certain, that the lengths of the bones of the three joints of a finger are nearly in proportion to each other, as three, two, and one; consequently, three,

* I would explain myself here by a better word, if I could find one; but if a *pause* or *silence*, fitly employed, makes a significant impression on an auditor, it may be admitted as an expression in the speaker.

the longest, is equal to the sum of two and one (the two shorter) added together. Now though I do not say there is, to my knowledge, any natural or necessary analogy between the proportions of our members and the measures of our words; yet, as *Aristides* says (δάκτυλος μὴν ὂν ἐκλήθη, &c. lib. I. p. 36.), "It is called "*dactylus*, because the order of its syllables is analogous to the "parts of a finger;" and the proportions I give the syllables in the *dactyl* according to my alteration, being agreeable to *Aristides*'s definition, I might stand upon this, as my authority. But it does not appear, the Greeks had any method of notation which set the *dactyl* in that order; and therefore I do acknowledge, I had no other authority for what I have done, than the judgment of my own ear, in estimating the *quantity* of syllables, and the *euphony* of language. I have taken the same liberty with the *anapæst* or *anti-dactyl*; and sometimes, under the same judgment, have put them both as the Greeks did.

I will set a few lines of the Iliad in like manner.

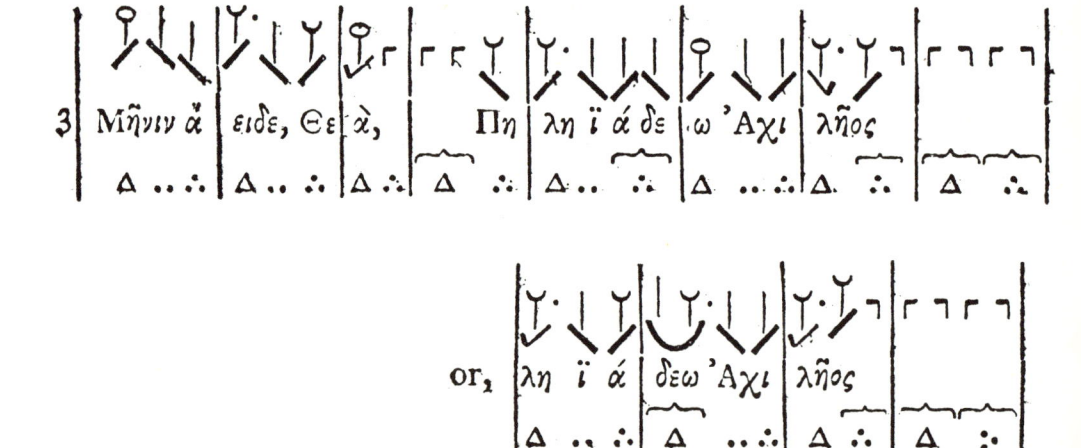

3| Μῆνιν ἄ | ειδε, Θε | ά, | Πη | λη ϊ ά δε | ω 'Αχι | λῆος

or, | λη ϊ ά | δεω 'Αχι | λῆος

Οὐλομέ-

Οὐλομέ | νην, | ἣ | μυρί' Ἀ | χαιοῖς ἄλγε' ἔ | θηκε·

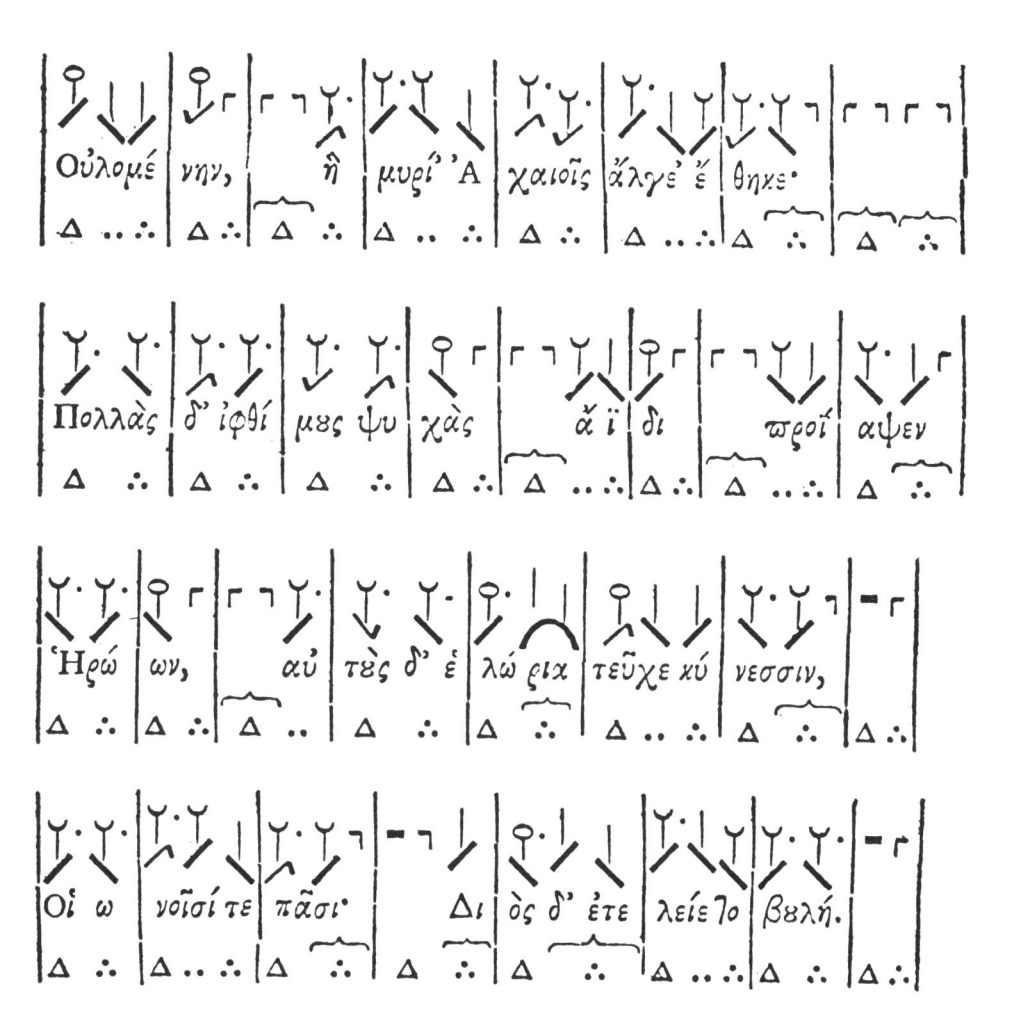

Πολλὰς | δ' ἰφθί | μȣς ψυ | χὰς | ἄϊ | δι | προΐ | αψεν

Ἡρώ | ων, | αὐ | τȣς δ' ἑ | λώρια | τεῦχε κύ | νεσσιν,

Οἰ ω | νοῖσί τε | πᾶσι· | Δι | ὸς δ' ἐτε | λείε]ο | βȣλή.

In setting these lines, I have followed authorities as far as I could find them; the rest I must take upon myself. We have Eustathius's authority for the two manners of disposing of the extraordinary syllable in Πηληϊάδεω; in either of which, ways, he says, " the tetrasyllable is to be considered only as a dactyl." However, it was strictly, in either way, a pæon, either a first or a second; and was a point of dispute among commentators: in our method it admits of no difficulty, whether it be tetra-

syllable

fyllable or trifyllable; in either way it is accommodated to the time of our cadence.

I think, from the examples I have given in the three languages, it may be inferred, either that the Greek and Latin poetry had not fo regular a *rhythmus*, fuch even *metres* (that is, *cadences*), nor fo great a variety in their *quantities*, as our language has; or that the ancient grammarians did not write the laws of their profody up to the genius of thofe learned languages; or that the rules of that art have been tranfmitted to us in a very imperfect ftate.

SOME FARTHER EXPLANATIONS, in ANSWER to the REMARKS and QUERIES made by the AUTHOR of the ORIGIN and PROGRESS of LANGUAGE.

† See Observations, page 57. § 1.

THE extent and form of circumflexes are very various in our language; two or three quarter tones more or less make little difference in the sense of their application. By the rules I have given, and the examples under them, I do not mean to give models of pronunciation; but to shew how any particular pronunciation may be fixed in characters, and transmitted to posterity.

I suppose there are as many different circumflexes as there are different tempers and features in men; to save words, I will exemplify some by notes:

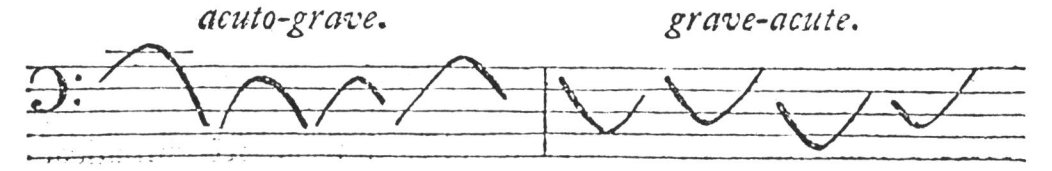

acuto-grave.   *grave-acute.*

The circumflexes, *acuto-grave*, are characteristic of the Irish tone; and the circumflexes, *grave-acute*, are characteristic of the Scottish tone.

The dialectic tone of the court and other polite circles rises but little above a whisper, and may be compared to that species of painting, called *The Chiaro Oscuro*, which is denied the vivacity of expression by variety of colours. There, the circumflex, though it cannot be left out of the language, is used within very narrow limits: frequently not rising or falling above

five

[86]

five quarters of a tone, and for the moſt part hurried over with great velocity, in the time of a quaver, or ſhorteſt note.

But, in the Court language, there is no argument; for in the Senate, and where that is uſed, the extent of the ſlides are enlarged to the extreme, though the circumflex is never ſo apparent as in the provincial tones.

Example of a familiar Engliſh interjection, uſed when a perſon is convinced by the relation of ſome new circumſtance not mentioned in the argument before. The whole extent of this interjective circumflex, between acute and grave, does not exceed 17 quarter tones (excluſive); whereas in ſome of our provincial dialects, the expreſſion on a ſimilar occaſion would run to an extent of 29 or 30.

‡ See page 58. § 2. " But ſtill it remains to be conſidered, " whether there be any difference with reſpect to tone, betwixt " the *accented* and *unaccented* ſyllables, &c."

Here I muſt take the liberty to diſcard theſe ſoleciſmatical terms of *accented* and *unaccented*, as they are notoriouſly repugnant to what we mean to expreſs; and, in their ſtead, to uſe the terms of *heavy* and *light*.

Then it is evident, from the ſeveral examples I have given, that in Engliſh the *heavy ſyllable* has ſometimes the *grave accent*, though oftener the *acute*; and that the light ſyllable has ſometimes the *acute accent*, though oftener the *grave*.

In

In our language, generally, the laſt ſyllable of any imperfect ſentence (while the attention is to be kept up, for the ſenſe of the whole, yet in ſuſpenſe,) ends in the *acute*; and all compleat periods end in the *grave*.

Queſtions, though in the ſame words, are ſometimes ſimple, and ſometimes tacitly implying a threat, or ſome condition, not otherways expreſſed than by *accent* and *emphaſis*. As for example,

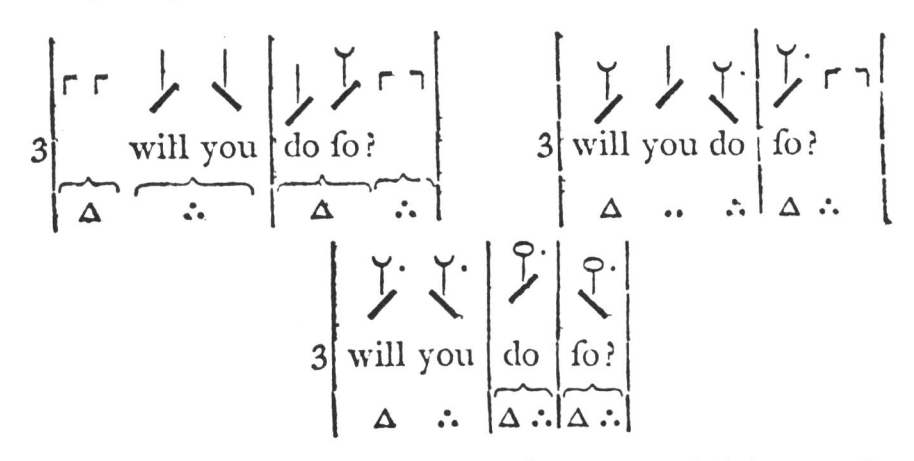

[musical notation: 3| will you | do ſo?   3| will you do | ſo?]

[musical notation: 3| will you | do | ſo?]

Now I ſay, that the affections of *heavy and light* are the moſt eſſential governing powers of *rhythmus*; for, ſince the accents, *acute*, *grave*, and *circumflex*, are common both to the *heavy* and to the *light*;

And ſince quantity, or the *long* and the *ſhort*, are likewiſe common to each;

And ſince the accidents of *loud* and *ſoft* are alſo common to each;

And laſtly, ſince the accidents of *accent, loudneſs,* and *quantity*, occur not periodically, but occaſionally, whilſt *cadence* is ſtrictly *periodical*, and divided into *heavy* and *light* alternately; which affections are to be accounted for in the mind, whether *ſounding or pauſing*, continued or articulated,

It

It follows, that *heavy* and *light* (as the certain alternate division of cadence) are the most essential governing powers of rhythmus both in poetry and prose.

The same thing, viz. *heavy* and *light*, which govern rhythmus in our language, governed it also in the Greek: for Aristides says, τὸν μὲν ῥυθμὸν ἐν ἄρσει κ̓ θέσει τὴν ἐσίαν ἔχειν· τὸ δὲ μέτρον ἐν συλλαβαῖς, κ̓ τῇ τέτων ἀνομοιότητι. (Meib. vol. II. p. 49.)

That is, " *Rhythmus* has its essence in (∴) *arsis* and (Δ) *thesis*; " but *metre*, in syllables, and in the variety of dissimilar sylla- " bles." I shall shew hereafter how far the Greek *metres* and our *cadences* are alike; and how they differ.

‖ See page 60. § 4. " Now as I am no musician, I am not able " to make the distinction between *light* and *heavy*, and *loud* and " *soft*, &c."

I have made several remarks, and have given musical exam- ples, in order to distinguish clearly the difference between *heavy* and *loud*, and between *light* and *soft*, which I will endeavour to illustrate further by a familiar example, in two words.

Suppose a man speaking to his mistress in the words, " MY " DEAR!" *Dear* being, in this place, put substantively, is abso- lutely affected to the *heavy*; therefore those words must be noted to be pronounced thus, " MY | DEAR." Suppose the conversation
∴ | Δ
to have begun in the ordinary degree of loudness, and at the instant he has pronounced *My*, a person appears in sight, who ought not to hear the next syllable, the speaker can instantly
soften

soften his voice, even to a whisper, though still the word will carry its proper emphasis, and remain *heavy*; so that to write those two words, as directory to an actor, they should be noted thus,

MY | DEAR!
forte. piano.

As the ancient Greeks, as well as their language, are all dead, I do not wish to be drawn into a comparative contest about them. I am sure I should be overborne by the number and abilities of their champions; for as nobody envies the dead, they have always, on these occasions, more friends than the living. I am ready to believe that they had many rules of art that are now unknown to us. If any persons of genius and assiduity think it worth their while to pursue the tracks my hints point out, they will perhaps find, that the just rules of melody and measure are as natively applicable to our language as to the Greek; though, from our too frequent terminations on mute consonants, and on the letters S and M, our language is far less melodious than theirs, and infinitely inferior, in that respect, to the modern Italian.

LETTER from the AUTHOR of the ORIGIN and PROGRESS of LANGUAGE to the AUTHOR of the TREATISE on the MELODY and MEASURE of SPEECH.

"April 6, 1775.

"I COULD not delay longer acknowledging the favour of
"your very polite and obliging letter, and thanking you moſt
"heartily for the attention you have been pleaſed to beſtow upon
"my work, and the excellent obſervations you have made upon
"it. It was chiefly with a view to ſet ſuch men as you a
"thinking upon ſuch ſubjects, that ſeemed to me new and
"curious, and to learn their thoughts upon them, that I came
"to the reſolution of publiſhing; and it has anſwered as to both
"volumes. For upon the firſt, I have got ſo many obſervations
"from different hands, as have enabled me to make a much
"larger, and, I think, a better book of it in the ſecond edition,
"of which I beg that you would accept of a copy, that I will
"order to be delivered to you; and if you will take the trouble
"to read it, and ſuggeſt to me your obſervations, I may profit
"as much by my errors in it, as I have done by thoſe in the
"ſecond volume.

"I have made ſome obſervations upon the valuable papers
"you have ſent me, and propoſed ſome doubts that ſtill remain
"with

"with me. * * * * The whole is exceedingly ingenious, and
" by the notation you have invented may be made very use-
" ful; particularly that part of it which marks the highest
" pitch of tone that the best speakers rise to in declama-
" tion without canting. To distinguish these two exactly is, I
" believe, a matter of great nicety, and what, I believe, some
" * * * * * * * * * * * are not well able to do. And
" one particularly * * * * * * * * *, I heard Mr. G— men-
" tion; who, he said, when he reasoned, pronounced better
" than any body; but when he declaimed, fell into an abomi-
" nable cant.

" What you have said of the pauses too, I think, may be of
" great use; for they certainly ought to be in just proportion to
" what is spoken, otherwise the speech can never be truly grace-
" ful and harmonious.

" I am very glad to hear from our worthy friend Sir John that
" your experiment upon Mr. Garrick's declamation succeeded so
" well. Actors are the only artists that cannot eternize them-
" selves by their works; but you have fallen upon a way to
" make Garrick live as long as his Shakespear.

" I am, &c."

TO THE AUTHOR OF THE ORIGIN AND PROGRESS OF LANGUAGE.

April —, 1775.

I AM favoured with your l—p's very obliging letter of the 6th inſtant, together with the two volumes; for which be pleaſed to accept my thanks.

A rumour of the ſubject of my little treatiſe having ſpread much farther than I could have imagined, * * * * I have laid aſide my intention of privately printing ſome copies, and have committed it to the public preſs. Lord — told me, he had heard of it at Geneva. * * * * * * I muſt beg your l—p's liberty to publiſh your paper of queries and obſervations, on which my laſt explanations were founded, as it will ſave me much trouble, and clear up the ſyſtem much better than it could be done without it. I hope your l—p's next queries will come in time, ſo that my anſwers to them may be able to compleat the whole. * * * Nothing can tend ſo much to elucidate any ſubject as the queries of an ingenious doubter.

I am, &c.

TO THE AUTHOR OF THE TREATISE ON THE MELODY AND MEASURE OF SPEECH.

"May 14, 1775.

"YOU have inclosed my remarks, which are too long; but
"as you defired them foon, I had not time to make them
"fhorter. I am glad that you are to give your fyftem to the
"public. * * * * * As to the queries and obfervations I fent
"you formerly, and have now fent you, you may make what
"ufe of them you think proper; and if they contribute in the
"leaft to make more compleat fo ingenious a performance, I
"fhall think they do me honour.

"I am, &c."

SECOND SET of OBSERVATIONS and QUERIES by the AUTHOR of the ORIGIN and PROGRESS of LANGUAGE.

"I WILL begin with stating those things in which we agree, or rather those things which I have learned from you; and then I will beg leave to propose some doubts that still remain with me; but which you may be able to solve, as you have done some of those I have already stated.

§ 1. "And in the first place, I am convinced that there is a natural propensity in the human mind to apply number and measure to every thing we hear; and indeed to every thing, as it is a necessary operation of intellect, being that by which intellect creates to itself its proper objects. For, though sense perceives things indiscriminately, and as it were in the lump, intellect apprehends nothing that is not reduced to number, measure, or order of some kind or another. And as this propensity of the mind is previous to any opinion or determination of the will, I think, you properly enough call it *instinctive*. This is undoubtedly the foundation of all rhythm; and as I have pretended to go to the bottom of things, and have for that reason taken a compass, which others, I know, as well as you, think too great, I ought certainly to have taken notice of what is the natural principle of all rhythm.

§ 2. "Secondly,

§ 2. "Secondly, I am therefore of opinion, that we cannot
"listen attentively, for any considerable time, to any sound,
"whether musical or not, without endeavouring to apply some
"measure to it, and to divide it into parts equal, or that have
"some other ratio to one another. For if we consider it only as
"continued, and without division, we have no idea of number or
"measure; for, as Cicero says, *Numerus in continuatione nullus*
"*est: distinctio, et æqualium et sæpe variorum intervallorum per-*
"*cussio, numerum conficit.* But the question is, how do we divide
"it? and what measure do we apply to it? To which I think it
"may be answered in general, that it must be some pre-con-
"ceived standard, or measure, of which we have formed an
"idea, and which we have been in use to apply to other things:
"thus we measure time by the usual standard of hours, half-
"hours, quarters, and minutes; and it is surprizing how accu-
"rately some persons will do this, merely from the idea they
"have in their mind of those measures, especially such as are
"not in use to consult clocks or watches. There are also other
"ways of measuring time, such as that which Horatio, in
"*Hamlet*, mentions, when he says, that the ghost staid with
"them, while one, with moderate haste, could count a hundred.
"But this, and every other way that can be imagined, of mea-
"suring time, must necessarily refer to some pre-conceived
"standard.

§ 3. "Thirdly, To apply this to music, I am now fully con-
"vinced, that every man, who considers a piece of music
"attentively, and with any degree of knowledge of the art,
"must necessarily divide it into parts, greater or smaller; and
"particularly

"particularly into *bars*, which is a measure by which every tune
"is divided into equal parts. And I am also convinced, both
"from the reason of the thing, and the experience of my ear,
"that the note which begins each bar, and which you call the
"*heavy note*, is not necessarily either a loud or a soft note, a high
"or a low, a long or a short note; nor does it appear to me to
"have really any pulsation or ictus, except what the mind may
"suppose it to have, when it makes it the leading note of the
"bar. But here I am at a loss to know how the * length is
"determined of these equal portions into which the mind is
"pleased to divide the tune. Why are they not greater? or
"why are they not less? To what pre-conceived standard does
"the mind refer in this division? It may be my total ignorance
"of the practice of music, that makes me have this doubt; but
"if you think you can satisfy me with little trouble, I hope you
"will be so good as to do it. In the mean time I would beg
"leave to suggest that of all the motions which you have men-
"tioned, as a natural standard for the measure of a bar, the step
"and pace appear to me the aptest; and where the bar consists
"of two notes, a light and a heavy; or of four, *viz*. two heavy
"and two light, the movement appears to me to be very like a
"step, or two steps, in ordinary walking. ‡ But I observe, that
"the mind naturally divides some tunes, particularly Scotch
"tunes, into many more notes, which are all connected toge-
"ther by one pulsation, real or supposed, and so make one bar.
"There I find it difficult to resolve the bar into steps or paces,

* This and the following marks refer to the answers hereafter given to these particular parts.

"whether

" whether of a sound or a lame man; and I should think, that
" in such a case the mind fixed upon some measure, suitable
" indeed to the genius of the tune, but such as has no standard
" in nature.

§ 4. " I am convinced, that the ancient music must have been
" divided, as well as the modern, into bars; and that the *arsis*
" and *thesis*, of which they speak so much, must have referred
" to such a division.

" I am obliged to you for your observation upon the inaccu‑
" racy of my expression, with respect to the harpsichord. If I
" had said, that there is no difference of length in the notes,
" while they continued invariably the same; that is, with the
" same degree of intenseness without dying away, I believe it
" would have been the truth; but I have expressed the thing too
" generally. I might have added further, in dispraise of the
" harpsichord, that it is incapable of what I think a very great
" beauty in music, and that to which it owes a great part of its
" expression, I mean the swelling of the note. But though I
" think it be not a pleasant music in itself, it is most useful for
" the purpose you mention, of keeping a concert in time.

§ 5. " As to what I have said of *time* in the passage you
" mention, I do not speak there of the time of music in parti‑
" cular; but I should think, that the duration of any sound may
" be called its *time*. I believe, indeed, musicians do not call
" the length or shortness of the particular notes, compared with
" one another, the *time of a tune*; but the length or shortness
" of syllables is, in the language of those who treat of the
" metrical art, the time of the syllables. In the language of

" music,

" music, I observe, that the word is used in a sense a good deal
" different from its natural and proper signification; for, instead
" of denoting the duration of the movement, it denotes the
" nature of it, according to the division which you have made of
" it into *common* and *triple* time.

" This is all I have to observe upon your music; in which if
" I did really differ from you, I should be ashamed to own it.
" As to language, your intention appears to be, to apply to it
" the rules of musical rhythm, and particularly to divide it into
" bars, without distinction, whether the syllable beginning the bar
" be a long or a short syllable, loud or soft, or whether the tone
" of it be high or low; and you compute the pauses, which the
" sense requires, to make part of the bars. It is, I think, a
" noble attempt; for as musical rhythm is exact and regular,
" being reduced to rule, and comprehended in the art; if we
" could apply it to speech, we should certainly measure it more
" exactly, and make it more truly rhythmical and numerous.
" That it may be done, at least in some degree, and that it will
" have this effect, I have little doubt; but that it hitherto has not
" been done, not even in the learned languages; and that it has
" been as yet made no part of either the grammatical or rhetorical
" art, I think I can take upon me to aver with some confidence.

" For as to the learned languages, and particularly the Greek,
" which was by far the most learned of the two, I mean the
" language of greater art, there are two things belonging to
" composition in that language, which their critics have distin-
" guished accurately, not jumbled together as modern authors
" have

" have done under the name of *profody* (*a*); I mean melody and
" rhythm. The firſt is, that muſic which was produced by
" the proper mixture of grave and acute tones in their language,
" ſo as to have a pleaſing effect on the ear. The other aroſe
" from the combination of long and ſhort ſyllables in what they
" called *feet*, by which they made their proſe, as well as their
" verſe, numerous, ſo as to affect the ear wonderfully, according
" to the deſcription they give of it.

§ 6. " As to their melody, you have convinced me that I was
" in an error, when I ſuppoſed that the acute accent roſe at once
" to a fifth upon one ſyllable, and fell down again precipitately
" upon the next. I now ſee clearly, both from the reaſon of
" the thing, and from authorities which I myſelf had collected,
" but not well underſtood, that their voice in ſpeaking was
" never at reſt as in muſic, but was conſtantly ſliding up and
" down, and was only at the higheſt upon the acuted or circum-
" flected ſyllable; after which it fell gradually, till it roſe again
" to the ſame pitch upon the next acuted or circumflected
" ſyllable. But I have ſome doubt, whether upon every grave
" ſyllable they began acute and ended grave. I rather incline
" to think, that upon the ſyllable next following the acute,
" the voice would begin to fall †, and continue falling upon that,
" and perhaps upon the next after that, till it came within a
" ſyllable or two of the next acuted ſyllable, and then it would
" begin to riſe gradually, till it arrived at its height upon that
" ſyllable. This ſeems to me to be the ῥύσις, or *flow*, of the
" melody of ſpeech mentioned by the ancient grammarians and

(*a*) See what I have ſaid upon this ſubject, vol. II. p. 271. 275. and 382.

" muſicians,

"muficians. But I fhall be very glad to be further inftructed by
" you upon this fubject

§. 7. " Before I leave this fubject, I muft repeat an obferva-
" tion I have elfewhere made (b), that when I fpeak of the accents
" or tones of the Greek language, I mean only fyllabical tones,
" which were appropriated to particular fyllables of each word,
" according to certain rules delivered by the grammarians; not
" the tones of paffion or fentiment, which did not belong to
" fyllables, but to words and whole fentences. Thefe made a
" principal part of the player's art, which was much ftudied,
" and in great reputation among them. But whatever the tone
" was that paffion or fentiment dictated, the accents or fyllabic
" tones were ftill obferved as an effential part of the grammar of
" the language. As to the variety of loud or foft, it muft have
" been in their language, as well as in ours; but it was not affected
" to fyllables ||, as with us, but belonged to words or fentences.

§ 8. " As to what they called the rhythm of their language,
" which was compofed of the quantity of fyllables, you feem to
" think, that the refpective length of their fyllables was not
" fufficiently fixed; and that the long fyllable was not to the
" fhort as two to one. And that it often was the cafe, that the
" long was not exactly in that ratio to the fhort, is certainly true;
" and we are fo told by their grammarians and critics. But then
" you are to confider, that the length or fhortnefs is properly in
" the vowel, on the vocal found, not in the confonants with
" which it was enounced. Now it is laid down, by all the
" writers upon the metrical art, and I have always held it to be a

(b) Vol. II. p. 277.

" rule

" rule that suffered no exception, that a long vowel was to a
" short as two to one. By the consonants indeed, either pre-
" fixed or following the vowel, the pronunciation of it will be
" so much retarded, as to make a long vowel longer; and if two
" consonants follow after it, they will, you know, make a short
" vowel long; or, to speak more properly, the syllable long.
" But the preceding consonants, and even a single consonant
" following, though they no doubt varied the quantity a little,
" yet that passed for nothing; and all hexameter verses were
" reckoned of the same length, though some of them necessarily
" must have been in reality longer than others. For you know,
" that there are many things in all arts, even in music, which I
" hold to be a more perfect art than language in this matter of
" rhythm, which affect the senses, and yet are not reduced to
" rule, and perhaps, by their nature, cannot be reduced to
" rule.

" It is by these feet that the ancients divided the continuity
" both of their verse and prose. These, if you please, you may
" call *bars*, and I think they would be peoperly so called; because
" I am persuaded, the beginning of them was marked, at least
" in their poetry, by the *supplosio pedis*, and from thence, as you
" very ingeniously observe, they had their name. But there
" was this difference betwixt those bars and such as we have, and
" I believe they had, in music, that they did not divide the
" speech equally, except in certain kinds of verse, such as
" hexameter; but on the contrary, the variety of feet of
" different times was reckoned a beauty in their prose compo-
" sition. That they had no other division or measure of the

" rhythm

" rhythm of their language than thefe feet, or bars, if you
" pleafe to call them fo, I think, is certain; otherwife, I think,
" it is impoffible but fuch writers as Ariftotle and the Halicar-
" naffian, who have all treated fully of the rhythm and numbers
" of their language, would have mentioned it.

" As to the paufes or refts which the fenfe require, I under-
" ftand they treat of them when they fpeak of the various
" lengths of periods, and their feveral members. But it feems
" they did not reckon filence any part of the rhythm of lan-
" guage, though, I think, it may be very properly fo confidered
" in language as well as in mufic: and I am convinced, that no
" language, whether profe or verfe, can be agreeable to the ear,
" if paufes are not properly adjufted and commenfurated to the
" words. The variety of paufes, even in their poetry, by which
" the verfe was broken into feveral parts, like a period in profe,
" is praifed by the Halicarnaffian *(c)* as a beauty, in the fame
" manner as the variety of paufes in Milton's blank verfe is
" commended by our critics.

" And in this way, I think, there muft have been a great deal
" of rhythm as well as melody in the Greek language, if rhythm
" be, as I have defined it, vol. II. p. 302. " A certain relation
" or analogy, in refpect of length or duration, which the
" mind perceives betwixt founds or motion of any kind." For
" the ratios of the metrical feet of the ancients to one another
" are various. The ratio of the *fpondee* to the *dactyl* is that of
" equality; the ratio of the *fpondee* or *dactyl* to the *pyrrhichius*
" is as two to one; of the *pyrrhichius* to the *tribachys* as two to

(c) See vol. II. Diff. iii. p. 560.

" three;

" three; of the *tribachys* to the *spondee* as three to four, &c.
" And if you want any other measure of the ancient poetry
" besides the feet, you have the verse itself, at the end of which
" there was always a pause greater or less; the consequence of
" which was, that the last syllable, though by its nature short,
" was considered as long. And this by the bye shews, that the
" pauses, according to your notion, stood for something in the
" measure of the ancient verse; and that perhaps, not only in
" the end of it, but in any other part of it, if the sense required
" a pause. And I have a fancy, that many difficulties in the
" versification of Homer might be solved in that way, though no
" critic, as far as I know, has thought of such a solution.
" Concerning this I will enquire further when I have more
" leisure. And so much for the melody and rhythm of the
" Greek language.

§ 9. " As to the melody of our language, I once thought that
" there was no tone in it, but what was either provincial, or
" what belonged to some passion, humour, or sentiment. But
" you have convinced me, that even when we speak in the
" plainest manner, and as much upon a level as possible, still
" there is not a perfect monotony; but the voice is perpetually
" sliding up and down, more, as you observe, in public speaking,
" or even the conversation of men from the country, less in the
" conversation of men bred at court. ✸✸ But our accents differ
" from the Greek in two material respects. First, they are not
" appropriated to particular syllables of the word, but are laid
" upon different syllables according to the fancy of the speaker,
" or rather as it happens; for I believe no man speaking English

" does,

[104]

" does, by choice, give an accent to one syllable of a word
" different from that which he gives to another; but he varies
" from necessity, not being able to keep his voice upon different
" syllables, perhaps not upon the same syllable, at the precise
" same pitch of tone. Secondly, the tone in common conver-
" sation in English, when we speak without passion or declama-
" tion, never rises so high as a fifth, at least as far I have
" observed; and, though some speakers may vary their voice
" so much, I am persuaded it is not common: whereas in Greek
" every man, who spoke the language properly, raised his voice
" to that pitch upon certain syllables and no other, whether he
" was speaking with passion or without passion, and whether he
" was haranguing or in ordinary conversation; for it was part of
" the grammar of the language, and a man would have been
" accounted a barbarian who spoke otherwise(d). From these
" so material differences, I think, it follows, that our accents
" never can be reduced to rules of art, as the Greek were, or
" made part of the grammar of our language; far less can they
" be made a beauty in our composition as they were in the Greek.
" Nay I do not think that we could venture to mark the accent
" upon any single word taken by itself, unless perhaps it were
" an interjection, such as *oh!* All we can do is to observe how,

(d) Relative to this there is a remarkable story told by the Scholiast upon the oration of Demosthenes περὶ Στεφάνυ. He tells us, that Demosthenes in asking the question of the judges, Whether Æschines was the *friend* or the *hireling* [μισθωτός] of Alexander barbarized on purpose [ἐβαρβάριζε], by laying the accent upon the last syllable instead of the first. Upon which the people, as was natural enough, corrected him by repeating the word properly accented. This he took for an answer to his question; and, says he, you hear, Æschines, what they say, ἀκύεις ἃ λέγυσι.

" in

" in certain compofitions of words, either in verfe or profe, the
" beft fpeakers accent particular fyllables. And even among the
" beft fpeakers it will be found, that as to the precife degree of
" the accent there is a great difference, and perhaps in the fame
" fpeaker at different times; fo that I fhould think it were almoft
" impoffible, even in compofitions of words, to mark precifely
" the accent of each fyllable, though, if it be poffible, you have
" fallen upon a very ingenious way of doing it. †† Upon the
" whole therefore, I am of opinion, that very little can be made
" of the accents of our language; and that to obferve them at
" all, is more a matter of curiofity than utility.

" There is in our claufules, or ends of our fentences, not only
" a fall of the voice, but alfo, I think, a change of tone. This
" may be accounted part, and it appears to me the principal part,
" of the melody of our fpeech: for if it be neglected, the ear,
" as you obferve, is cheated, and it really is very offenfive. An
" exact notation how much the voice is let down in the con-
" clufion of periods, with refpect both to loudnefs and tone,
" according to the practice of the beft fpeakers, might, I think,
" be very ufeful; for I have obferved, that many fpeakers offend
" in this article; fome keeping up their ends too high, to ufe a
" phrafe of Mr. Bayes; fome letting them down fo low as not to
" be diftinctly heard; fome changing the tone too much, and
" others too little. And fo much for the melody of our
" language.

§ 10. " As to the rhythm of it, I think it muft confift in one
" or other, or all of the four following things: the quantity of
" the fyllables; the variety of loud and foft; the paufes; and

" laftly,

" lastly, your division into bars. And I shall consider all the
" four; first with regard to our prose, and then with respect to
" our verse.

§ 11. *(vide answer to § 7.)* " As to quantity; though we have
" undoubtedly in our language some syllables much longer than
" others, yet I have always been of opinion, that it made no part
" of the rhythm of our language; and that it was a vain attempt
" to endeavour to reduce our compositions to metrical feet. And
" I am much confirmed in this opinion by observing, that you
" lay no weight upon the quantity with regard to rhythm,
" though you have taken the trouble to note it. Two reasons,
" I think, may be assigned for this. The first is, that the ratio
" betwixt the short and long syllables is by no means ascertained,
" as it was in the ancient languages. The second is, that by far
" the greater number of our syllables appear to be of the same
" length, as much as the different beats of a drum. I say,
" *appear*, for I would not be understood to mean, that there is
" not betwixt most of them, some small difference of lengths,
" discernible by a nice ear, like yours, but is altogether imper-
" ceptible to a common ear, and therefore must go for nothing
" in the composition either of our verse or prose; whereas in
" the learned languages the difference was so great, that a false
" quantity in pronunciation was, as we are told, offensive to the
" meanest of the people.

§ 12. *(vide answer to § 7. ||.)* " As to the variety of loud and soft
" in the syllables of the same word, it is a distinction which I see
" you admit; and indeed it is in English so perceptible to every
" ear, as to distinguish our language most sensibly not only from

" the learned languages, but, I believe, from every other modern
" language in Europe, as I am sure it is from the French. It
" has not, however, been attended to in our prose composition;
" and though, I think, it might even there make some kind of
" rhythm that might be agreeable, yet I do not know that it
" would be a beauty worth studying.

§ 13. *(vide my answer to § 10.)* " It is the third thing I men-
" tioned, namely, the pauses, that, in my opinion, make the
" chief, if not the only, rhythm of our English prose. If these
" be not properly attended to, and the style properly divided into
" periods, and members of periods, of different lengths, varied
" likewise by pauses, shorter or longer, the composition will be
" altogether without numbers, and will never be approved by a
" good ear; and, as speaking is the best trial of composition, this
" defect will chiefly appear when the performance is read or
" spoken. But though I insist so much upon the variety of the
" pauses, as well as the whole structure of the composition, I do
" not deny, that there should be likewise sometimes an uni-
" formity; and that sometimes periods, and members of periods,
" of the same length, sometimes with words answering each to
" the other, will now and then be agreeable. This was a figure
" well known to the ancient masters of art, and was too much
" practised by some of their orators, particularly Isocrates; but
" was more moderately used by Demosthenes, who has joined in
" his style great variety, and at the same time uniformity, with
" respect to his pauses, as well as every other part of his com-
" position.

"The last thing belonging to the rhythm of our language I
"proposed to consider, was your method of dividing our prose
"into equal parts, which you call *bars*. That this has hitherto
"never been practised in English is a fact most certain; but that
"it is practicable I have no doubt, as I can see nothing in the
"genius of our language that forbids it. And if it be true, as
"it undoubtedly is, that there can be no rhythm without
"measure, a method which contrives to measure the whole
"composition, the pauses or intervals, as well as the sounds,
"should contribute very much to make the composition rhythmi-
"cal and numerous. Of such a rhythm, I believe, every person
"who had an ear would feel the effect, though very few would
"be able to assign the cause, which you know is generally the
"case in all the popular arts. And so much with respect to the
"rhythm of our prose.

§ 14. "As to our verse, there is one part of its rhythm
"which every body perceives, and that is the equal length of
"the verses. That arises from their consisting of the same
"number of syllables; ten, for example, in our hexameter verse.
"Nor can this be dispensed with; for even a pause, however
"long, will not supply the want of a single syllable.

"2dly, In our rhyming verse, and particularly in Mr. Pope's,
"there is a kind of rhythm produced by the stop or cæsure,
"about the middle of the verse, of the same kind with that of
"the French long verse. This I have always thought a blemish,
"both in our verse and the French; for it makes the compo-
"sition, which was before too uniform, by being in sentences
"of a certain determined number of syllables, still more tediously
"uniform.

"　uniform. And I approve much more of our blank verse, which
" only stops where the sense requires it, besides the advantage it
" has of running the sense of one line into another; a privilege
" which our rhyming poets of former times used, but which is
" now given up. This division, therefore, of verse into hemi-
" stiches is not an essential property of our versification, any
" more than the rhyme; but the first I mentioned; *viz.* the
" number of syllables is essential, so that there cannot be verse
" without it. And I am now to mention another, which I
" likewise hold to be essential; and that is,

(*The same as* § 7. ‖.) " 3dly, The mixture of loud and soft
" syllables, and the percussion at certain stated intervals of the
" loud syllable. This is so essential to our verse, that, if the
" sense require that an emphasis should be laid upon the soft
" syllable, it evidently mars the verse. Thus, if in reading the
" first line of the *Paradise Lost*, you were to lay an emphasis
" upon the word *first*, which by no means is necessary, the verse
" would plainly halt, and be different from the succeeding verse,
" where the syllable *for*, of the word *forbidden*, which answers
" to the word *first* in the preceding line, must necessarily be
" sounded soft. And it is a beauty in our versification, when
" the emphasis, which the sense requires, and the *forte*, which
" is necessary to the verse, coincide, as I have observed (*e*) in those
" famous verses of Denham upon *Cooper's Hill*, " Though deep,
" yet clear, &c." And as this mixture of loud and soft is peculiar
" to our verse, so it is also peculiar to our language; distinguishing
" it, as I have observed, not only from the learned languages, but

(*e*) Vol. II. p. 389.

" from.

" from every other modern language in Europe, as far as I know.
" I should therefore have thought it strange, if it had not entered
" into the composition of our verse.

§ 16. " The two things, therefore, that, in my opinion,
" constitute our verse are, the number of syllables, and the
" mixture of loud and soft, according to certain rules. ‡‡ As to
" quantity, it is certainly not essential to our verse; and far less
" is accent.

" As to your method of dividing our poetry into bars, like
" music, it is exceedingly ingenious; and I have no doubt that
" it will be useful in poetry, as well as in prose, towards forming
" a just ear. But it is to be observed, that the rules of music
" will not apply to our verse in this respect ||||; that the pauses,
" as I have observed, cannot stand for any part of the verse, nor
" supply the place of a single syllable; whereas in music, the
" pauses make bars, or parts of bars. At the same time, these
" pauses are a very great beauty, particularly in our blank verse,
" filling up a considerable part of the time; and therefore are
" very properly considered as a part, at least, of the time of the
" verse, if not the verse itself ✱✱✱.

" As to the comparison you make betwixt the melody and
" rhythm of the English language and those of the Greek;
" although you have shown that there is more of each in the
" English language than is commonly believed, yet I cannot
" think, that our language will bear comparison with the Greek
" in this any more than in other respects. As the excellence of
" their grammatical art admitted of a great variety of arrange-
" ment; ††† and as certain syllables of certain words had parti-
" cular

" cular tones appropriated to them, they had it in their power, by
" different compositions of those words, to mix those tones, so
" as to make a music agreeable to the ear, and which accordingly
" is observed by their critics as one of the beauties of their com-
" position. Now, I think, it is certain, as I have already
" observed, that our composition can be little or nothing im-
" proved in that way. And as to rhythm, we have not what
" they called *rhythm* ‡‡‡, arising from a certain composition of
" long and short syllables; and therefore we are obliged to make
" our verse in a manner quite different from theirs; that is, by
" the number of syllables, and the mixture of loud and soft: a
" way which we may think preferable, because our ears are not
" formed to their rhythms; but which I cannot bring myself to
" think, is near so numerous as their versification. ||||| In short,
" the Greek language was the work not only of grammarians and
" philosophers, but of musicians; for the Greeks excelled no less
" in music than in other arts, and applied it very much to the
" improvement of their language: whereas the Romans, whose
" musical parts (to use an expression of my lord Shaftesbury)
" were not near so good, though they spoke originally the same
" language, did not cultivate it so much in any respect, and
" particularly did not improve the sound of it so much as the
" inhabitants of Greece did. Our language, on the other hand,
" is the production of unlearned, popular use, corrupting a
" better language, out of which it has grown; I mean the Saxon,
" which again is a corruption of the Gothic. This degeneracy
" of the art of language, as well as of other arts, is, I think, to
" be accounted for from the nature and history of man; and I

" will

" will endeavour to do it, in the laſt part of my work, wherein
" I am to treat of the decline of language, if ever I ſhall execute
" it. For the preſent it will be ſufficient to obſerve, that in the
" art of muſic, which you underſtand ſo well, if we can believe
" the teſtimony of all the ancient authors who treat of it, there
" is a wonderful falling off; for the *diatonic,* which we now uſe,
" was only the muſic of the vulgar among them; whereas the
" muſic of the connoiſſeurs and the men of taſte was the *chro-*
" *matic,* and particularly the *enharmonic.* If you think it worth
" while, you may ſee what I have further ſaid upon this ſubject,
" vol. II. p. 288."

PART IV.

ANSWERS TO THE SECOND SET OF OBSERVATIONS AND QUERIES, BY THE AUTHOR OF THE ORIGIN AND PROGRESS OF LANGUAGE.

IN order to answer so accurate and subtilizing a querist as your l—p, I have endeavoured, from the beginning, to reduce my subject to system. This required a set of pertinent appropriated terms, which were not easy to find, to my intire satisfaction, considering the misapplication of several important words, and particularly of *accent* and *measure*, confirmed by immemorial vulgar use.

ACCENT, I was obliged to compel, as it were, by rude force to its proper duty.

MEASURE, I unwillingly left, in compliance with the vulgar idiom, as a term of the same import with *rhythmus*; and yet, in truth, it should have been confined to the Greek sense of *metre*.

But having adopted CADENCE instead of *metre*, as a word which seems to explain itself to our senses, by intimating the pulsation of time, I shall still continue it in that place; because, though I frequently shew, that *metre* is almost synonymous with

CADENCE, yet they are not quite the same, as I shall explain hereafter.

RHYTHMUS, as it signified with the Greeks *number*; that is, the *number* of *metres* contained in a *line* or sentence; so it may signify with us, the *number* of CADENCES in a *line* or sentence: but I use it also as the general term under which CADENCE is a division, and QUANTITY a sub-division. And when I describe this sub-division of a CADENCE, I say, it is *metrically* divided into such aliquot fractional parts; that is, long and short QUANTITIES, as make up the *intirety* of the CADENCE.

But before we come to the fractional division of the CADENCE, there is an integral division of it to be considered, properly called its METRE, according to which the aliquot QUANTITIES are *metrically* computed and disposed. That is, the CADENCE is either equally divided by the *integral* even number two, or the *integral* odd number three which constitute the two general modes of *metre* (or MEASURE), these two, being the first numbers possible, that occur, for the division of matter. That is, the first possible division of any length is into two parts; and the next possible division is into three parts. But further than these *two modes* of *equal division* nature has never yet gone in the *equal division* of *sensible time*.

For if a CADENCE be divided into four integral equal parts, the number two will still be the divisor, and it will *sensibly* become two CADENCES.

A division into *five equal parts* nature will not admit. (Vide p. 23. and 26.)

A division

A division into six equal integral parts is either the double of three, or the triple of two; and consequently, may be mentally reduced or sub-divided into two *cadences*, or into three *cadences*. And the like of all other admissible divisions; for the divisions of 7, 11, 13, 17, 19, &c. equal parts, are not admissible (P. 23. and 26.)

I have shewn the similitude between the Greek *metres* and our CADENCES; *videlicet*, that the *rhythmus* or number of *metres* made lines, thence called hexametres, pentametres, &c.; so with us, the *rhythmus* or number of cadences make lines, such as octometres, hexametres, &c.

Now I must shew how they differ.

CADENCES, under the same RHYTHMUS, are exactly equal in duration of time to each other, and are commensurable by even steps, or by the pulses of a pendulum.

But the Greek METRES, though nominally under the same RHYTHMUS, are not always of equal length; some being simple METRES of one *foot*, and others compounded by *copula* of two *feet*, of various lengths; consequently, not always reducible within the compass of equal periodical pulsations like our CADENCES.

For CADENCES always begin with *thesis*, or ∆ the *heavy* syllable, and end with *arsis*, or ∴ the *light*; consequently, between step and step, or, musically speaking, between *bar* and *bar*, the whole of each CADENCE is included.

But some Greek *feet*, of which their METRES are composed, begin with *arsis*, or ∴ the light, and some with *thesis*, or ∆ the heavy. And consequently, the Greek METRES cannot always be included,

included, as our CADENCES may be, between the pulses of equal time, such as our *steps*, and such as we mean to mark by musical *bars*; because the pulses, always coincident with thesis, or △ the heavy, would sometimes fall in the middle, sometimes on the beginning, and sometimes obliquely, neither on the beginning nor in the middle, which is the case in almost all the METRES by *copula*, the *bacchic*, the *cretic*, the *pæons*, and the *epitrites*.

The space of time between each pulsation and the next succeeding pulsation, I have called a CADENCE or *bar*, because I usually mark a *bar* at every CADENCE, though in common music, two or more CADENCES are often comprised in one *bar's* length.

The whole time of the CADENCE or *bar* (as aforesaid) must be capable of being equally divided either by the number two, the essential and distinguishing mark of the genus of common measure, or by the number three, the essential mark of the genus of triple measure.

The whole quantity of the time or duration of a CADENCE or *bar* (whether *common measure* consisting of two *integral units*, or *triple measure* consisting of three *integral units*), may be subdivided by *metrical articulation* (in *sound* or in *silence*) into any unequal fractional *quantities* of time, provided their sum altogether be neither more nor less than the *integral quantity* of the said *cadence* or bar. (Vide page 24.)

The term QUANTITY is appropriated to discriminate the relative value of sounds in duration of time, being either the QUANTITY of whole CADENCES, or the QUANTITY of each of the sub-divisions of a CADENCE; that is, it refers to the distinction of *longer* and *shorter* notes or *syllables*, or of longer and shorter *pauses*.

Consequently,

Confequently, the time or duration of every individual found, fyllable, or paufe (in the fub-divifion of the equal or integral numbers of a cadence into unequal though aliquot parts; or the re-union of fuch unequal or aliquot fractions into whole numbers), is called its QUANTITY.

The *inftinctive* fenfe of *pulfation* gives the mind an *idea* of *emphafis* and *emphatic divifions*, independent of any actual increment of found, or even of any found at all. But emphafis and emphatic divifions imply, that there are fome founds of a different nature; that is, that there is a difcontinuance or diminution of emphafis with or without difcontinuance or diminution of found; or, in other words, independent of found. And hence we have the mental fenfation of *emphatic* and *unemphatic*, which I diftinguifh and reprefent by the words and fymbols of ∆ *heavy* and ∴ *light*. (Vide p. 20.) And as a common term to fignify both, I appropriate the word POIZE, in like manner as ACCENT is ufed as the common term for *acute* and *grave*, and QUANTITY for *long* and *fhort*. (See note, p. 77.)

It is the office of RHYTHMUS, aided by the *influence* of this *inftinctive* POIZE, to regulate the whole duration of any melody or movement by an exactly equal and periodical pulfation, until it is thought proper to change the meafure, for fome other uniform pulfation, either quicker or flower.

In the time of the world, a natural day (night included) is a fingle *cadence*; the fetting and rifing of the Sun are the *thefis* and *arfis*; feafons and years are rhythmical claufes: the real beginning and the ending of this melody are out of our fight; but to human apprehenfion, the apparent are birth and death, and life is our part in the fong.

See Obfervations, p. 96. § 3. *. " How is the length of thofe " equal portions, into which the mind is pleafed to divide the " tune, determined? Why are they not greater? or why are " they not lefs? To what previous ftandard does the mind refer " in this divifion? &c."

The beating of our *pulfe*, which we muft feel whenever we are filent and inactive, prones us to *rhythmical divifions* even in the feries of our thoughts; as foon as we begin to move, our *fteps* fucceed in the government of *rythmical pulfation*, and the *meafure* may then be at our *option* fafter or flower; for while we were filent and motionlefs, the *meafure* of our thoughts muft have been regulated by the *cadences* of our *pulfe*, which is an involuntary motion.

Every fingle *ftep*, or every pace, may mark a *cadence*, the putting down the foot being ∆ *heavy*, and the lifting it up being ∴ *light*.

Now it is obvious, that a man walks fafter or flower, either for convenience or pleafure; but I think it as needlefs here as it would be endlefs, to look for the caufes that might be the firft movers in his mind, either of his conveniency or his pleafure in fuch a cafe.

If our *pulfe* is to govern the time or length of a *cadence*, the *thefis* ∆ and *arfis* ∴ muft keep pace and coincide with the *fyftole* and *diaftole* of the heart.

[119]

If the *step* or pace, then between walking and running there is a latitude for a great variety.

But in the *rhythmus* of language, all polysyllables are affected to their *poize* of *heavy* and *light* so positively (and the *poize* determines the *cadence*), that nothing remains in doubt except the difference between the slowest and the fastest speaker. However, that doubt is of no consequence in this argument, since every speaker, if he preserves the proportions demanded by the natural *quantity* and *poize* of the words, must adopt that measure of quickness that the *poize* of the words points out; that is, he must allow himself time to make the difference between long and short syllables: for, as it has been often repeated before, a *cadence* must begin with △ the *heavy* and end with ∴ the *light* (the ∴ *lightest* being only an inferior species of the *light*); or, in other word, as every *cadence* begins with △ the *heavy*, of course the whole of every *cadence* lies between △ *heavy* and △ *heavy*, as often as they occur. For example,

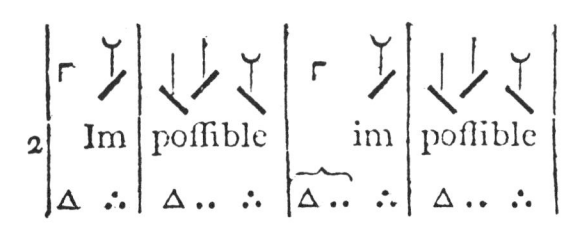

This word in common measure cannot be twice repeated without leaving the *quantity* of half a *cadence* in silence under the △ *heavy*, as the first syllable *im* is under the *light* ∴ *poize*.

In triple meaſure it may be noted thus:

[musical notation with "im | poſſible im | poſſible" in 3 time]

But ſuppoſe a perſon of opinion, that *accent*, *quantity*, and *poize*, were quite arbitrary in modern languages, ſhould deſire them to be varied on this word; for example thus:

[musical notation with "impoſ | ſible | impoſ | ſible" in 2 time]

it is no longer an *Engliſh*, but clearly a *French* word.

Now to return to the anſwer of the queſtion before us, theſe examples ſhew, that though a rapid ſpeaker may repeat three *hexameters*, while a deliberate ſpeaker pronounces only one; yet if they both underſtand the language, and give it its due, each of them muſt allow ſix *cadences* to each *hexameter* line; for it is evidently the language, and the words themſelves, that meaſure and point out the *cadences*.

Theſe examples may alſo ſerve to illuſtrate what is ſaid (in p. 115. and 116.) concerning the difference between Greek *metres* and our *cadences*. For the *Engliſh* words, *impoſſible*, *impoſſible*, are *metres* of two *choriambic feet*; but the *cadences* are *anapæſts* in *common meaſure*, and *Ionici à minore* in *triple meaſure*; as *French* words they are ſpondaic, *metre* and *cadence* all the ſame.

But

But as I propose these new marks of notation to be written with prose or poetry, in order to prescribe any such manner of enunciation to a reader, as the writer shall think proper; the writer may follow his judgement or fancy in fixing the degree of velocity, by marking it for two steps to a second of time, or one step to a second, or more, or less; or he may leave a greater latitude, by marking it *slow walking time, moderate walking time, quick walking time,* or *running time.*

I have shewn in several examples, how easily the two general modes of times, *common* and *triple,* may be intermixed, by varying the *metrical* sub-division of the *cadences,* and without making any alteration in the *rhythmus;* as, suppose a piece marked for *common measure* thus,

Here the mark ⌒3 denotes that the three quavers under that arch, are to occupy only the time of two quavers; consequently, though all the *cadences* are of equal length in time, yet the first and third are in *common* measure; the second in *triple* measure; and the fourth *mixed,* half *triple,* half *common.* Again, suppose a piece marked for *triple measure,* as,

Here the second and 4th bars or *cadences* have evidently the effect of being in *common* measure, as each of them consist of only two

notes of equal length; the first and third *cadences* are evidently in *triple* measure; but all the *cadences* are of equal length, and under one *rhythmus*.

Now suppose a line written and noted, and at the pleasure of the writer the measure to be governed by that of a moderate walk, wherein each step occupies a second of time;

3| Arma vi|rumque ca|no, | | Tro|jæ qui|primus ab|oris

(Here, though the measure is marked *triple*, yet as the two genera are virtually intermixed, the quantity allowed to the *arsis* or the *light* part being by the mark ∴ (which in this case comprehends as many notes as are equal to half the *cadence* or *bar*) made equal in duration of time to (Δ) the *heavy* part, the whole *bar* or *cadence* consists only of one *step*.)

Then let the reader walk and pronounce, putting down (suppose) the right foot to *ar*, lifting up the other with *ma vi*, down again on *rum*, right foot up to *que ca*, down to *no*, the left up under the *pauses* ⌐ ⌐, and down under the *pauses* ⌐ ⌐, the right up to *Tro*, down to *jæ*, left up to *qui*, down to *pri*, right up to *mus ab*, down to *o*, left up to *ris*, left down and the right up to the pauses of ▬ minim and ⌐ crotchet.

‡ See p. 96. § 3. " But I observe, that the mind naturally " divides some tunes, and particularly Scotch tunes, into many " more notes, &c.——There I find it difficult to resolve the *bar* "-into

" into steps or paces.——A meafure,—fuch as has no ftandard
" in nature."

In anfwer to this, I fay, that the (∆) *heavy*, and (∴) *light*, in *common* meafure, where two is the divifor; or the (∆) *heavy*, (..) *lighteft*, and (∴) *light*, in the pure *triple* meafure, where three is the divifor, are to correfpond with thofe integral monads, which determine the genus of the meafure, and not with their various fractional fub-divifions; which, though I think it has been fhewn by examples before, I will here endeavour to illuftrate farther by fome others.

EXAMPLE I.

Very flow walking-time.

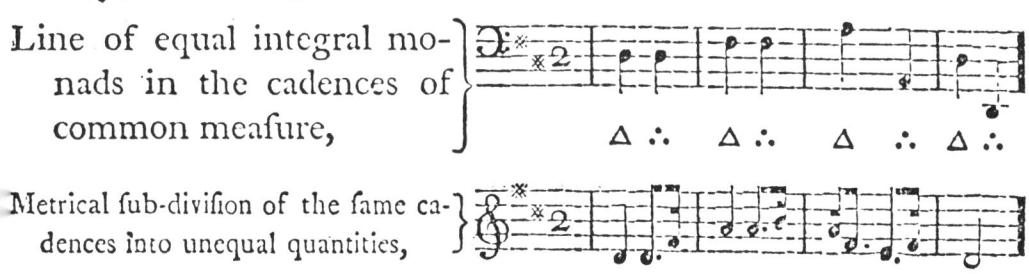

Line of equal integral monads in the cadences of common meafure,

Metrical fub-divifion of the fame cadences into unequal quantities,

EXAMPLE II.

A ftep to a fecond of time.

Or the fame melody thus,

The line of equal integral monads,

[124]

EXAMPLE III.

Example where two steps or a pace make a cadence of triple measure, corresponding with the walk of a lame man.

Three seconds of time equal to a cadence; the thesis of the lame leg equal to △ ..; and that of the sound leg equal to ∴ ...

Line of 3 equal integral monads corresponding with this example,

EXAMPLE IV.

Example of the *pure* triple measure, *one step only to a cadence*, and the time three-fourths of a second to each step.

Vent' anni   fono   foste tro vata qui' abbando nata   da' un Colonello.
△ ... ∴   △ ... ∴   △ ... ∴ △ ... ∴ △ ... ∴   △ ... ∴   △ ... ∴ △ ... ∴

If your l—p had pointed out to me what particular tunes you found, that would not submit to your measurement by steps, I would have given you a demonstrative answer on those very

tunes;

tunes; for I will venture to affert, that there are none in nature that will not fubmit to thefe rules.

When our modern method of notation was firft introduced, and for a long time after, there were no bars thought of; and alfo for many years after the divifion by *bars* was found ufeful, they were rather applied as the marks of *rhythmical claufes* (vide p. 23. and p. 30.) than of *individual cadences*. In Corelli's compofitions they were, for the moft part, fo fparingly ufed, as to be only the marks of *rhythmical claufes:* for inftance, the allegro, called *Giga,* in the eleventh fonata, opera fecunda, of that author, (the meafure of which feems fo difficult to young performers, that it has got the name of the Devil's fonata), has its *bars* marked only at every *fourth cadence;* and the difficulty of keeping the meafure arifes firft, that the *bars* feem as if they were marked, not at the beginning of each apparent claufe, but either on a *cadence* too foon or too late; fecondly, the claufes appear as if they were unequal, as there feems to be in the firft part, three claufes of four *cadences* in each *claufe,* and two of ten *cadences* in each. But the fecond part, which is eafier to be played, is divided into eight *claufes* of four *cadences* in each: however, it cannot be doubted, that the author intended this as a piece of rhythmical drollery; for had the *bars* been marked at each real *cadence,* which in this air confifts of three quavers, the meafure would appear to be the fame as that now ufually marked in the triple meafure *preftos* of modern compofers, and would remove the difficulty fo puzzling to young performers.

The Scotch airs, called *Lovely Nancy, Thro' the wood, laddie,* the Englifh air, *As near Porto Bello lying,* and many others in the like

like ftile, are fet in flow triple meafure of three monads in a *bar* (vide foregoing example, N° III.). But in fact, each *bar* of that flow meafure may be confidered as a *rhythmical claufe* of three *cadences* or fteps of common meafure, each *cadence* or ftep including its △ and ∴ in the fpace of a fecond of time. Thus,

[musical notation with markings: 1ft. 2d. 3d. 4th.]

" *How can you, lovely Nancy, &c.*"

I have marked the beginning of each claufular divifion by thick *bars*, numbered 1ft. 2d. 3d. and 4th. in thofe places where *only* BARS are marked in the ufual way of writing this air in triple meafure, each of thofe *thick bars* comprehending three of our *cadences*; and thefe are truly the natural *cadences* of this air, which demands the △ emphafis as often as I have marked it.

Whether, by what I have faid, I fhall be able to fatisfy your l—p in this point or not, I cannot tell; but I am quite clear myfelf, that every fpecies of rhythmical found can be afcertained by the ftandard of our ftep. And though the various paces of quadrupeds furnifh us with rhythmical movements of jig triples and double *cadences*, fuch as the *ra ta pat* and the *ra ta pa ta* which are not naturally made by bipedes, yet our habit of riding makes us almoft as familiar with the meafures beaten by the paces of horfes as if they were our own.

P. 97. § 4. "I am convinced, that the antient music must "have been divided, as well as the modern, into bars, &c."

If your l——p has found any antient authority to convince you of this, it must convince me too; but until that is pointed out to me, I must remain of a different opinion.

Though the INSTINCTIVE SENSE of *periodical pulsation* is certainly coeval with our animal frame, yet the invention of the *pendulum* has made the moderns more accurate and expert in divisions of time than those antients who had no such help.

I think, if the Greeks had had the same idea and use of *bars* in their music as the moderns have, Aristides Quintilianus would not have been totally silent about them. When he is explaining rhythmus, he says, Μέλος μὲν γὰρ νοεῖται, καθ' αὐτὸ μὲν τοῖς διαγράμμασι, ᾗ ταῖς ἀτάκτοις μελῳδίαις· μετὰ δὲ ῥυθμοῦ μόνου, ὡς ἐπὶ τῶν κρεμάτων ᾗ κώλων.——Ῥυθμὸς δὲ καθ' αὐτὸν μὲν ἐπὶ ψιλῆς ὀρχήσεως· μετὰ δὲ μέλους, ἐν κώλοις. (Meib. vol. II. p. 32.) Which I understand thus: "Song, simply by itself, appears in *written characters* "and in unmeasured melody. And joined with rhythmus alone, "in *pulses* and *feet*.——Rhythmus by itself appears in * naked "(or silent) dancing; but joined with song, in *feet*." I take the word κρέμα (or *pulses*) to signify here the throbbing sounds of instruments struck like the lyre, which could only mark the quantity of each note, but not measure *cadences*. And κῶλα must mean *feet*, the members into which their music and poetry were divided: for if it meant the members made by the cæsure, it was departing from the true meaning of rhythmus, which is number;

* The movement of dancing without, or abstracted from, music.

that

that is, the number of metres or feet in a line. Surely, if they had had any διαγράμματα like our *bars* for marking the (divisions of *rhythmus* into) *metres*, this author would have mentioned them, as well as the *diagrammata* or written characters for the song or melody.

The invention of our modern notes, the figures of which declare accurately their *metrical quantities*, together with the *bars* to mark the *pulses* or *rhythmical divisions*, have rendered the Greek feet totally useless in the practice of our music.

As mechanical instruments for the composition of poetry, the *Greek feet* were ingenious, though intricate and inaccurate when compared with our musical rhythmus; but now, if joined with ours, I conceive, the two together may become useful for the better reading of the antient classics, and perhaps for modern compositions in our own language.

According to our method of *rhythmical* divisions, by *bars* or *cadences*, and by the *metrical* sub-division of those *cadences* into *sub-duples*, *sub-triples*, or any such mixed fractional numbers as are aliquot parts of the whole *cadence*, there are no words or form of words, but what, by the aforesaid rules and the aid of measured *pauses*, may be reduced to an exact *rhythmus*.

Aristides's division of *times* into *rhythmical* and *non-rhythmical*, I understand as meaning to say as I have done (p. 11. 21. 23. 26.); that is, that *rhythmical* time is only capable of being generically divided either by the even number two, or by the odd number three; but that the numbers seven, eleven, thirteen, seventeen, nineteen, &c. are *non-rhythmical* divisors. And perhaps his *rhythmoides*, or *apparently rhythmical times* may correspond

[129]

correspond with the exception which I have made for the number five in *clausular divisions* (page 23.). His sentence, τέτων δὲ οἱ μὲν ϛρογγύλοι καλẽνται, &c. That " some of these are called *round*,
" because they run too fast; and others, *superabundant*, or over-
" measure, because by their composition of sounds they move
" too slow," shews that they had not the use of marked *bars* and marked *pauses* for regulating their rhythmical *cadences* as we have. For in the example so often repeated,

| Oh, | happiness! | our | being's | end and | aim! |

I take *happiness* to be, according to Aristides's sense, a *round* word, as it runs off the tongue before it reaches the end of the cadence; the vacant time of which, however, is made up by the crotchet pause (𝄽), and the *rhythmus* thereby continued without interruption.

The *superabundant* was very likely to happen in Greek in many of their long polysyllabic compounded words, because their *metrical* proportions of *quantity* were thought to be only *two* and *one*; but in our language, according to our system, which admits a much greater variety of *proportional quantities*, I can think of no word not reducible both to *metre* and *rhythmus* in *cadences*.

It seems clear, that the Greek *metres* were raised both in their music and poetry from *syllabic feet*; so that they could admit of no *quantity* of sound, longer or shorter, than what was (as I

S   may

[130]

may say) the *statutable length* of some *syllable*, and that syllable must have been a portion of some *legal foot*. So that, though in their *dactylic measure*, the *cadences* might have been as equal as if they had been marked by *bars*, and measured by a pendulum or steps; yet in their *compound* or *mixed measures*, the *cadences* were unequal, which plainly shews they had not a notion of *bars* like ours, which divide all *rhythmi* into equal *cadences*.

P. 97. § 5. " As to what I have said of time, &c."

Time being a general word of great extent, is used by modern musicians to distinguish the two modes, *common* and *triple*; next to those it distinguishes also the species, *allegro, adagio, largo,* &c. and more particularly minuet, jigg, allemand, ciacone, saraband, &c.; therefore having carried the term *time* far enough, for the rest, it is well to follow the distinction made by the latter commentators, by appropriating the term *quantity* to denote the duration or length of a single tone or syllable. It is certain the Greeks used the word time in music, in a manner directly opposite to the moderns; for they fixed a minimum or shortest note as their standard measure, which they called *one time*; their next greater was two times, the next three times, &c. But they did not conceive any syllable, within the rules of rhythmus and metre, to be of $1\frac{1}{2}$, or $2\frac{1}{2}$, or three times; their Ἡμιόλιόν τε ᾗ ἐπίτριτον (that is, sesquialterate and supertertian), relate only to the division of their *metres* by *arsis* and *thesis*; for example, in a *metre* of five times, giving two to *arsis* and three to *thesis*, or *vice versâ*: and in a *metre* of seven times, giving three to *arsis* and

and four to *thesis*, or *vice versâ*. Still insisting, that for syllables, they had only two measures; *videlicet*, of *one time*, or of *two times*.

Whereas, when the modern musicians refer to any thing like a *standard for time*, it is to a *maximum*, which they suppose may be subdivided to infinity by *sub-duples* or *sub-triples*.

However, in settling a standard for the *metrical quantities* of language, it is most proper to adopt the *minimum*, or *shortest syllable*, for that purpose, as no sound in speech can be shorter than the shortest syllable; and therefore, in this system I have made no mark for any note shorter than (|) the *quaver*, which, according to the Greek manner of computing, stands for *one time*.

P. 99. § 6. †. " I rather incline to think, that upon the
" syllable next following the acute, the voice would begin to
" fall, and continue falling upon that, and perhaps upon the
" next after that, &c."

Your l—p's opinion in this matter is, in general, very right, as you will see in the word *happiness* in my first example and many others.

It would require but little practice, with the help of an instrument (as directed p. 16.), to be able to mark all the accents of any speech or poem: for, in general, the distinction between *acute* and *grave* is so obvious, it can seldom or never be mistaken. The only difficulty lies in the *circumflex tones* (either ∧ or ∨); for as they are confined within a small extent, and pronounced exceedingly rapid in the polite tone of our language, and yet have in themselves both the sounds of *acute and grave*; if not accurately attended to, they may pass for either, though they are, simply, neither: therefore, whenever the ear is much puzzled to know whether an accent is *acute* or *grave*, it will be a good rule to suspect it to be a *circumflex* of one or the other sort. Our English sound applied to the vowel u, which in most cases is really a diphthong, as in *you, use, cure, pure, muse*, and the like, is always under the *circumflex* ⌢ *acuto-grave*. And the English sound *I* in the first person, in *idle, iron, try, fly*, and the like, is always made by a *circumflex* ⌣ *grave-acute*.

P. 100. § 7. " When I speak of the accents or tones of the " Greek language, I mean only syllabic tones which are appro- " priated to particular syllables of each words, according to " certain rules delivered by the grammarians, &c."

When rules are delivered dogmatically as universals, without marking the exceptions and exemplifying all the varieties to which they are liable (a matter difficult to do, and very rarely done), they often lead into errors, either by too limited or too loose a construction. And this, we have great reason to think, has been the case, in regard to the prosodical rules of the Greek language.

I have no doubt, that the antient Greeks had nearly the same ideas annexed to *thesis* and *arsis*, as I have given to *heavy* and *light*; but not having used any marks for those expressions, is, I believe, the cause why *accent, quantity*, and *emphasis*, have been confounded together, as one thing, by the commentators of the middle and latter times.

The

The grammatical rules for fixing the *accents* in all *Greek words* are certainly not followed by the modern Greeks in the pronunciation either of their vulgar or of their antient language; though the learned among them are very correct (under thofe rules) in marking them in their writings; yet in their fpeaking (like all other nations), they make a manifeft difference in the profody of the fame fyllables when in a queftion, and when in an anfwer, or in other different intentions.

I think there can be no articulated language without *emphafis*, *accent*, and *quantity*. And any language (if any fuch there be) which wants the power of diverfifying the application of each of thofe accidents in all its words, on particular occafions, muft be fo far deficient in the elegance, force, and aptitude of its expreffions.

The few words, called by the Greeks *enclitics*, had, as we are told, this convenient quality, in fome degree, by changing and giving up their *accent* to the word they clung to; but furely this was not enough.

Our *monyfyllables* are much more pliant than their *enclitics*. I cannot recollect one that is not capable of changing to the complexion that will beft fit the meafure and intention of the fpeaker, and affuredly this is a perfection in language, which the commentators would fain perfuade us the Greek language had not, by laying down rules that abfolutely excluded it; however, I rather impute this to their errors or neglect, than to real defect in the language.

To elucidate what I have faid, I will give a familiar inftance in our own tongue, to fhew the utility of changing thefe accidents

of

[134]

of syllabic expression. In which I shall introduce two of our monosyllables that seem most obstinately affected to the *light poize*; notwithstanding which, they readily submit to the *heavy*, when their position and the sense requires it. These are the prepositions *to* and *from*.

EXAMPLE.

3| As Peter was | going to the | hall, | he met | John.

Sure, you mis|take; | you must | mean, | Peter |-coming from the| hall.

or thus, | you must | mean, as |Peter was| coming from the| hall.

Coming | from! | no, | no, I | say going | to.

In this example, the monosyllable TO is, in the first line, *short, acute,* and *light*; in the last, *long, acuto-grave,* and *heavy*.

FROM,

FROM, in the second and third line, is *short, acute,* and *light*; in the last, *long, acute,* and *heavy*.

HALL, in the first line, is *long, heavy,* and *acute*; in the second and third, *long, heavy,* and *grave*.

Here also it may be observed, that the two syllables of the word GOING being joined together by vowels, without the intervention of a consonant, pass off almost as a monosyllable, and the word, in regard to its *poize*, is also as pliant as a monosyllable; for in the first line it is *heavy,* and in the last, *light*.

Every one of these varieties makes a significant difference in the expression. A significant variety, without which no language can be compleat, either in speaking or in writing; but which, if applied to the Greek, must deviate frequently from the letter of the rules as commonly received and understood.

The variation, on the latter part of the second line, shews, that though the words AS and WAS were not expresly required to explain the sense, they were useful as expletives for the *euphony*; and that their addition made no alteration either in the *rhythmus* or in the *metres* of the *cadences,* since their quantities, when omitted, passed in silent pauses.

I have said in my answer to § 4. p. 128. " That perhaps the " Greek method of composing by feet, joined with ours, might be " of some use in modern compositions." In this view I shall here set down several English words, the first that occur to me, marking them with my notes of *accent, quantity,* and *poize*; and likewise give them the names of such *Greek feet* as their *quantities* seem to refer them to.

[136]

This specimen, I hope, will shew that our language has the same title to syllabic accents, and perhaps as fixed, as those of Greek; for it is not probable, that the *Greek tongue* should have been denied the convenient power of marking the *difference*, between an *interrogative* and a *positive* expression, by the change of *accent*.

WORDS MARKED WITH PROPER ACCENT, QUANTITY, AND EMPHASIS.

constant?	constant.	careless?	careless.
willing?	willing.	wicked?	wicked.
maxim?	maxim.	wonder?	wonder.
succeed?	succeed.	success?	success.
(to) accent?	(to) accent.	(an) accent?	(an) accent.

} spondees.

(to)

[137]

(to) *insult*,
(an) *insult*, } spondee.

music, trochee.

or, *music*, spondee.

ager, trochee.

agerly, dactyl.

able, trochee.

a bi li ty, choriambic.

ever,
never, } pyrrhic.
sever,

compensate, molossus.

compensation, choriambus.

compose, iambic.

composition,

[138]

composition, third epitrite.

variety, choriambic.

wonderfull,

curious, dactyl or spondee.

absolute? ⎫
⎬ dactyl, or anapæst
absolute. ⎭ à majore.

curiosity, ⎱ iambus and anapæst
⎰ per copulam.

terrify, anapæst.

impossible? ⎫
⎬ choriambic or
impossible, ⎭ 1st pæon.

exterminate, choriambic.

exquisite, anapæst.

various, dactyl or spondee.

deliberate, choriambic.

avarice,

avarice, anapæst.

aver, iambus.

average, anapæst.

confess, iambus.

confession, dactyl.

or, *confession*, 1st pæon.

confessor, dactyl.

or, *confessor*, cretic.

succession, 1st pæon.

successor, dactyl.

or, *successor*, cretic.

beauty, spondee.

beautifully, proceleusmatic.

beautiful, cretic.

consider,

[140]

consider, cretic.

consideration, cretic-iambic.

declare, iambus.

declaration, diambic.

(to) *demonstrate*, bacchic.

(a) *demonstrative*, 2d pæon.

demonstration, diambic.

necessary, proceleusmatic.

necessity, choriambic.

musical, dactyl.

musician, dactyl.

differ, pyrrhic.

defer, iambus.

deference, anapæst.

difference,

difference, anapæst.

delicate, anapæst.

delinquent, bacchic.

(a) *project*, iambus.

(to) *project*, spondee.

respect, (in suspense)

respect, (final)

} iambics.

res|*pective*, (English) molossus.
proper

|*respective*,| (Scotch) anapæst.
error

miser, spondee.

misery, anapæst.

species, dactyl or spondee.

specific, dactyl.

compare, iambus.

comparison,

[142]

comparison, choriambic.

comparable, proceleusmatic.

instant, spondee.

instantaneous, spond. and dact.

communicate, choriambus.

communication, dact. and spond.

continue, cretic.

continual, choriambus.

continu | ation, dact. and spond.

constitution, dis-spondee.

constituent, choriambus.

constanti | nople, molossus and spondee.

instruct, spondee.

instruction, molossus.

instrument,

[143]

inſtrument, dactyl.

(to) *produce*, iambus.

(the) *produce*, ditto.

product, ditto.

production, bacchic.

ſyllable, anapæſt.

ſyllabic, dactyl.

(to) *frequent*,

(adject.) *frequent*, } ſpondee.

inſpire, iambus.

inſpiration, diſ-ſpondee.

or, *inſpiration*, ionicus *à minore*.

vibrate, ſpondee.

vibration, moloſſus.

occupy,

[144]

occupy, dactyl.

repetition, proceleufmatic.

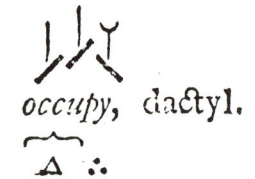

occupation, ionicus *à minore*.

or, *repetition*, diambic.

or, *occupation*, diambic.

obdurate, anapæft, or with the paufe ionicus *à minore*.

or thus, according to Milton, P. L. b. I. line 58.

repeat, iambus.

obdurate, amphibrachys.

The POIZE of fyllables is the moft determined accident in our language.

QUANTITY (or the *long* and *fhort*) is occafionally varied, more or lefs, in all words that may be fpoken, either in common or in triple meafure, which is probably derived from our language having four times as many different quantities as the Greeks had rules for *.

The

---

* The Greeks gave rules for the long quantity equal to two times, and the fhort quantity equal to one time. Only two proportions in all. The Englifh language has at leaft eight different

The ACCENTS muſt always be liable to be changed according to the poſition of words, whether in *queſtion* or in *anſwer*, in a *ſuſpended* or in a *final ſenſe*.

Beſides theſe neceſſary licences of variation, there is alſo a manner of *gracing* the *tones ad libitum*, as in ſinging; by the uſe of what the Italian muſicians call the *appoggiatura*, or *ſupporter*; which is a little (as it were ſuperfluous) note, that the ſinger introduces, to ſlide up to, or down to, the real preſcribed note of the ſong, and therefore might be called an *inſinuator*. This *appoggiatura* being a grace *ad libitum*, the ſinger varies it in different ways at different times in ſinging the ſame tune. For example:

The upper line ſhews the *real* preſcribed *notes* of the tune; the middle and bottom lines have exactly the ſame *notes* in *large* characters, beſides the little *appoggiaturas* or inſinuating notes, in two different manners; and that there ſhould be no breach in the meaſure, the *quantities* of theſe *little notes*, be they more or leſs, are to be *ſtolen* out of the *great* ones.

different proportions of quantity; videlicet,

|=1; |·=1½; Y=2; Y·=3; ?=4; ?·=6; ♯=8; ♯·=12.

Or thus,

|=1; |·=1½; Y=2; |+|·=2½; Y·=3; Y+|·=3½; ?=4; Y+Y=5; ?·=6; Y+Y+Y·=7; ♯=8, &c.

For all theſe and more different proportions of time are employed either in ſyllables or pauſes. And whatever is either taken from, or added to, the pauſes, is either given to, or taken from, the ſyllables; ſo that all theſe various proportions may be neceſſary in well meaſured languages.

[146]

So in *speech*, instead of a plain *acute*, one may use a little *circumflexed grave-acute*, thus ✓, or sometimes *acuto-grave*, thus ⋀; and sometimes, instead of a plain *grave*, thus ⋀, or thus ⋁.

I make this remark in order to shew, that different speakers, or the same speaker at different times, may all be essentially in the same *accentual tones*, though a little disguised by the use of graces or *appoggiaturas*; that is, like musicians severally playing the same air, though some grace it with variations, while others play only the plain notes.

Many of our words, especially those which consist of syllables joined by vowels, without the intervention of a consonant, may be pronounced either in two or in three syllables, and consequently may be either *dactyl* or *spondee*, as *various*, *curious*, *species*, in the foregoing list of words. Others also may be rated either as *choriambics* or first *pæons*, as *impossible*, having the first syllable longest, and the other three, though of different quantities, all shorter than the first, may be considered as a first pæon; but if written thus, *impossible*, it will be a choriambus. Now to note it under the Greek description of proportionate quantities, it could only be marked in this latter manner, since they only admitted their longest syllables to be valued as double to the short ones; but in the first manner of noting this word, the first syllable is in the proportion of three, the second of one, the third of one, and the fourth of two.

This, however, is a minuteness, and I may say an accuracy, which the Greeks did not enter into, though they knew their syllables were *long* and *longer*, *short* and *shorter*. And yet, in our method of dividing time, it is just as easy to be correct in marking every syllable to its true and just *quantity*, as it would be to follow the Greek method of rating *quantities* as equal, which they allowed at the same time were not equal.

In the foregoing list of words it will be seen, that the syllables in some *verbs* are of a different POIZE from the same syllable in the kindred *noun*. This useful distinction is, I believe, not of very long standing. I remember when it was in fewer words than it is now; and, I think, it is a good deal in the power of the learned, by art, to make it almost, if not quite, general.

P. 100. § 7. ‖ " As to the variety of *loud* and *soft*, it must
" have been in their language as well as ours; but it was not
" affected to *syllables*, as with us, but belonged to *words* or
" *sentences*."

I know of no syllables in our language affected to *loud* or *soft* otherways than as the nature of the subject in discourse may occasionally require; and then assuredly it will be applied to whole *words* or *sentences*. I have taken some pains in sundry parts of my essay (p. 23. 29, 30.), and in my former observations (p. 88.), to shew, that heavy △ and light ∴ being obstinately and periodically fixed, are affections quite different from loud and soft; for no sentence can be pronounced without distinguishing the *poize* of syllables; whereas a whole narrative or reasoning discourse may pass without any variation of force respecting loud and soft (vide p. 47. Mr. Garrick's manner of delivering *To be* or *not to be*).

P. 100. § 8. " As to what they called the *rhythm* of their " language, which was composed of the *quantity of syllables*, " &c."

I understand that the Greek *rhythmus* was composed of *metres*; that *metres* consisted of *single* or *copulated feet*; and that feet were composed of syllables, according to their quantities, long or short: and therefore, that the business of *rhythmus*, in gross, went no farther than to number the *metres*; and that it was the office of these latter to regulate *feet* and their *quantities*, in detail.

The Greek ideas of the duration of sound were derived from the actual lengths of their syllables. The shortest syllable was their standard for measuring all their other sounds. This standard was so much an object of immediate sense, that when they heard no articulate sounds, they seem to have had no rule or standard for measuring silence beyond the length of one syllable; and this happened more particularly, because their *rhythmical divisions* or *metres* always embraced a whole *foot* at least. And their *feet* being of various and *varying* lengths, their rhythmical divisions could never have been generally comprised, as ours are, within the periodical swings of a pendulum, or the equality of steps, which enables us to measure silences as accurately as sounds. But also from the same cause, the unequal length of their *rhythmical divisions*, they were unable to make an accurate measurement of syllables, and therefore were content to let them pafs as if they were always in the proportion of two to one, though they, knew very well they were otherways. Whereas our *rhythmical divifions*, or *cadences*, confifting either of founds or filences, being equalized by a pendulum or by our fteps, enables us to compare and compute the proportions both of founds and filences to a great exactnefs.

P. 103. § 9. ** " But our accents differ from the Greek in
" two material refpects. Firft, they are not appropriated to
" particular fyllables of a word; but are laid upon different
" fyllables, according to the fancy of the fpeaker, or rather as
" it happens, &c."

I fuppofe there was a time when the Greeks had no rules either for *punctuation* or *accentuation* in their language, when perhaps the invention or the practicability of fuch rules were not thought to be poffible, or to be ufeful if they were; nor, when they were firft introduced, was it probably forefeen, to what perfection, by their affiftance, their language might arrive. The foregoing lift of words, *poized*, *meafured*, and *accented*, fhews that our language is as determined as the Greek, to have fixed accents. It is not in the indecifive ufe of thofe properties that its imperfection lies. Time, aided by learned men with mufical ears, may perhaps rub off fome of its unneceffary, uncouth confonants.

As to the extent of our flides, fo far from being generally lefs than a fifth, I obferve, the common error is the other way; for there are few people that, without great attention, can confine themfelves to fuch narrow bounds.

P. 104.

[150]

P. 104. § 9. note *(d)*. " Relative to this there is a remarkable
" story.———Demosthenes, in asking the question of the judges,
" whether Æschines was the friend or the hireling [μίσθωτος] of
" Alexander, barbarized on purpose, by laying the accent upon
" the last syllable instead of the first, &c."
To shew the possibility of a similar instance in our language, let us suppose a patriot, in a popular assembly, saying, " Sir, I
" would ask, whether we ought to look upon this peace-making
" minister as the disinterested friend of mankind, or the

" *pensionaire* of our rivals?" To which the shouts of the assembly would probably answer *rapidly* in plain English pronunciation,

" *Pensioner, pensioner.*" From which, I think, no other grammatical or critical consequence could be justly drawn, except that the patriot had slily affected a Gallicism in the pronunciation of a word, which, independent of * accentuation, was the same in both languages.

* Here, for want of a better word, I put ACCENTUATION, as a general term to include *accent, quantity,* and *poize.*

P. 105.

P. 105. § 9. †† " Upon the whole, therefore, I am of
" opinion, that very little can be made of the accents of our lan-
" guage; and that to obferve them at all is more a matter of
" curiofity than utility."

If we have no accents in our language, our difcourfe muſt be monotonous; but, I thought, it was proved (p. 15.), that it was not monotonous, not even on a fingle fyllable. Or if it be admitted that we have accents, but that they are ufelefs, vague, and arbitrary; then any provincial clown may accent his words as properly as Mr. Garrick.

But if it be admitted, that a change of accent may alter the fenfe of an expreffion (vide *interrogative* and *pofitive*, p. 136.); and that Mr. Garrick may accent his words with more grace and fignificant propriety than a clown, it ſhould feem that a method of accenting words and fentences, as pronounced by the moſt correct fpeakers, ought to promife fome future utility.

I hope thefe additional explanations, together with a review of the whole treatife, which your l—p will find now more
enlarged

enlarged, and more correct than the sketches of last year, will give you reason to alter your opinion.

We have a recent example of the powerful effects of musical rhythmus in the improvement of an art, with which, in the eyes of moderns, music was as little connected as with language.

Thirty years ago, military men considered music in no other light than as an amusement of parade to their corps; when one officer of uncommon genius, who still lives the ornament of his profession, began to use it as an engine of discipline, by engaging the minds of a body of men, through the force of melody, to attend to one thing; and after having so attached their attention by their ears, then to make them perform all their motions and evolutions under the instinctive power of whatever rhythmus he had prescribed to his musicians. It required no less than the unremitting perseverance of this able officer to stem the prejudices of vulgar minds against what appeared to them a puerile and visionary innovation. A few years, however, convinced the most obstinate; and ever since the commencement of the late war, not only the British regulars, but the militia also, perform their manœuvres and evolutions under the influence of melody and rhythmus, as well as the antient Greeks. Aristides says (lib. II. Meib. vol. 2d. p. 71.):
Ἔν τε τοῖς πολέμοις, ἐν οἷς μάλιϛα εὐδοκίμησε ᾗ εὐδοκιμεῖ, προσθήσω δὲ ᾗ εὐδοκιμοίη, τὴν μὲν καλὰ πυρρίχην τῶν τακτικῶν μελέτην, ὡς διὰ μυσικῆς ποιεῖται, τί δεῖ λέγειν; πᾶσι γὰρ δήπυ ταῦτα φανερά· ἀλλ' ὃ τοῖς πλείϛοις ἄδηλον, ἐν αὐτοῖς τοῖς ἀγῶσι, ᾗ τοῖς κινδύνοις, τὰ μὲν διὰ λόγων πολλάκις ἀποδοκιμάζει παραγγέλματα, ὡς βλάψονͭα εἰ τοῖς ὁμοφώνοις τῶν πολεμίων διαγνωσθείη· διὰ μυσικῆς δὲ ποιεῖται τὰ σύμβολα· ὀργάνου

ὄργανον μὲν Ἀρήϊόν τε, ᾗ καταπληκτικὸν μεταχειριζομένη τὴν σάλπιγγα ἑκάστῳ δὲ παρεγγυήματι μέρος ἴδιον ἀφορίζεσα. Ἐπιδρομῆς ἓν τῆς κατὰ μέτωπον ᾗ ἐφόδε τῆς κατὰ κέρας ἰδιάζοντα κατατέτακται μέλη· ᾗ ἀνακλητικὸν ἕτερον· ἐξελίξεών τε τῶν ἐπ᾽ Ἀσπίδα ἢ ἐπὶ δόρυ πάλιν ἑκάστης ἴδια· ᾗ πάντα ὅτως ἐφεξῆς περαίνει τὰ σοφίσματα, συμβόλοις τοῖς μὲν πολεμίοις ἀδήλοις, τοῖς δὲ φιλίοις σαφεστάτοις τε ᾗ δι᾽ εὐχερείας γινωσκομένοις. Οὐ γὰρ κατὰ μέρος τέτων διακέεσιν, ἀλλ᾽ ἠχῇ μιᾷ τὸ σύμπαν ἔπετι σύνταγμα.

" Also in war, it was, and is, in the greatest estimation; and
" I may add, that so it ever will be; of the pyrrhic exercise in
" tactics, which is performed by music, what need I speak?
" Though it is openly seen by all, yet this (part) is from many
" concealed; that, in engagements and hazardous enterprizes,
" it often disapproves of giving verbal orders, from the danger
" of discovering them to the enemy, if they should be of the
" same tongue; therefore it gives symbolic signs by music, mak-
" ing use of the trumpet, a martial and alarming instrument,
" and appropriating a peculiar piece (as a signal) for every dif-
" ferent (order or) admonition. So for a charge in front, and
" for an attack in flank, particular tunes are appointed; and
" another for the retreat. Again, when they are to turn to the
" left or to the right, there is a different air for each. And so
" for the rest, it performs them all by signals unknown to the
" enemy; but to their friends most manifest and intelligible.
" Not (waiting) to be heard from man to man, but (warned)
" by one sound, the whole regiment moves on together."

As I have cited the whole passage in the original Greek, it will not be suspected that I have copied this from the discipline of our light cavalry, among whom, it muſt be confeſſed, this pyrrhic exerciſe ſeems to be thoroughly eſtabliſhed. But if any one thinks it was much more excellently performed by ancient Greeks than by modern Britons, he may uſe his endeavours to prove that fact as well as he can, without taking away from the preſent profeſſors of the art, the merit which they really have in improving our tactics. In like manner, I would intreat all paſſionate lovers of the *Greek* language, to content themſelves with admiring the elegance of their miſtreſs's dreſs;—how gracefully ſhe *lengthened* or *ſhortened* her robes;—where ſhe pinned her *accent*;—and how ſhe *poiſed* her *emphaſis*. But why muſt they attempt to ſtrip our poor *mother tongue* of thoſe neceſſary parts of her cloathing, to which ſhe has as natural a right as the *Grecian lady?* The native rudeneſs of her ſhape, and the hitherto neglect of her education, were not her faults, but her misfortunes; which it is the duty of her learned ſons to endeavour, rather to correct, by inſinuating arts and gentle admonitions, than to diſpute her legal rights, and to diſparage her by humiliating compariſons.

P. 105. § 10. " As to the rhythm of it, I think it muſt conſiſt " in one or other, or of all the four following things; the quan- " tities of the ſyllables; the variety of loud and ſoft; the pauſes; " and laſtly, your diviſions into bars, &c."

In my anſwer to your lordſhip's former remarks, I certainly pointed out in manner of a demonſtration (ſee p. 87.) that *cadence* being *emphatically* divided into the *heavy* and the *light*, was the ONLY *eſſential* governing power of *rhythmus*.

Quantity

Quantity, which is only subservient to *metre*; or, as I may say, to the *metrical* division of *cadence*, has no more to do in the definition of *rhythmus*, than a closet has to do in that of a house, which may be either as a barn, without any interior division, or as a church with a hundred pews, or as a dwelling-house, divided according to the conveniency of the master: therefore, the *essence* of *rhythmus* does not lie in *quantity*. Nor in *loud* and *soft*; for a whole discourse may pass without any such variety (see remark on Mr. Garrick's speech in Hamlet, p. 47.).

Nor in *pauses*, which are only as portions, or a portion, of *quantity*, not employed in sound, but in a silence, like an empty room in a house, or a vacant house in a street.

As to *bars*, though I have frequently made use of the word as synonymous with *cadence*, in order to be the better understood by musicians; yet, I must own, it was an error against precision, for which I hope I shall be excused by philosophers; who will perceive, that a *bar*, properly speaking, is only the graphical mark of the beginnings and endings, or of the boundaries, of *cadence*: whereas *cadence* itself is an essence, co-existing with articulate sound, the subject both of sense and intellect, independent of any mark on paper: and in this sense, *bars*, as the typical marks of *cadence*, may figuratively be said to be the essential or constituent parts of *rhythmus*; which I would have always understood to be an instinctive sense and idea of dividing the duration of all sounds and motions, by an equal periodical pulsation, like the oscillations or swings of a pendulum.

P. 106. § 11. " As to quantity, though we have undoubtedly
" some syllables in our language much longer than others; yet I
" have always been of opinion, that it made no part of the
" rhythm of our language; and that it was a vain attempt to
" endeavour to reduce our compositions to metrical feet, &c."

RHYTHMUS takes notice of no *quantity* less than that of a whole CADENCE. The several examples which I have set, with the notes of *accent, quantity,* and *poize,* are as strong proofs as any we have from the Greeks, that our compositions are reducible both to *metrical cadences* and *feet*.

A person not initiated in the practice of music will not easily perceive the difference in *quantity* between *crotchets* and *quavers*; nevertheless, their proportion to each other is as two to one; much less will such a person be able to distinguish the difference between the *specked crotchet* and the *plain crotchet,* which are to each other as three to two. But notwithstanding this want of distinction in a person unpractised in the art, the art itself is perfect, and those who are versed in it find no difficulty to distinguish and evaluate notes so minute as twenty-four or thirty-two to a second of time. It would be very unjust to say there could be no distinct power of description in the language of Japan, because I did not understand it, and that all their words seemed to my ears to sound exactly alike. Your lordship has well proved, that language is an art; but it is an art that we learn (to speak in the vulgar phrase) very naturally; that is, by *rote*. Many people learn music nearly in the same manner, especially singing; and both those who talk by *rote,* and those

who

who sing by *rote*, are often proficients in practice, without knowing that those arts are capable of rules and of very subtil analyzation, any more than a child of five years old comprehends, or can explain, how he stands and walks. All the languages in modern Europe have a plain traditional descent from those of two or three thousand years ago. The organs of mankind, their faculties, and their aptitudes, are still the same. The chain of communication from Aristotle to your l—p consists only of forty links of about fifty years for each. What ground have we to suppose, that those necessary materials of language, *accent*, *quantity*, and *poize*, so remarkably cultivated by the Greeks, should be lost in so short a passage, as through a line of forty lives? Instead of losing, we might have acquired more properties, if language had been capable of more than what we have; since it is almost clear, that ours is a compound of all that existed within the extent of the Greek, Roman, and Gothic empires.

Our pedestrian performers on the harp, pipe, and fiddle, are seldom farther advanced in the literate art of music, than Europe is in the musical part of language; that is, unconscious of notes or any scientific method, they are all talking and playing by *rote* and by *ear*, or, in the more vulgar phrase, by *air*.

There was a time when the Greeks, in regard to their language, were in the same situation; for we are told, *accentual* notes were not used by them till long after the days of *Homer*.

Now when an unlettered harper or piper, though perhaps of extensive fancy and great execution, meets with an inferior player possessed of the art by notes, it humbles the pride of

his

his native talent, and he submits to the lettered man as his master.

This, then, is the state of the art between these two men: we will suppose the ignorant player to be the best performer, but that he conceives not the possibility of reducing his musical ideas to rules of art, or of communicating them to others by words or writing; while the other, by setting down all the wild notes of the unlettered man, convinces *even him*, that the rules existed, although *he* knew them not.

P. 108. § 14. " As to our verse, there is one part of its " rhythm which every body perceives; and that is the equal " length of the verses. That arises from their consisting of the " same number of syllables; ten, for example, in our hexameter " verse: nor can this be dispensed with."

The lengths of verses or lines of poetry are no necessary constituent part of *rhythmus*; for though every line should be composed of regular *metres* or *cadences*, yet the *rhythmus* will be good, whether the number of *cadences* in each line are equalized or not, as in the species of poems called *Odes*. But a line may consist of *ten syllables*, which, for want of the proper *poize* or the proper *quantities*, cannot be reduced to *metrccal cadences* without great assistance from pauses, or changing the position of the words, and of course will not be a *rhythmical verse*.

As instances of this, I will here give some lines from the first book of Milton's Paradise Lost, which assuredly want

the

the assistance I have mentioned, to make them rhythmical verses.

Line.

122. | Irrecon | cileable | to our | grand | foe. |

159. | To | do aught | good, | never will | be our | task. |

Or thus, *transpose* NEVER,

| To | do aught | good, will | never | be our | task. |

160. | As | being | the con | trary | to | his high | will. |

But in modern language, this method of pronouncing CONTRARY is only used among vulgar people; therefore it should be thus:

| As | being | the | contrary | to his | high | will. |

248. | Whom | reason | hath | equall'd, | force hath | made su | preme. |

402. | His | temple | right a | gainst | the | temple | of | God. |

406.

406. Next Chemos, the obscene dread of Moab's sons.

452. Of Thammuz yearly wounded; the love-tale.

470. He also against the house of God was bold.

472. Ahaz, his sottish conqueror, whom he drew.

490. Belial came last, than whom a spirit more lewd.

499. Of riot ascends above their loftiest towers.

509. Gods, yet confessed later than heaven and earth.

554. Deliberate valour breath'd, firm and unmov'd.

558. Anguish, and doubt, and fears, and sorrow, and pain.

562.

[161]

562. Their | painful | steps | o'er the burnt | soil: and | now.

584. Da | mafco, | or Mo | rocco, | or | Trebi | fond.

592. All her o | riginal | brightnefs; | | nor ap | peared.

594. Of | glory ob | fcured: | as | when the | fun new | rifen.

622. O! | myriads | of im | mortal | fpirits! | O! | powers.

632. That | all | thefe pu | iffant | legions, | whofe ex | ile.

682. The | riches of | heaven's | pavement | trodden | gold.

704. Severing each | kind, | and | fcumm'd the | bullion | drofs.

Or, Sever'd each | kind, | &c.

Y

710.

[162]

710. | Anon, | out of the | earth | a | fabric | huge. |

735. | And | sat as | princes; | whom the su | preme | king. |

737. | Each | in his | hierarchy | the | orders | bright. |

753. | Of | sovereign | power, | with | awful | ceremony, |

756. | At | Pande | monium, | the | high | capital. |

758. | From | every | band, | and | squared | regiment. |

Measured lines of whatever lengths, are, or may be, what I call *rhythmical clauses*; and are otherwise distinguished both in antient and modern language by the names of *hexametres, pentametres, tetrametres*, &c. If it were not for the rhymes in modern poetry, the ear would never discover the ends of verses, when properly pronounced; because the *rhythmus* never stops, not even at * pauses, which would be tiresome and offensive if we

* For though there is a discontinuance of sound, the rhythmus is continued to the end of the piece; and by that continuance every *pause* is measured.

always

always found them at equal and periodical diſtances; and hence it is, that the cæſure is never offenſive in blank verſe (ſee lines from Milton, p. 77.). If the *octometres*, which I have given (p. 80, 81.) from the *Æneid* and *Iliad*, are read by my notes, the ear will not diſcover the ends of the lines by an equality of periods.

Our language which (to ſpeak according to the Greek proſody) abounds with *iambics, trochees, ſpondees, dactyls,* and *anapæſts,* makes agreeable *hexametres* with five cadences of words, and the quantity of one more left for pauſes.

But the preciſe number of TEN ſyllables are not always the neceſſary complement of the five *cadences* of words; for if there are dactylic feet, the number of ſyllables may be increaſed without any injury to the meaſure. As for example,

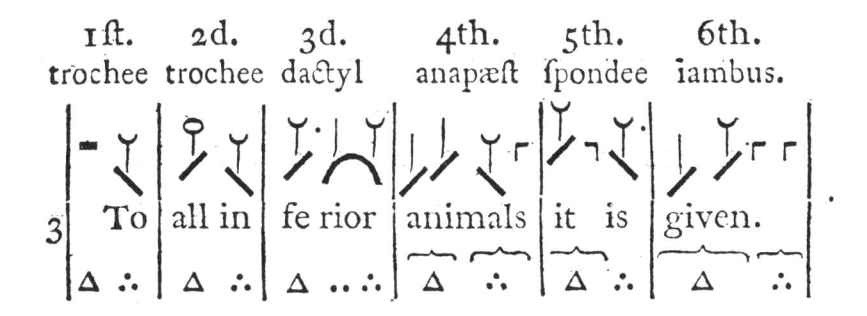

    1ſt.   2d.   3d.   4th.   5th.   6th.
trochee trochee dactyl anapæſt ſpondee iambus.

3 | To | all in | fe rior | animals | it is | given.

A *minim reſt* or ſilence, together with the ſyllable TO, makes the firſt cadence a *trochee*. In the fourth cadence, the word ANIMALS, by itſelf, is an *anapæſt*; but to give a denomination to the whole cadence, which includes a *reſt* or ſilence of a *crotchet*, it ſhould be called an *ionicus à minore*. The word GIVEN in the ſixth cadence is an iambus; but to give a denomination to the whole cadence, which has a *trochee* in silence, we muſt call it an antiſpaſt.

The above line, if read as noted, is a good *hexametre*, not *alexandrine*, and yet has THIRTEEN ſyllables. And as a proof that our language has ſyllables affected to *quantity* as well as to *accent* and *poize*, the word ANIMALS, though of three ſyllables, was not long enough to make up the meaſure of the *cadence* without the *crotchet reſt* which follows it; and the monoſyllable ALL in the *ſecond cadence* is exactly as long as the three ſyllables of ANIMALS. Again, the monoſyllable IT in the *fifth cadence* was not long enough to ſtand for half the *ſpondee*, without the aid of the *quaver reſt* which follows it.

If authorities can be quoted againſt theſe opinions, to ſhew, for example, that IT may be *long* and ALL *ſhort*, we muſt be obliged to acknowledge, we have many examples of bad writers, and bad readers, and bad men, who pay no regard to *accent, quantity, poize,* decency, good order, or common honeſty; but, notwithſtanding all violences and irregularities, *accent, quantity, poize,* order, decency, and honeſty, have ſtill an eſſential exiſtence, in the language and manners of mankind.

Several of our monoſyllables, ſuch as *our, hour, torne, worn, borne,* and the like, are ſo long as that any one of them with eight other ſyllables will make an unexceptionable *hexametre* line. However, theſe long ſyllables ſo employed have evidently the effect, and nearly the ſame ſound, as two ſyllables, though in other lines they can be ſounded as mere monoſyllables.

EXAMPLE

EXAMPLE OF A LINE OF NINE SYLLABLES IN SIX CADENCES, COUPLED WITH AN ALEXANDRINE OF EIGHT CADENCES.

So | Britain, | worn | out with | crops of | men

Muſt | now be, | ſtock'd with | brutes, | a | wilderneſs | a | gain

P. 109. § 15. "The mixture of loud and ſoft.——This is "ſo eſſential to our verſe, that if the ſenſe require that an "emphaſis ſhould be laid upon the ſoft ſyllable it evidently mars "the verſe, &c."

In this obſervation, two things, diſtinct in their nature, ſeem to be confounded together, *poize* and *force*.

Loudneſs of ſpeech, whether on ſyllables, words, or ſentences, muſt always be *ad libitum*, and is therefore an *accident* different from, and independent of, *emphaſis* or the △ *heavy poize* of a ſyllable, which is never *ad libitum*, but poſitively fixed in all words, except monoſyllables. For if *loudneſs* be required on a particular word or ſentence, it ſhould continue uniformly on all and every one of the ſyllables of that word or ſentence; whereas *emphaſis* or the △ *heavy poize* is confined to a ſingle ſyllable, or to

half

half *a cadence* at moft, the next fyllable or next *half cadence* requiring abfolutely the *unemphatic* or ∴ *light poize*. We have proved by a clear example (fee p. 88. *my* ∴ *dear* △), that the △ *heavy* fyllable may be (**,**) *foft*, and the ∴ *light* fyllable (**"**) *loud*.

Now all our *polyfyllables*, except thofe which may be contracted into *monofyllables*, have their *poize*, for the moft part, unalterably *fixed*; fo that wherever they are employed in poetry or profe, whether intended to be fpoken *loud* or *foft*, the words fhould be fo arranged, that they may be pronounced, without violence, according to their proper *poize*. And a writer muft have but little fkill or a bad ear, who cannot always affect this, fince almoft all the *monofyllables*, with which our language abounds, are fo *pliant* as to fubmit, according as the cafe may require, to either the ∴ *light*, or △ the *heavy*. But the words SOIL, TOIL, and fome others feem abfolutely heavy; for which an exception fhould have been made in p. 133.

I obferve your l——p thinks the word *firſt*, in the firſt line of the Paradife Loft, fhould be read (∴) *light*, which I have marked △ *heavy*. As it is not my intention in this treatife, to decide magifterially on the certain pronounciation of any word, which, in the feveral parts of this ifland, may be underftood to be the fame, though very differently founded, I will not infift on the rectitude of the expreffion which I have applied to that or any other fyllable; my defign being principally to fhew, that all the neceffary expreffions, or accidents of elocution, may be reduced to rule, and committed to writing, by thefe legible fymbols.

However,

However, if my judgement was erroneous in the above mentioned instance, I will just mention what led me into it.

I thought so great a poet as Milton would not have put an unmeaning expletive in the | first | line of his | poem; | but that, on the contrary, he meant to point out *emphatically (not loudly)* what particular act of | man's diso | bedience | it was, which had drawn on him and his race so | heavy a | punishment, | and therefore I marked it, of | man's | first diso | bedience |; neither do I see any reason for bringing the accidents attending the syllables in the first line of a distich to tally numerically with those of the second: for in that case, the cæsure must always be in the same periods of both lines, which your l—p justly remarks as a great fault in French and English poetry; though, I think, it does not necessarily happen in the latter. And M. Voltaire

has

[168]

has avoided it, in some degree, since he has adopted our ten syllable measure *.

P. 110. § 16. ‡‡ " As to quantity, it is certainly not essential " to our verse; and far less is accent."

If your l——p's opinion prevails here, it will destroy my whole fabric. But having laboured to ascertain and explain these essential accidents of our language by legible notes; and to prove the truth of their existence, by experiments submitted to our vulgar senses, by the aid of a bass viol or *pitch-pipe*. I must now call the several examples, which I have made the subjects of those experiments, FACTS; and those *facts* only, without farther words, are all I shall here oppose to your l——p's opinion on this head.

* The greater number of monosyllables in English, being in proportion as 3 to 2 more than in French, gives our language a considerable advantage over theirs, in changing the place of the cæsure, as well as in the disposition of cadence and quantity. And considering how much both languages are embarrassed with necessary consonants (besides the useless ones), if they had not had a great proportion of monosyllables, their versification would have been much worse. In English, the proportion of monosyllables to polysyllables is more than as 5 to 2. In French something less than as 3 to 2. But in Italian, which having more vowels has less occasion for monosyllables, their proportion to polysyllables is not quite 3 to 4, or 1½ to 2. The superior melody of one language over another will be nearly in proportion as the one exceeds the other in the number of (vowels or) vocal sounds. The number of vocal and consonantal sounds in Italian are nearly equal, or 54 consonants to 53 vowels; in Latin 5 consonant to 4 vowels; in French, supposing the orthography not as written, but as sounded in pronunciation, the consonantal to the vocal sounds are as 4 to 3; and in English, in the like manner, the proportions are as 3 to 2. Therefore, in this view, the French has an advantage over the English in the proportion of 9 to 8; but this is over-balanced by the English advantage in its monosyllables, which it has more than the French in the proportion of 5 to 3 or 10 to 6.

P. 110.

P. 110. § 16. |||| and ※※※ "The paufes, as I have obferved,
"cannot ftand for any part of the verfe, nor fupply the place of
"a fingle fyllable.——At the fame time thefe paufes are a very
"great beauty, particularly in our blank verfe, filling up a
"confiderable part of the time; and therefore, are very properly
"confidered as a part at leaft of the time of the verfe, if not
"of the verfe itfelf."

Your l—p fays enough here to fhew the ufe and importance of paufes; they certainly have the fame ufe in rhyme as in blank verfe. The foregoing examples give proofs.

P. 110. § 16. ††† and ‡‡‡. "Certain fyllables of certain words
"had particular tones appropriated to them.——Our compo-
"fition can be little or nothing improved in that way.—And as
"to rhythm, we have not what they called rhythm, arifing
"from a certain compofition of long and fhort fyllables, &c."

The fpecimens I have given (in p. 136. *& feq.*) prove, that we have our appropriated tones as well as the Greeks. But in order to know whether our tones in general are, or are not, capable of improvement, let any man, in his travels through this ifland, take down, by thefe rules, the feveral provincial tones. Then, comparing them with one another, and with that of the metropolis, he will find a confiderable variety among them; and fome, he will probably think better than others: furely then it will follow, that the tones which he does not approve of, may be altered for the better, by adopting the moft approved accentual founds in their ftead.

As to *rhythmus*, there is not the least room to doubt, but that we have as absolute *quantity* in our language as the Greeks had in theirs; and that their *rhythmus* was governed by the *poize* of *arsis* and *thesis* is testified by all their writers, as ours is by the same thing, only changing the form of the members from *metres* to *cadences*, which are more exact (see p. 113, 114, and 115); and in that we have the advantage of effecting the same thing with less labour. *Quantity* never governed *rhythmus*; but was as subservient to it as materials are to the building of an edifice: wherein it is the business of the workman to chuse the materials that will fit, and not to accommodate the size of the apartments to the dimensions of the bricks and stones. And here we may shew one of the uses of our *pauses*; for if a syllable is too short, we may supply its deficiency by a *pause*, by which means an *iambus* or *trochee* may answer to fill a *cadence* as well as a *spondee*. Of this examples may be found among the foregoing. I make no doubt, but many instances may be adduced, where both *poize* and *quantity* have been violated by our best poets; but a poetical licence, the offspring of hard necessity, is not a sufficient authority to deny or disown the laws of nature. For though speech is artificial; yet *accent*, *quantity*, and *poize*, are natural principles, without which it could not be constructed.

P. 111. § 16. ‖‖‖. " In short, the Greek language was the " work not only of grammarians and philosophers, but of " musicians, &c."

I do not pretend to set up *our language* as any thing like a rival to the *Greek* in its *grammatical, etymological,* or *orthogra-*

phical

phical frame and conſtruction; but certainly, the accidents of *melody* and *rhythmus* are not peculiar to the *Greek:* they are *common* to the *Engliſh* and to all the languages that I know any thing of, or ever heard pronounced.

When a man ſtudies the character and manners of an ancient worthy, the utility he may and ſhould draw from that ſtudy, is to form his own morals, as near as the difference of times and places will permit, by the imitation of ſo excellent a model. It is not in our power to make the Greek our national language; but it is certainly in the power of learned men to make great improvements in that we have. Your l—p's maſterly obſervations on the Greek language give us room to think, you underſtand it more critically than even your native tongue; which is far from being my caſe. I juſt know enough of it to perceive how much better its properties were underſtood, cultivated, and methodized, by its grammarians, poets, and muſicians, than has happened to any other language within my knowledge. But as, in compariſon with the Greek, all the languages in modern Europe are involved in the ſame diſgrace, among which our own holds at leaſt a middle rank, let me preſume to offer the following hypotheſis as their apology.

While the Greek poet and muſician was one and the ſame perſon, he took great care to make his muſical fancy ſo far ſubſervient to his poetical, that neither the *accent*, *quantity*, or *poize* of a ſyllable ſhould ever be violated. But when the two profeſſions came to be ſeparated, then, I can ſuppoſe, the muſical compoſer, more partial to his own, than to the compoſition of the poet, gave preference to a pretty muſical idea, though it might run counter to every accentual property. This abuſe, I preſume, was ſo thoroughly eſtabliſhed before the revival of the arts and the invention of our modern ſcale and modulation, that no mere compoſer of muſic felt, or feels, any concern about *lingual accent, quantity*, or *poize*; but is quite indifferent whether, in compliance with his muſical whim, he extends a ſingle ſyllable to the length of 20 *cadences*, either on a ſingle tone, or articulated into 160, through all the extent of the voice; or whether he crams 8 or 12 ſyllables (which might in their natural quantities be ſpondaic) into the narrow compaſs of one cadence (ſee p. 66. *folly*). Now, admitting this ſuppoſition, let us ſtate the natural conſequences of the ANTIENT and of the MODERN poetico-muſical compoſition. The ANTIENT Greeks, always accuſtomed to hear the ſame accentuation of their language, both in common diſcourſe and in muſical melodies, were never led aſtray; but became, by habitude, to know as familiarly the *accentual* and *rhythmical* properties of every word, as we do, now-a-days, the like qualities of every common hacknied tune; in which nobody, that has any ear for muſic, is materially miſtaken. But as to MODERN languages, their *accentual* and *rhythmical* properties being continually violated by muſicians, it is no wonder, that even learned men have been hitherto ſo far miſled as not to perceive that they have preciſely every *accentual* and *rhythmical* property that the Greeks had; properties which muſt neceſſarily belong to all languages whatſoever.

Thus, when things arrive at a certain point of perfection, luxurious refinements in great communities ſeldom fail to lead them

them into error and confusion. The physician, quitting his pharmacy, trusts the life of his patient to the hazardous handling of a second-hand profession. The lawyer, no longer composing his own pleadings, lifeless in the cause, blunders through the blunders of a subaltern blunderer.

So the Attic or Roman poet, who first submitted the *poizing* and *accentuation* of his language to a mere musician, laid the foundation of our lingual disgrace. To rectify which, there is no method so sure as to adopt, in that particular, the *ancient Greek* prudence, under which the study of music and letters were intimately blended together. For if we think it necessary to instruct our children by a dancing-master, in the rhythmical art, to enable them to move and walk more gracefully than the untutored peasant; why, since language depends both on rhythmus and melody, should we not also teach them to read under the rules of music, that their speech may be as graceful and as proper as their movement? All that part of language which belongs to its utterance, is intirely to be regulated by the rules of music; that is, of melody and rhythmus: how then is it possible, to bring that part of it to the perfection it may be capable of, if our men of letters are so ignorant of it, as to doubt or deny its existence?

In | fine, | if we | would | *know,* | we must | first | *learn* | ; and if we wish to improve our language, the grammarian, the poet, and the musician, must again be united in the same person.

POSTSCRIPT.

POSTSCRIPT.

WHILE the fourth part of this Essay was in the press, the old proof sheets of the three first parts were sent to the Author of the *Origin and Progress of Language*, with a letter, observing, that as there were in those three parts some additions and corrections beyond what he had seen, his l——p, might on the perusal, find something to answer the objections, and remove the doubts expressed in his last observations. To which his l——p replied:

SIR,

I HAD the favour of your letter by Mr. —— with your printed sheets; for which I think myself much obliged to you. You have added, I see, more examples and illustrations; and the public is obliged to you for your fair dealing, in publishing what may be said against your system as well as for it; so that every man may judge for himself. Whether what I have said by way of objection, will be thought to have any weight, I know not; but I am sure, that I am obliged to you for the honourable mention you have made of the Author of the Origin of Language. What further has occurred to me, upon reading your printed sheets, you have in the enclosed paper.

I am, with great regard and esteem, &c.

To J—— S——, Esq; Margaret Street, Cavendish Square, London.

THE

THE OBSERVATIONS INCLOSED IN THE FOREGOING LETTER.

"THE nature of your work, as I undestand it, is to com-
"pare the melody and rhythm of music with the melody
"and rhythm of language; and to try how far the rules of both
"these in music may be applied to language. A speculation
"certainly very curious, and which, I think, may be also useful;
"inasmuch as the melody and rhythm of music are more accu-
"rate, and governed by more certain rules, than those of even
"the most perfect languages. As to the *melody* of language,
"there is a difference, which you acknowledge, betwixt it and
"the melody of music; namely, that the latter proceeds by
"greater intervals, distinctly marked, and therefore is what the
"Greek writers call *diastematic:* whereas the music of speech
"proceeds by very small and inappretiable intervals, the voice
"never resting upon any one tone, but going on in a continued
"flow, or ῥύσις, as they called it; and from thence they gave it
"the name of συνεχὴς, or *continued*, in contra-distinction to the
"*diastematic*. And so far you are certainly in the right. As to
"*rhythm*, you seem to think, that there is no material difference
"betwixt the rhythmus of music and that of language. For,
"according to your system, there is *common* and *triple* time in
"each; they are both divided into bars, and the pauses of each
"make part of those bars. And here, I think, lies the great
"objection

" objection to your system: for, till I shall have seen what you
" have written, I must still continue to doubt, whether there be
" any other division of the sound of language than, first, what
" is common to all languages; *viz.* the pauses which the sense
" requires; secondly, the division into feet, consisting of certain
" combinations of long and short syllables, which is peculiar to
" the learned languages; and, thirdly, the combination of loud
" and soft syllables, which makes what we call the *feet* * of our
" English verse, and may, I think, also be applied to the rhythm
" of our prose. Besides these, I, for my part, perceive no other
" rhythm in speech. At the same time, I am far from setting
" up my perceptions as a rule: for I am sensible how much they
" are governed by custom, of which we need no other proof
" than that we certainly have not the same perception of the
" division of language into combinations of long and short sylla-
" bles (that is, metrical feet), as the ancients had†; because
" having no such rhythm in our language, our ears are not
" accustomed to it (*a*). ‡ That language may be divided into bars
" as well as music, you have shewn very evidently; and it is
" likely, that a well-taught ear, such as yours, will perceive
" that division, and will measure speech by it as well as it does a
" tune. It may also perceive, that those bars proceed either by
" common or triple time. But I much doubt, whether any
" man, that is not a musician, can be made to perceive it; the
" consequence of which is, that it will be of no use. It may,
" however, be true, that though the division itself may not be

* This and the following marks, in these observations, refer to the answers which follow them.

(*a*) Vide p. 119 to 121. 136 to 144.

" perceived

"perceived by any but those of learned ears, yet the effects of it
"may be felt by all. For this is generally the case of the
"popular arts, of which every body feels the effects, but only
"the learned know the causes which produce them. As to
"music, I am convinced, that the division of a tune into bars,
"whether in common or triple time, is absolutely necessary.
"Now if the reason of this could be shewn, we should be able
"to judge, whether that reason would not likewise be applicable
"to speech. You seem to think it difficult, if not impossible,
"to discover this reason; and if it be impossible to you, I am
"perswaded it is to every other. But it is certainly possible to
"be sure of the fact;—I mean, || whether a speech, composed
"in such a way as not to be capable of a division into bars, will
"not offend the ear as much as music so composed. And if
"that be the fact, I shall be satisfied, without knowing the
"cause; though I should be obliged to confess, that I have
"spoken all my life in musical bars, without knowing that I
"did so, like the *bourgeois gentilhomme* you mention in Moliere,
"who had spoken prose all his life without knowing it.

"Before I quit this subject, ** I must own myself fully con-
"vinced, that the pauses make an essential part of the rhythm
"of speech; and that if a man in speaking, stops where he
"should not, or stops too long or too short, he will not only
"offend the understanding, but the ear; and our notation of
"these stops in writing is imperfect, inasmuch as they only
"mark that one pause is greater than another; but do not let us
"know by how much, or in what proportion, the one is longer
"than the other.

"As to the Greek language, the knowledge of its accents and "rhythmus does not belong to your general system, any farther "than as it may serve to explain and illustrate your theory. "Till I see more of your sheets, I shall believe, that the tones of "the Greek language were altogether different from the tones of "English, or of any other language now spoken in Europe, in "this respect, that each word in Greek, pronounced by itself, "and without the least degree of passion or sentiment (*b*), had an "acute accent upon one particular syllable of it, just as much as "any English polysyllable, pronounced by itself, has one syl- "lable sounded louder than the rest. The modern Greeks have "lost those tones, and in place of acute and grave have substi- "tuted loud and soft ††; for they constantly sound every syllable "loud which is marked in the Greek books with an acute accent, "which makes their pronunciation resemble more that of the "English than of any other language in Europe. In this man- "ner, I imagine, the single Greek word was pronounced; and "in composition, whether the speaker spoke loud or soft, or in "whatever tone or passion, still the elevation of the tone upon "the accented syllable was observed (*c*).

"And here there occurs a problem well worthy the considera- "tion of such a musician as you; *viz.* wherein the difference "consists betwixt the tone of passion ‡‡ and the musical tones of "acute and grave? That there is such a difference I hold to be a "certain fact. ‖‖ For one man will sing a tune so as to make it "touch the heart of every body who has any feeling; while

(*b*) Vide p. 136. English words have the same.
(*c*) It is the same in English.

"another

" another shall sing the same tune, the same notes, the same
" rhythm, and in the same key, but without any expression.
" Now I should be glad to know, what makes this difference.
" Is it, that the one voice is clearer, sweeter, or more liquid
" than the other? Or is there something more than all that?

" There is another thing concerning the Greek language, of
" which I should be glad to have your opinion; *** whether I
" do not carry the doctrine I have learned from you, of the slides
" of the voice in speaking, too far, when I suppose, that the
" Greek acute accent did not rise at once upon the accented
" syllable; but was rising gradually upon the preceding syllables,
" and only came to its greatest height upon the acuted, and fell
" down again in like manner upon the succeeding syllables.
" This is a conjecture I proposed in the last observations I sent
" you, and I hope you will favour me with your opinion of it (d).

" I have only to add, that I am very sensible of the truth of
" what you hint in your last letter, that I know not enough of
" the practice of music to be able to judge rightly of your system.
" But though my curiosity be very great, I am afraid that I am
" too late in life to learn that, or any thing else, of which I
" know nothing at all. I have a very high opinion both of the
" theory and practice of music. As to the theory, I am clearly
" of the opinion of the Pythagoræans, that all nature is music;
" that is, numbers and proportions. Every philosopher, there-
" fore, should study the theory of it: and as to the practice,
" I hold it as a part of a liberal education to be taught it more or
" less. This, at least, was the opinion of the ancients. In

(d) See p. 142. the words *comparable, constituent, Constantinople,* and p. 143. *syllable.*

" Athens,

" Athens, every gentleman learned grammar, mufic, and the
" exercifes of the *palæstra*; and, I believe, it was fo likewife
" among the Romans, after they ceafed to be barbarians. In
" this country we are taught grammar at fchool; but not near fo
" well as you are in England. The exercifes are almoft gone
" quite out of fafhion among us; and, I believe, it is no better in
" England. And as to mufic, it never was any part of a liberal
" education here; and for that reafon I know nothing of it,
" except a little of theory, which I have taught myfelf."

LETTER TO THE AUTHOR OF THE ORIGIN AND PROGRESS OF LANGUAGE.

* * * *, Margaret Street, Sept. 23, 1775.

YOUR l——p's favour of the 21st *ult.* with your last observations, is come to my hands; to which I have given the best answers in my power. But as they refer to many passages in the fourth part, which your l——p has not yet seen, I send you six more of the proof sheets, and I hope I shall be able to present your l——p with the whole in about a month. My printer, careful to avoid errors, does not finish more than a sheet in a week; notwithstanding which, several have escaped our vigilance.

I have mentioned in a former letter to your l——p, that " nothing can tend so much to elucidate any subject as the " queries of an ingenious doubter." And it is natural to suppose, that some or all those which your l——p has made, would have come into the minds of other ingenious men: therefore, as my design was to find out and establish *a truth*, I was very well pleased to have them fully stated, that I might have the opportunity either of correcting myself, or of obviating all other probable objections by my answers to *them*. In doing which, I have experienced the infufficiency of my abilities to explain new ideas that required the utmoſt clearneſs and precifion of words: for having ſet out at firſt too concife to be intelligible, I am now under the neceffity of making repetitions to clear up the obſcurities of my former brevity.

I am, with great refpect, &c.

ANSWERS TO THE OBSERVATIONS IN THE POSTSCRIPT.

PAGE 176. * " The combinations of loud and soft syllables, " which makes what we call the feet of our English " verse, &c."

My system admits of no such *rhythmical* distinction as that of loud and soft syllables, nor of feet so formed. I was in hopes what I have said in p. 12. 19, 20. 22 to 24. 27 to 32. 68. 77. 86 to 89. would have convinced your l—p of the necessity of calling these perceptions, being manifestly different, by different names (see also p. 115. 117 to 120.). Your l—p cannot think that the Greeks meant THESIS to signify *loudness*; or ARSIS, *softness*. The emphatic distinction among syllables, which I call the POIZE, occurring periodically, and divided alternately into *heavy* and *light*, was certainly what they understood by THESIS and ARSIS. They felt the emphatic power of the THESIS, which I call *heavy* Δ; and by that feeling, or *impulse*, they were governed in the Ἀγωγὴ ῥυθμική (a), or *rhythmical* DRIFT of the tune or verse; that is, in the quality of the *metres, triple* or *common*, as well as in the degree of velocity; and this was clearly pointed out by the words Ἀγωγὴ ῥυθμικῆς ἐμφάσεως, the DRIFT of *rhythmical emphasis*.

Now if this THESIS, or *emphatic impulse*, which is *sensibly* *expected* in every *metre*, and which, in my system, lies on the

(a) Aristid. Quint. lib. I. Meib. vol. II. p. 42.

first *found* or *silence* of every CADENCE, is not distinguished from *loudness*, which means a *force of sound* uniformly exerted, and not a periodical and alternate change by intermissions, such as the POIZE of *heavy* and *light*; I say, if two affections, so palpably different, cannot be distinctly comprehended and described by appropriated terms, I cannot see how it is possible to explain them in words.

In treating of arts, there are important and significant distinctions concealed in words of vulgar use and appearance, which escape the observation of all except those who are skilled in the arts described; and therefore, notwithstanding the excellent translation and commentary of Meibomius, it is absolutely necessary to understand both Greek and *music*, in order to comprehend what the ancient writers on that subject have said; in which search, the *virtuosi* will find more help from their knowledge of the art than even of the language.

That the *emphatic impulse* of THESIS has been generally confounded with ACCENT by the moderns, has certainly been owing to their misunderstanding and misapplying what has been said by the ancients; which furnishes us with a convincing proof that the grammatical rules of *accentuation*, hitherto followed, are not only defective, but have led all those who strictly adhere to them, into an erroneous application of both ACCENT and QUANTITY; from which they are not likely to recover, till they acquire a clear understanding of the POIZE, as a peculiar and essential property, or accident *sui generis*. For, notwithstanding the resemblance in some cases, between FORCE and EMPHASIS, may contribute to make your l——p think them to be *one and the same*,

same, they certainly have nearly as much difference in their application and in their effects, as exists between and among our several senses. So, though seeing, feeling, tasting, &c. can all be reduced, under one general term, to sensation or perception; yet, as each of these five sensations have different objects and effects, they require distinguishing terms. I perceive by my eye, by my ear, by my finger, by my nose, and by my tongue; but is it not better to have the distinct powers of expression by saying, I see, hear, feel, smell, and taste? By my tongue, I may in the same instant perceive bitterness, sweetness, and heat; which, if I were denied those several distinguishing terms, I could never express so clearly and distinctly by the simple verbality of perception or sensation: I might say, I had three different perceptions; but, for want of distinguishing terms, could not explain myself farther.

In language and music, a *sentence*, or *clause*, of twenty or more *cadences* may be *loud*, and the twenty next following *soft*; but at the same time, every *cadence*, both of *loud* and *soft*, must begin under the *heavy poize* (△), and end under the light (∴ or ..): from which it must appear, that FORCE and POIZE are two different perceptions; the one being, by necessity, uniformly periodical, and alternately *heavy* and *light* within each period; the other occurring casually or *ad libitum*, and continued or interrupted at the option of the speaker.

P. 176. †. " We certainly have not the same perception of the
" division of language into combinations of *long* and *short* syllables
" (that is, *metrical feet*), as the ancients had; because having

" *no* such *rhythm* in our own language, our ears are not accus-
" tomed to it."

In speaking, there is, or may be, a measure of time chosen in such just proportion to the subject and circumstance of the discourse, as that either faster or slower would seem to fall below perfection, in comparison with that just proportion; yet it is notorious, that various speakers, whose elocution, as to the *quantity* of syllables, either in the learned or the vulgar tongues, passes without censure, do all speak in very different measures of time; that is to say, some of them much faster, or twice as fast as others; but as every one of them preserves an *unity of measure* in his own discourse, so the syllables of each, singly speaking, will hold the proper proportions of *long* and *short,* each to each, among one another: though if we were to compare the *quantity* of any certain syllable pronounced by the slower speakers, with the *quantity* of the same syllable as uttered by the more rapid, we might, among the many, find this syllable of such various lengths as to suppose there was no such thing as *quantity* in the syllables of any language. But the relative proportional *quantities* of syllables, in both learned and vulgar languages, are as fixed and certain as the *steps* of a *minuet,* or any other regular dance, wherein, whether the *agoghe* or DRIFT be faster or slower, the proportional lengths, of each to each, must be preserved under the *impulse* of *rhythmical* CADENCES (see p. 119 to 121.).

P. 176. ‡. " That language may be divided into bars, as well
" as music, you have shewn very evidently.———But I much
" doubt, whether any man, that is not a musician, can be made
" to

" to perceive it; the consequence of which is, *that it will be of*
" *no use.*"

I think, the hardness of this decision, " *that it will be of no use,*"
might be softened by adding the words, " to (the *amousoi*) those
" that do not understand music." For why need an art be
cried down, because some people do not understand another art
on which it depends? With the same justice it may be said,
" The invention of letters is of no use, because some people
" have never learned to read." *Quintilian* says, " Grammar
" cannot be perfect without music, as it must treat of *metres* and
" *rythmus*(b)." And therefore, as I have endeavoured to shew,
that our language has precisely every one of the *rhythmical,
metrical,* and *accentual* accidents attributed to the learned languages, I should hope, that Quintilian's opinion will have some
weight here; and that the learned who happen to be *amousoi,*
and consequently not competent judges of the facts, will think
it just to stand neuter, when this question comes to the vote, if
their taste and native ear for music does not incline them to be of
our side.

P. 177. ||. " Whether a speech composed in such a way as
" not to be capable of a division into bars, will not offend the
" ear as much as music so composed?"

Neither music nor speech can be so composed as not to be
capable of a division into bars; but a bad musician, or a bad
speaker, may pronounce so as to keep no certain measure. And

(b) Institut. Orat. lib. I. c. 4. De Grammaticâ. Tum nec citra musicen grammatica potest esse perfecta, cum ei de metris rhythmisque dicendum sit.

a speech written down by the help of our notes, according to the bad manner of such a speaker, would appear to be divided *unrhythmically*; that is, by no equality of METRES or CADENCES. Even poets of great character sometimes write lines that, without great management of the reader, appear to be not divisible by *bars* or CADENCES of equal measure; but, by our rules, the worst can be reduced to METRICAL CADENCES and RHYTHMUS. (See the examples from the first book of Paradise Lost, *p.* 159.)

The syllabic articulations of speech are distinctly formed by the change of our organs, in expressing the several *literal sounds* of language: but the different *meanings* of *words*, formed by the same, or nearly the same, literal sounds and syllables, are distinguished by ACCENT, QUANTITY, and POIZE.

The POIZE being divided alternately into *heavy* △ and *light* ∴, and the *heavy* △, or *emphatic*, occurring uniformly, during the whole continuance of the same measure, at equi-distant periods, answers the same end between a speaker and his audience, as beating time does among musicians. For in whatsoever measure the speaker delivers himself, still the *agoghe*, the *emphatic impulse* of the POIZE, will keep both him and his audience in time together, and compel him to preserve the just *metrical proportions* of *quantity* in his *cadences*, according to *his* habitual dialect or tone.
△
For example:

Suppose two persons of the same habitual dialect or tone, differing only in velocity; the one quicker, the other slower; If the first should speak a sentence in the proportion of *six times*, or *six quavers*, in each CADENCE, allowing *one time* or *quaver* to

the

the *shortest syllable*; and the other should repeat the same words in the proportion of *twelve times*, or *six crotchets* in each CADENCE, that is, allowing *two times*, or *one crotchet*, to the *shortest syllables*: it is evident, these two speakers would separately preserve the same ratio or proportion in the lengths of their syllables, each to each; so that, in that respect, the words would carry the same meaning, though the first speaker would pronounce twice as quick as the last; for the first would utter two CADENCES in the same space of time that the second would pronounce only one. As thus, the proportions marked in numbers:

First speaker, in cadences of six times.

3.	1. 2.	3.	1. 2.	4.	2. 4. 2.	2. 2. 2.	3. 1. 2.
Light as the	lightening	glimpse,		they	ran, they	flew.

Second speaker, in cadences of twelve times.

6.	2. 4.	6.	2. 4.	8.	4. 8. 4.	4. 4. 4.	6. 2. 4.
Light as the	lightening	glimpse,		they	ran, they	flew.

But if the same words were uttered in the following manner by a third person, where, by the inequality of the *metres* or CADENCES, the RHYTHMUS is quite destroyed, and the POIZE misplaced,

False

False cadences, or metres, of unequal time.

1. 4. 8.	4. 8. 8.	4. 8.	4. 2. 4. 4.	4. 4. 4.
Light as the	lightening	glimpse,	they ran,	they flew.

we should perceive the language so altered, as that it would scarce seem to be the same; it would be ridiculous or disagreeable, like the most uncouth mixture of different provincial manners; and the dislocated order of the POIZE (if any one could pronounce so) would give pain to an audience.

People who stutter, pronounce partly in this latter manner; but it is notorious, when such persons sing,' they never hesitate or stutter; whence it may be supposed, the most easy and effectual method of curing them, would be to accustom them to beat time to their reading and common discourse, by which means they might learn to speak in just time to the proper measure of their words and phrases. For it should seem, the cause of their hesitation and stuttering arises from some inaptitude to fall in immediately with the *rhythmical pulsation* or *poize* befitting their words; but which, in singing, they are enabled to do, by the additional influence of the *diastematic melody*, wherein the CADENCES are more certainly pointed out, than even in poetry, or any language without additional music.

P. 177. ※ " I must own myself fully convinced, that the
" pauses make an essential part of the rhythm of speech, and
" that if a man stops ——— too long or too short, &c."

As your l—p is convinced of the necessity of measured *pauses*, you will easily conceive, that neither *syllables* nor *pauses* can be measured or duly proportioned without a certain uniform *pulsation*, either actual or in the mind; and this brings us to the necessity of the division by CADENCES or *bars*, the beginning of each CADENCE being marked almost as sensibly by the △ *heavy* POIZE, as if the measure was beaten by the hand or foot.

P. 178. †† " The modern Greeks have lost these tones, and
" in place of *acute* and *grave* have substituted *loud* and *soft*; for
" they constantly found every syllable *loud* which is marked in
" the Greek books, with an *acute accent*, &c."

Allow me here to put my terms of *heavy* and *light*, in the room of your l—p's words *loud* and *soft*; and then we shall agree, that the modern Greeks, misunderstanding what their ancestors meant by THESIS and ARSIS, and misled by the grammarians and commentators of the barbarous middle ages, are now in the same error with ourselves, by not considering that " the POIZE " of syllables is the most determined accident in language" (p. 144.), though all nations must feel it, and by not making a proper distinction between that and ACCENT.

∴ △ ∴ △ ∴ △ ∴

P. 178. ‡‡ " Wherein (does) the difference consist betwixt
" the tone of passion and the musical tones of acute and grave?"

The tones of passion are distinguished by a greater extent of the voice both into the *acute* and the *grave*, and by making the *antithesis*, or diversity between the two, more remarkable. Also
by

by increasing the *forte*, and making contrasts occasionally between the *forte* and *piano*; and by giving an extraordinary *energy* or *emphasis*, and blending the *forte* now and then with the *heavy poize*; and lastly, by sudden and desultory changes of the measure and of its modes; that is, from *fast* to *slow*, and *vice versâ*; and from *common* to *triple*, and *vice versâ*.

P. 178. |||| " One man will sing a tune so as to touch the " heart;———another———without any expression."

A great deal of this difference lies in the tone of voice, but a great deal more belongs to art, which comes under the head of taste, and is done by adding *insinuating graces* (see p. 145.) and by the discreet use of the *staccato* and *sostenuto*, the *piano* and *forte*, the *swell* and *dying away*.

P. 179. ✷✷✷ " Whether———the Greek *acute accent* did (or " did) not rise at once upon the *acuted syllable*, but was rising " gradually upon the preceding syllables, &c."

This depended generally on the subject, attendant circumstances, or the humour of the speaker, and sometimes, I conceive, on particular words; for so it is in our language. A review of the several examples which I have given will shew, that the *accent* rises or falls, sometimes at once, and at other times gradually.

And let it be remembered, as it is said in p. 30, " that " drawing the *accents* simply over the syllables, without the *five* " *musical parallel* lines, but with some regard to higher or lower " by position of the marks, was so certain a guide, &c."———

I say,

I say, let it be remembered, that in the several examples, where the *accents* are drawn some higher or lower than others, as ╱╱ it means to shew, that the second *acute* continued ascending gradually higher than the first; and if thus, ╱╱ it means to shew, that the second *acute* did not begin from so low a tone as the first, but surpassed it in going higher. The same observations, being reversed, will apply to the *grave*, as ╲╲ or ╲╲; a little attention will make this familiar, especially as great accuracy is not absolutely necessary in the dawn of this art, for we are allowed a great latitude in the pitch and extent of our *accents*.

ADDITIONS.

September, 1779.

SINCE the first publication of this essay, the author having received several remarks of learned correspondents, containing doubts, queries, and objections, and among other things observing that some of the terms made use of in the treatise, as well as some of the examples of accentuation, do not agree with such rules, as have been laid down by antient writers and their commentators: He answers in general, that he collected the materials, of which this system is composed, from repeated experiments on his own language; for which purpose, he was obliged to appropriate a set of terms, under special definitions, to guard, as much as he could, against their being misunderstood, as some of them have been heretofore variously misapplied: Now, as far as any of his terms, propositions, or rules, agree with those laid down by the antients, or their commentators, for the Greek or Latin languages, he considers them as lucky incidents that tend perhaps to prove their truth, which however he did not designedly provide for; and where they differ, he must submit to be censured by the champions of those old authorities; but hopes, they will always remember, that his principal view was only to settle a mode of noting an accentuation for the English tongue, and that, therefore, he is not bound to agree with any of those writers, either antient or modern, who did not separate *quantity* from *emphasis*, and both of these from *accent*, and all three, each from the other, according to the nature of those *accidents* in the English language, nor with those Greek or Latin authors (however high in fame) who, thinking it necessary to mark an acute *accent* only to one syllable in a word, have led strangers to conclude the other syllables were positively to have none.

Some of these remarkers take notice, that this new system admits two or three acute accents immediately following each other in the same word, which the antient rules did not. In answer to this, let it be observed, that the antients had no distinct mark for emphasis; for, their commentators have generally supposed that *acute, emphasis*, and the *long syllable*, always went together, or at least that the acute should not fall on a short syllable; but this English system, which has distinguished *accent, quantity*, and *emphasis*, by separate marks, shews that the *emphasis* or *poize*, divided into the heavy △, and the light ∴, is the most important and the most characteristic in our language; and I will add, perhaps and probably, upon further enquiry, may be found to have been the same in the Greek; for though two or three acuted, or two or three long syllables may immediately follow each other, two △ heavy syllables can never follow in the same word, line, or sentence, without the intervention of a ∴ light syllable in sound, or, a pause for it, in silence.

I have the most reverential respect for the general learning of the antient Greeks; and though I am sure we have not, in many points, derived all the knowledge from their remains, which may still be in our power; yet I believe their mathematics, their politics, and their ethics, or moral philosophy, have been tolerably well explained to us; and we have adopted as much of them as our own particularities could hitherto bear. But after acquiring so much of the useful, we have undoubtedly thrown away a great deal of time and pains in discussions concerning the pronunciation of their antient, now a dead language, and in endeavouring to explain the tones, properties, and affections of their letters and syllables; while, for want of bestowing the like labours in analysing and separately examining the several elementary properties and accidents of our living languages,—and whilst every illiterate peasant is in the constant and distinct use of such *accent*, *quantity*, and *emphasis*, as is peculiar to his native tongue,—our men of letters are composing treatises to shew that all those elegant distinctions died with the old Greeks and Romans; and are putting words on paper to prove, what the first sentence they pronounce before a sensible audience, will most forcibly contradict.

I believe the organs and faculties destined for the utterance of speech are and have been generally of the same structure and power, in all the human species, at all times.—Under this persuasion, I was of opinion, that by employing my thoughts in and upon my native language, I should sooner be able to discover, to analyse, and to describe separately, what appeared to me to be the essential properties or accidents in enunciation, than if I had determined, in the first instance, to take nothing but what I could derive from the writings of the antients, or, in defiance of my senses, reject any discovery of my own, unless I could make it bend to the vague and discordant rules of commentators.—I therefore resolved to depend neither on hypothesis, nor on antient authorities, for any facts which I could ascertain by actual experiment;

experiment;—by a pendulum, or by my steps, I can measure the *quantities* of time;—by an instrument of music, or by my ear, I can distinguish between *acute* and *grave*;—by the same means, I can discover the manifest difference between the *emphatic* △ and the *unemphatic* ∴ *poize:*—and by the use of these simple tools, if I may so call them, I think, I have rendered this subject something clearer than it was left to us by the antients; and, I hope, I have recovered it from the confusion and perplexity some parts of it were involved in by the moderns.

Having premised so much, candor obliges me to present my reader with the principal of the above-mentioned critical doubts and observations, in the words of their very respectable authors; who, I am persuaded, lay under no prejudice against the new system, except what they derived from their profound erudition.

Extract of a Letter from Glasgow, 27th January, 1776.

' 1. THE first of the observations I alluded to, is with re-
' gard to the *imperfection* of the scheme of notation, in as far as
' *tone* is concerned. The scale itself is only accommodated to
' quarter tones as the most minute divisions—even this quarter-
' tone-scale is abandoned for the common scale of tones and se-
' mitones—and even that also is (in many of the instances ad-
' duced) relinquished, and a still more general measurement of
' ascent and descent adopted, viz. a simple ascending and descend-
' ing line (╱ ╲) which gives no intimation, or at least but a very
' general one, how to estimate the lowest and highest of the
' slide—that although the inclined and curved form of the
' symbols

' symbols (/ \ ⌒ ✓) is a noble contrivance to mark out the
' *anomalies* in the progress of the slide, yet they may perhaps
' not come up to all the variety necessary to be represented, and
' leave the performer too much at liberty in his execution—
' that therefore an attempt towards a nicer and more minute
' graduation would contibute much to the utility of the system—
' and to the general conviction of its foundation in truth. It is
' doubted whether the notation given of the speech in Hamlet,
' would enable an expert performer to execute it as you, from
' your nice ear, and memory combined with it, can do. If so, it
' must in part detract from the evidence of the system.

' 2. You seem to consider the antient way of dividing verse
' into *metres* as imperfect when compared with a division by *ca-*
' *dences* or *bars:* and your idea grounds itself chiefly upon this,
' that these *metres* (meaning by them such as are capable of
' being constructed by feet of different quantities) cannot be re-
' duced to any common measure. Now, in the first place, may
' we not conceive some such common standard to which the
' metres may be reduced by filling up the deficiencies with
' pauses, as you have done the passages in ordinary discourse,
' which surely have an appearance not less anomalous—or, se-
' condly, may they not in many cases be defended by the general
' conduct of even modern musicians?

' Keeping in the same piece of music to *one key*—to *one loud-*
' *ness*—to *one duration* for a note of the same kind—to *one mode*
' *of time*—is so far from being a rule prescribed, that a piece
' composed on such principles would be scarce capable of being
' attended to —In proportion as our *ears* become more refined,

' and

‘ and our minds capable of greater mufical *verfatility* (fo to fpeak)
‘ we are able to *endure* greater deviations from *famenefs* in all
‘ thefe articles; and even feem to *require* them. The fame man,
‘ who in the infancy of his mufical training, could not enter into
‘ a tranfition from *common* to *triple* time, till after fuch an inter-
‘ val of filence as made them appear two different pieces, will,
‘ after his progrefs and experience is increafed, be able to go
‘ along with this tranfition, when it goes on in the way of in-
‘ fertion—ftill, however, it will be neceffary that the tranfition
‘ be not quickly nor frequently made, he will perhaps bear them
‘ at firft after 20 bars—then fixteen—then 12, and fo on—now
‘ where muft this end? could not an exquifite ear not only en-
‘ dure, but at laft receive a kind of regale from a piece where
‘ there was an alternate tranfition from common to triple every
‘ fingle bar? could you not, for inftance enter eafily into that
‘ fragment of antient mufic, fet to an ode of Pindar, given by
‘ Rouffeau in his mufical dictionary, where many of thefe tran-
‘ fitions occur? I myfelf can go along with it as far as the time
‘ is concerned.—Now, many of the antient metres were nothing
‘ more than this; if, for inftance, a tragic verfe went on in pure
‘ iambics—it was all triple—if in metres where the fpondee, or
‘ dactyle, or anapeft, was admitted, then there was this rapid
‘ tranfition from the one time to the other.’

Extract

Extract from the Answer, 30th May, 1776.

AS you mentioned in your letter that you intended to give the essay another reading, I was in hopes you would find your two objections were already provided for in the book itself.

For the 1st, see what I have said in page 30; by which, however, I did not mean to hinder any person, who will take the pains, from using the accurate scale by quarter tones (as described in p. 6, and p. 13.) or from noting any poem or speech in that manner. I intended no more in my essay than to shew demonstratively, that there was a *melody* or *accentual* variety of extent, *acute* and *grave*, of the human voice in common speech, the manner of which was by slides; and I thought the *notes* I gave were sufficient to support my propositions by experiments visible and audible: but I do not conceive we can require any division for that purpose more minute than quarter-tones; for I believe no human ear is at present capable of estimating any interval in the tones of speech smaller.

If any one can invent better and more accurate *notes*, such an improvement will give me great pleasure. In the mean time, I am very glad to know that my small attempt is so well received as to inspire the notion of a farther improvement; considering that two years ago, all former opinions concerning the *accentual melody* of speech, though dogmatically asserted, yet being unsupported by auricular experimental proofs, were, by many learned men, as dogmatically denied.

2. As to your second observation concerning the difference, I have supposed to be between the *Greek metres* and my division by

cadences

cadences or *bars*, when I marked this difference, I confidered the Greek metres as they are authoritatively defined; but you will fee in p. 82 and 83, that I have fet the firft five lines of the Iliad exactly according to your idea, having accommodated the antient metres and my cadences together by means of paufes; but, for this, you know, I had no authority from our received rules of profody. Viz. p. 78.

The definitions of rhythmus* and metre have been left in fuch a cloud of confufion by all commentators, that I have feen, (not excepting even Mr. Fofter, whofe effay has however a great deal of merit) that I thought it neceffary to give my notions of their nature, their fimiliarity, and difference as clearly as poffible. See p. 72, 73. 78. 114, 115. 121. 128, 129. 135, 136. 148. 163. 170. 183. 188.

The mixtures of the different meafures *common* and *triple*, are accounted for, explained, and exemplified, p. 25. 28, 29. 40, 41. 121. and in feveral other parts: Nothing is more eafy; for ♩·♩· make a cadence or bar in common meafure, and are exactly equal in length or duration to ♩♩♩ which make a cadence or bar of triple meafure; the duration of each cadence or bar being determined by the fwing of the fame length of pendulum; as in p. 28, the meafure changes from 2 to 3, but the times or lengths of each cadence or pulfation, are fuppofed to be exactly equal, notwithftanding the diverfity of the fubdivifion into 2, or into 3.—But in p. 42, where the meafure changes from 3 to 2, with *allegretto*

---

* Rhythmus being an appropriated term in this effay, it was neceffary for the author to give a clear definition of it, according to his meaning, efpecially as he does not mean to be governed by the various fenfes given to this term by commentators.

wrote over the change, it is intended to quicken the pulsation, as if made by a shorter pendulum, and to lengthen it again in p. 43, where it returns to triple measure; but these changes of pendulum or pulsation are never required, or indeed admissible in speech, only on occasion of expressing some degree of passion, of joy, grief, despair, anger, &c. and will not be more frequent than the changes of such emotions in the mind; whereas the changes or mixture of the measures, triple and common, without altering the pulsation or length of pendulum, happens continually, independant of any passion; being necessarily governed by the natural poize and quantities of the words and syllables made use of, as will appear through all the examples given in the essay —The pious composer of the celebrated exhortation put into the mouths of all our parish clerks, " *Let us sing to the* " *praise and glory of God!*" had certainly the idea of a dance in his heart at the time he conceived them; for it is impossible to pronunce them otherwise than in jig measure, giving the sentence its natural *agoghe* in our language.

Extracts of Letters communicated by a Friend.

I.

'I received Mr. Steele's book; his notion of the melody of
'speech is to be found in Aristophanes, p. 8, 9, where he de-
'fines it to be produced by continued sounds, whereas that of
'long is produced by distinct intervals; but I believe Mr. Steele
'is the first that ever attempted to reduce it to a regular system.
'I cannot

'I cannot at prefent execute his flides on the violoncello fo as to
'imitate language, and I doubt whether I ever fhall, for it feems
'to require much practice.

'Mr. Garrick's objection, page 54, feems to me unanfwerable;
'for I have heard Correlli's jig in the famous 5th folo, played
'very differently by two eminent mafters, though both played
'the notes, *come flavano* (without gracing) on fine inftruments.
'And if a piece of mufic, where the founds are perfectly defined,
'can be played in different taftes; much more one where flides
'require a peculiar neatnefs (or delicacy) of expreffion.

'I cannot approve of Mr. Steele's manner of dividing the
'Greek and Latin heroic verfe for recital, it feems totally incon-
'fiftent with the Greek doctrine of Rhythm, whereby they fup-
'plied the want of our manner of marking meafure by bars;
'their mufical notes having no dinftinction of long and fhort like
'ours. In page 153, there are fome errors, &c.'

2.

'I am far from thinking that Mr. Steele's notion of the me-
'lody of fpeech was not his own difcovery, though it is as old
'as Pythagoras, and mentioned by almoft all the Greek writers
'on Mufic now remaining, and particularly defcribed by fome.
'But Mr. Steele has certainly the merit of having reduced it to
'a practical fyftem. It feems, however, to require fo much
'practice to obtain a facility in executing the flides, and efpeci-
'ally the circumflexes, with the velocity and neatnefs requifite to
'imitate common fpeech, that I defpair of its ever coming into ufe.

I wish Mr. Steele had seen the section on versification, in Dr. Pemberton's Essay, or *Observations on Epic Poetry*.'

Answer to the foregoing Extracts.

I AM much obliged to you for communicating to me some paragraphs of your letters from your learned and ingenious friend.

The system of the *melody and measure of speech*, was many years in my head before I put any thing on paper; and it was not till after I had made the first sketch of it, that I looked into the antient Greek authors; when finding that I had fortunately wandered into the same paths with them, I was encouraged to hazard the publication.

I imagine that after a perusal of my essay, so great a master of the Greek tongue as your friend, may find many interesting passages in the antient Greek musicians and grammarians which have long escaped general notice.

He observes, " he cannot yet execute the slides on the violon-" cello so as to imitate language:" To do that to a degree of perfection would be very difficult; but my directions intend no more than to make use of that means as a sliding scale, in order to find out, on every occasion, whether a syllable is *acute, grave,* or *circumflex*, (acute grave, or grave acute), and also to measure the extent of each accent, how much in degree of ascent or descent; and to do this will not be found very difficult after a few trials.

I cannot

I cannot agree to the inftance your friend adduces againft the poffibility of a correct and certain notation, when he fays, " he " heard *Corelli's jig* played very differently by two eminent maf- " ters, though both played the notes *come ftavano* (exactly as they " were written, fimply and) without gracing."—In the editions which I have feen of Corelli's folos, there are no other characters expreffed, except thofe of the meafure, with the quantity, and quality (*acute* or *grave*) of the notes, and alfo of the *flurs*; which laft, if they have any precife meaning, are to determine fuch parts to be played *foftenuto* and not *ftaccato*; there are no marks of *forte* or *piano*, except to the laft claufe of the whole tune, which is marked *piano*; therefore there feems to be no licence for variation, fub- mitted to the pleafure of the performer, who fhould undertake to play the notes *come ftanno*, except in the degree of contraft that he may chufe to make between the antecedent loudnefs, and the fubfequent foftnefs of this *piano*; for the quantity of *al- legro* may be fixed by a pendulum.—Now, I fay, if three fimilar copies of this tune, as here defcribed, are fent to be fet by three barrel organ-makers, one in Germany, another in France, and the third in England, I will anfwer for it that their three inftru- ments will play the tune, as to manner, exactly the fame way; nor will the variety of ftops, employed by each maker (high or low pitch, reed ftops or flutes, though much greater than the variety of violins, or of human voices) make any difference in the correct identity of the tune. And although from the want of more accurate marks than were known in Corelli's time, or than are yet generally ufed by muficians, a great variety of ex- preffion (in the degrees of *piano, forte, crefcendo, diminuendo, ftac-*

cato,

cato, sostenuto, &c.) may or may not be applied, by people of peculiar tastes, where no marks of such expression have been written; yet in such cases those expressions must be admitted to be *graces ad libitum,* and consequently that the performer who employed them did not play the notes simply *come stavano.*

For the liberty I have taken in offering a new manner of prosodiac notation for poetry of any language, and particularly for Greek and Latin, I have made an apology in my essay, with some reasons in support of my opinion.

I do not think the Greek method of defining their measures of time was so accurate as their natural sensation of those measures must have been; and though we do not know of any symbolic marks used by them to distinguish between the *long* and *short* notes of a tune, without the accompanyment of words, it is certain, when the tune was so accompanied, that then each note assumed its proper *quantity* from the known length or shortness of its correspondent syllable; therefore, as far as appears to us, we should suppose the Greeks had not such smybolic marks for *measure* and *quantity* (in orchestra music unaccompanied by words) as the moderns have invented; though they certainly must have observed and kept those measures in their performances, in like manner as our vulgar unlettered musicians do, who play only by ear.

But, admitting the Greeks probably governed, the time and measures of their orchestra music only by ear, having had no marks of *quantity* to their musical notes; they were, however, very accurate in the quantities of their words and syllables.— Contrary to them, the moderns are very accurate in making the
quantities

quantities of their musical notes, but have abandoned the *quantity* and measure of language to be governed entirely by ear.—The lengths of antient musical notes in a song were limited by the lengths of the syllables: the lengths of syllables in modern songs are extended or curtailed by the accidental lengths of the notes.—And whereas in modern songs, the principal attention, both of the singer, and of the audience, is given to the tune, and little to the words; I am of opinion, that in Greek music, the chief attention was to the words, and little to the tune.—From hence it may happen, that when many of the languages of this age may be neglected and forgotten, its music may be preserved and esteemed.

Since the publication of my essay, I have found in *Bacchius Senior*, a passage, which I wish I had discovered before*: in Meibom. Bacch. Sen. p. 23, he says, "They had three sorts of "measure for time, *short, long,* and *irrational*: The *short*, the "least in quantity, and incapable of division; the *long*, double "the quantity of the *short*; the *irrational* longer than the *short*, "and shorter than the *long*; but because it is difficult to explain "in what ratio it is longer or shorter, it is therefore called *irra-* "*tional.*"

I acknowledge again, I had not remarked or attended to this passage in Bacchius when I took the liberty of applying my notation to a few lines of the Æneid and Iliad.—But whether Bacchius would think that I had thereby reduced the *short*, the *long*, and the *irrational*, to one certain, intelligible, and practicable rule;

---

* I confess myself subject, like other travellers, to ride post through a book, and consequently liable sometimes to run by objects without discovering all their importance.

or whether I had rather confounded them all; for want of his personal appearance, I must submit the decision to the judgment of those who are more intimately acquainted with him and his countrymen than I am.

I shall be much obliged to your friend for his corrections and observations on every part; for, whether I agree with him or not in them all, they will greatly contribute to throw a farther light on a subject which is yet very obscure, and hardly distinguishable in the modern world.

I shall be glad to see Dr. Pemberton's essay, and particularly his section on versification, mentioned by your friend: at present I know nothing of it, but on his recommendation I shall peruse it with attention.

REMARKS on Mr. Steele's *Treatise on the Melody and Measure of Speech.*

' Page 24. Emphasis or Cadence; Heavy △, Light ∴.

' Here emphasis and cadence are supposed to be the same, but
' the former is competent to a single sound, whereas cadence (in
' melody) consists in the succession of one sound to another.—
' Rousseau, in his musical dictionary, defines cadence in melody
' to be " a quality in good music, where the performer or the
" hearer immediately discovers the measure as it were by in-
" stinct."—' This must be by a different succession of sounds
' proper to different measures; and when once the ear has caught
' the measure, the mind seems involuntarily to lay an emphasis
' on

' on the repetition of it at the beginning of every bar, which
' may have given occasion to musicians to call the beginning of
' the bar its accented part, not distinguishing between accent and
' emphasis.—And this emphasis, whether expressed or imagined,
' seems to be what Mr. Steele calls heavy.'

ANSWER.

The author of the essay, having given special definitions of all his appropriated terms, has defined emphasis, cadence, or poize, as comprehending the two affections of △ heavy, and of ∴ light; and in some cases the three affections of △ heavy, .. lightest, and ∴ light, and sometimes thus, △ heavy, .. lightest, ∴ light and .. lightest; examples of all which are in the essay*. But having defined and appropriated a set of terms to a new system, it is in this essay, and not in prior dictionaries, those definitions are to be sought.

Rousseau's dictionary gives the definitions of four genera, besides several species of the term *cadence* among musicians: happily one of them nearly agrees with our author's sense of it.— Almost all the terms necessary to be used on this occasion, have been so variously applied and confounded among commentators, antient as well as modern, that nothing less than special definitions could keep us from falling into the same confusion: wherefore, though we have, as far as we could, made use of the same materials, we thought it more adviseable to erect a new, than to attempt to repair the old building.

* See p. 34. 41. 43. 45.

REMARKS.

' The Greek and Latin accents were regulated by the quantities of the syllables; they never placed the *circumflex* on the last syllable but one, nor the *acute* on the last but two, when the last syllable was long: and the Romans did not place the *acute* accent on the last but two, if either of the two was long. Quintilian, treating of the Latin accents in his first book, says, "Evenit ut metri quoque conditio mutet accentum, ut

"———— *pecudes pictæque volucres*,

"nam *volúcres*, media acuta legam; quia etsi brevis natura, tamen positione longa est, ne faciat Iambum, quem non recipit versus heroïcus."—' Which implies either that the accent lengthened the syllable, or that the want of it shortened it.'

ANSWER.

This observation brings on a trial, in which both Virgil and Quintilian are necessarily brought to our bar.

I will set the whole line, marking the feet, and the quantities in the word *volucres*, as Quintilian says, they legally were or should be in any other position.

| Et genus | æquore | um | pecu | des | pic | tæque Vo | lu cres |

To avoid any dispute about the form of the dactyls, I have marked them in the old way; but to save Virgil's honour, in respect to the *short* and the *long*, I have helped out the short syllable *lu* with a crotchet rest, in order to make the last bar or cadence equal to the time of a spondee*; and as I suppose Quintilian felt, though he did not say so, that, by position, *lu* required to be pronounced emphatically, I have marked △ the heavy poize under it.—Now I conclude this application of *volucres* could only be excused as a poetical licence; for, Quintilian says, in any other position, vo | lu cres | must have been | volucres | or | volu | cres | ; but where was the △ heavy poize or emphasis to be? he is silent: he talks only of *acuting lú*, and of making it *long*, but seems not to have comprehended that *thesis*, or the *heavy* emphasis was the distinguishing mark, which, in the utterance, was to accompany that syllable in that place: the words of Quintilian imply, that the *acute* lengthened the syllable; but if length of time was the requisite wanting, the crotchet *rest* which I have marked, fills up the time, though it leaves the syllable still a short one: and Mr. Foster, in his 4th chapter, proves authoritatively, that an acute accent may lie on a short syllable; therefore we must conclude, the liberty taken by Virgil in this place, was not, accurately, what Quintilian says, but was precisely putting the syllable (*lu*) in *thesis*, whereas it naturally should have been (*lu*) in *arsis*; or in other words, Virgil put it in a place where it must be pronounced *emphatically*, though by its nature it was *unemphatic.*—I have appealed on this occasion

* See p. 170, and 163, 164.

to Mr. Foster, only to support me with his learned authorities, in proving how this matter stood in the Greek and Latin languages: for the many examples which I have given in the essay, shew undeniably to those readers who will take the trouble of examining them experimentally, that the *acute* accent, in our language, though most frequently joined with the *heavy* and the *long*, is sometimes with the *short* and the *light*; and that the *heavy poize* △, though oftenest with the *long* and the *acute*, is sometimes with the *short* and the *grave**.

The last or tenth syllable, of what is commonly called an English heroic line of poetry, should be △ heavy, in like manner as the penultima, or last syllable but one, of the Latin or Greek heroic or hexameter line; against this rule, in the instance above-mentioned, the great *Virgil* has erred; so our great *Pope*, as well as all our other poets, under the hard necessity of writing smooth sense, in rugged words, and clogged with barbarous rhyme, frequently force *light* syllables to fill the places of *heavy*;

In faith and hope | the world will disagree

But | all man | kind's con | cern | is | chari | ty:

Which, according to its proper poize should be | charity | ; but then the line would want above half a cadence or half a bar of its due length; and yet I apprehend a judicious reader would

* See p. 76. 119. et passim.

rather

[213]

rather deliver it so as to give the just sound to the word charity,
△ .. ∴

and make up the deficiency of time by a silence, than to vitiate the pronunciation in compliment to the strict measure and the rhyme. (See p. 188.)

The following arrangements of the poize may be applied to a line of the celebrated Gay;

 The peeping fan in modern times shall rise,
 Through which, unseen the female ogle flies;

3 | This shall in | temples | the shy | maid con | ceal,
 △ .. ∴ | △ ∴ | △ ∴ | △ ∴ | △

 And shelter love beneath devotion's veil.

Or thus, for these words run very naturally into jig measure;

3 | This shall in | temples, | the | shy maid con | ceal
 △ ... ∴ | △ .. ∴ | △ ∴ | △ .. ∴ | △

Or if both these were offensive, the words might be thus transposed;

3 | This, the shy | maid, | in | temples, | shall con | ceal
 △ .. ∴ | △ ∴ | △ ∴ | △ ∴ | △ ∴ | △

But after all, I suppose, Mr. Gay would have read this line thus;

3 | This shall in | temples | the | shy | maid con | ceal
 △ .. ∴ | △ ∴ .. | △ ∴ | △ ∴ | △ .. | △ ∴

The significancy of which manner is probably lost on the generality of readers, through want of some such notation.

REMARKS.

REMARKS.

'Are not the two following rules obferved in our own and in
'fome other languages?

'Firft, In all polyfyllable words that have one or more long
'fyllables, the accent fhall fall on a long fyllable.

'Secondly, In polyfyllable words that have no long fyllable,
'that on which the accent falls, may occafionally fupply the
'place of a long fyllable in verfe. I think we obferve both
'thefe rules, and they may have been the occafion of our con-
'founding accent with quantity.'

ANSWER.

This queftion, with the two rules and the remark upon them, are all derived from the prejudices of our antient learning; the truth is, that by not diftinguifhing the *emphatic poize* from *accent*, we have confounded our whole profody antient and modern. In both thefe queftions if the learned remarker had confulted his ear, inftead of his grammarians, he would have put the word *emphafis* in the room of the word *accent*. I can, however, with great certainty anfwer, that neither of the rules are fuitable with our language; for in the words 2| im | poffible |, 3| con | feffion |, 2| deference |, | de | liberate | | delicate, |, and in many others, the *thefis*, heavy △, or emphatic poize, lies on the fhort fyllables, and the

arfis,

arſis, or ∴ light, on the long ſyllables; I leave accent entirely out of the queſtion, as it has nothing to do with rhythmus or metre.——And here I muſt repeat, that it is emphaſis, cadence, or the poize of △ heavy and ∴ light (by the Greeks called *theſis* and *arſis*), which alone governs, by its periodical pulſation, that part of muſic and poetry (as well as of dancing) properly called rhythmus. (See p. 87.) The whole time or duration of each cadence, of which the rhythmus conſiſts, is made exactly equal, each to each, but the metrical ſubdiviſion of each cadence may vary as to the quantities or number of the notes and ſyllables, provided the ſum of the quantities of one cadence does not exceed the ſum in each of the other cadences. See p. 116.

Whether a cadence begins with a ſhort or a long ſyllable, or note, or with a reſt in ſilence, is quite indifferent to rhythmus; but that firſt ſyllable, or note, or reſt, muſt invariably carry with it the △ heavy poize, or *theſis*.

REMARKS.

' 1. There can be no greater proofs of the uncertainty of the
' meaſure of the Engliſh language (or perhaps of the inaccuracy
' of my ear), than the liſt of words marked with proper accent,
' quantity, and emphaſis, from p. 136 to p. 144; in many of
' which I have the mortification to find I differ from Mr. Steele.
' P. 139, *beauty*, is, in my opinion, a *trochee*, like *duty*.——*Beauti-*
' *ful*, a *dactyl*.——*Beautifully*, a firſt *pæon*, or a double *trochee*; and
' the like in many more.

' 2. In this liſt many of the words are made to carry two
' acute accents, ſome two circumflexes; others one, or more
' acute

'acute accents, and a circumflex; the word *neceſſity* has two con‑
'tiguous acute accents; all this contrary to the antient doctrine
'of accentuation.'

ANSWER.

1. This criticiſm is very flattering to our author, as it proves that the ſymbols made uſe of in this eſſay are ſufficient for marking any mode of pronunciation, ſo as not to be miſunder‑ſtood by a reader.

It is not very material, whether the author was right or wrong in his application of the marks of quantity to the words *beauty* and *beautiful*, or whether he aſcribed them juſtly to thoſe Greek feet to which they properly belong; as his intention was not ſo much to ſhew how theſe words ſhould be pronounced, as how that pronunciation, whether right or wrong, ſhould be marked. The difference between a *dactyl*, an *anapeſt*, and a *cretic*, or between a *ſpondee* and a *trochee*, or an *iambus*, is very unimportant at preſent in our language, provided the *theſis* or △ heavy poize is not put out of its proper place. What a degree of nicety we may attain hereafter I cannot judge of; it is a great point gained now to have it admitted that we have the varieties of accent, quantity, and emphaſis, in any modern tongue.

2. The antient doctrine of accentuation called that affection in ſyllables, *accent*, which was and is really *emphaſis*.—I have marked acutes and circumflexes as I found them by experiment, and they often follow each other without interruption: but the ſame experiments have compelled me to lay it down as an in‑variable rule, that two △ △ *theſis*, or heavy poized expreſſions,

can never immediately follow each other, without the intervention of ∴ *arſis*, or the light, whether in ſound or in ſilence: and I apprehend this ſhould have been the rule of the antients, if they had, on this occaſion, explained themſelves with their uſual preciſion and perſpicuity.

REMARKS.

' In p. 51, the ſpeech of Demoſthenes is ſet to one regular
' movement, all through, which Cicero reckons a great fault in
' oratory.—In p. 53, and elſewhere, there ſeems to be an in-
' congruity in placing two prickt crotchets in a bar where the
' movement is by three crotchets, for two prickt crotchets in a
' bar is common time, the *arſis* and *theſis* being equal.'

ANSWER.

The mixture of the two genera of common and triple meaſure is employed in the example, p. 51, as well as in p. 53. In computation of meaſure, ſilence being as ſignificant as ſound, the reader will ſee that the 5th, 10th, 12th, and 13th bars or cadences, having the quantities of their △ heavy and ∴ light equal, give the diverſity of common meaſure mixed with triple, without, however, being incongruous either there or in page 53, ſince the rhythmus is not diſturbed by this variety of metrical ſubdiviſion within the cadences, while the whole times of the cadences are moſt ſcrupulouſly equal, each to each. It will be found alſo, on a cloſe examination, that the triple cadences are otherways variouſly diverſified; ſo that we imagine that ſpecimen does not in this inſtance fall under the cenſure denounced by Cicero.—To those who are better acquainted with arithmetic than with music, the diversities in the measures of the speech of Demosthenes, p. 51 and 53, will be more apparent when exhibited in the numbers, of which the bars or cadences are composed, as thus, p. 53.—Let the quaver $|$ = 1, and $\curlyvee$ = 2, then $\curlyvee\cdot$ = 3, and $\curlyvee\!\!\!\!\curlyvee$ = 4, and $\curlyvee\!\!\!\!\curlyvee\cdot$ = 6. the cadences contain as thus,

| 2, 2, 2, | 6, | 3, 3, | 2, 2, 2, | 3, 3, | 6, | 2, 2, 2, | 3, 1, 1, 1, | 2, 2, 2, | 3, 3, | 2, 2, 2, | 3, 3, | 3, 3, | 6, | 4, 2, | 4, 2, | 3, 1½, 1½, | 2, 2, 2, | 3, 1, 2, | &c.

REMARKS.

' 1. It is commonly supposed that all notes of equal value ' in the same piece are to be played as exactly equal as the beats ' of a clock; if so, common time could not be distinguished from ' triple, but by some affection either of emphasis or of melody. ' Both of which will be found to take place, in some degree, in ' every musical composition.

' 2. But a regular rhythmus was reckoned such a fault in ' oratory by the antients, that Cicero and Quintilian look upon ' a single verse as a blemish in prose: and an emphasis, recurring ' at equal intervals, must be tiresome and disagreeable: there-' fore prose does not seem to admit a division by *arsis* and ' *thesis*.'

ANSWER.

1. Here follows a series of notes, which, without any particular application of *emphasis*, may be either *common* or *triple measure* or *metre*.

Suppose a crotchet to be equal in time to one step of walking,

But if this series be repeated, without intermission, the finger or player will be led instinctively to lay the *emphatic pulses* so as to divide it into *cadences* or bars of *common measure:* or if the last note be made a specked minim, or be followed by two crotchet rests, then the finger or player will be instinctively inclined to divide it into cadences of triple metre.

Now let it be observed, that this determination of the mode to *triple* or to *common metres*, does not arise from the *harmonic* order of the series; that is, from the melodious, or the harmonic relation of the notes that compose it, but merely from their rhythmical or numerical relation or congruity; for if the series were not to be marked with any emphasis, and not to be repeated, its mode would be entirely equivocal; but if repeated without addition of sound or *rest* to the last note, it would force the finger or player into the emphasis of common metres or cadences: therefore it may have its cadences or bars marked in either of the two following modes:

Cadences of common metres.

Cadences of triple metres.

For though a perſon, in contradiction to his inſtinctive ſenſe of cadence, might continue the ſeries contained in this clauſe repeatedly in *triple meaſure* (without lengthening the laſt note to the time of a ſpecked minim, or without the addition of two crotchet reſts) he would find ſome uneaſineſs and difficulty in doing ſo.

1ſt clauſe.   2d clauſe.

3d clauſe

4th clauſe.   Becauſe

the inſtinctive ſenſe of the ear would be immediately ſhocked, in the firſt repetition, or ſecond clauſe, to find the heavy impulſe △ ſhifted from the firſt to the third note of the original cadence in the ſeries; and in the next repetition, or 3d clauſe, the ſame heavy impulſe △ again ſhifted to the ſecond note of the original cadence; and though at the 3d repetition, or 4th clauſe, the ear would be pleaſed to find the heavy impulſe △ or emphaſis again returned to the firſt note of the original clauſe, yet

yet it would still be dissatisfied in some degree for want of the uniformity, or congruity of clausular divisions: for the instinctive ear would remember that the series which made the first clause, consisted of six whole cadences; whereas the first and second repetitions, by changing the emphasis, could allow no more than five cadences in each of the 2d and 3d clauses, and the number of five cadences in a clause, unless lengthened out by an additional cadence in silence, is certainly incongruous and displeasing to our instinctive sense of musical rhythmus.— However, it must be admitted, that a judicious composer may sometimes designedly endeavour to puzzle his audience by changing the emphatic impulse (as in this example) and also to disturb their feelings by incongruous clauses in his measure, as well as by discords in his harmony, in order to prepare them to be more exquisitely delighted by a return to uniformity, congruity, and concord.

Now, admitting that such doubts and uncertainties may occur in determining the measure of a piece of music, written without any marks, by bars or otherwise, to direct the player where to lay his emphatic poize, which should correspond with a periodical pulsation, I will observe, that the like doubts and difficulties will frequently occur in reading language, and always in an unknown one, unassisted by some such notes as those proposed in this essay, but principally for want of the marks of the poize △ heavy and ∴ light.

But when a piece of music is properly played, or a speech properly spoken, the senses of the auditors are immediately influenced and carried along with the player, or the speaker, in

whatever

whatever is the proper measure of his tune or of his speech; and the effect of this instinctive communication of periodical impulse is more immediate and more certain in speech than in music, in as much as we are all more perfect in our understandings of speech than of music: many people are not musicians, but all use their tongues, and listen to the discourses of others.

2. To the second Remark I cannot think of a better answer than to set the very words of the learned remarker to my notes of quantity and poize, leaving it to the issue of this experiment to determine, whether prose can or cannot admit of a division by *arsis* and *thesis*.

3. But a | regular | rhythmus was | reckoned such a | fault in | oratory | by the | antients | that | Cicero | and Quin | tilian | look upon a | single | verse | as a | blemish in | prose | and | an | emphasis re | curring at | equal | intervals | must be | tiresome | and disa | greeable | | | Therefore | prose | does | not | seem to ad | mit | a di | vision by | arsis and | thesis.

I would

I would not have it underſtood that theſe periodical pulſations of ſpeech muſt always be ſtrictly confined, as it were, to the ſwing of the ſame length of pendulum: that certainly is not the caſe, either in proſe or in poetry, nor yet in ſuch diaſtematic muſic as pretends to expreſs any thing either narrative or characteriſtic: the length of the bars or cadences may be occaſionally increaſed or ſhortened at the pleaſure of the ſpeaker, but always the new metres of the rhythmus muſt be preſerved after every change till it be found proper and agreeable to make another change; and this we ſee continually exemplified in dancing, by changes in meaſure both quicker and ſlower, as well as in diverſity of modes, triple and common; though ſtill under all theſe changes the movement is rythmically governed by the *agoghe* or drift of *theſis* and *arſis*.

REMARKS.

'I am not ſatisfied with the anſwer to Mr. Garrick's queſtion
' in p. 54.—It is well known that the ſame piece of muſic may
' be played in different taſtes by different performers.—If, then,
' a piece of muſic, whoſe tones and movement are ſo preciſely
' determined, can be played in different manners, muſt not an
' imitation of the vague tones of ſpeech be much more liable to
' ſuch variety?

'I can eaſily believe that Mr. Steele may imitate a ſpeech he
' has heard with great exactneſs; but I cannot perſuade myſelf
' that one who did not hear it can do the like from any notes
' or ſymbols whatſoever.

‘ It must, however, be acknowledged, that Mr. Steele's notation, well executed, may give an idea how a speech ought to be pronounced.’

ANSWER.

In answer to the first objection in this remark, the reader is referred to what is said on this head in page 205, to which I will farther observe, that when in ordinary music a performer adds any graces or peculiarity of manner, not expressed in the notes set before him, such addition or alteration is as peculiarly his own, and as unexpected from those notes, as if a taylor, under the prescribed orders for making a plain suit, guided by his own inclination, should generously compliment his employer, by adding the ornaments of lace or embroidery to it.

However, the like incidental graces are not as applicable to speech as to diastematic music; the variety of natural tones in voices, such as the nasal, the guttural, the lisping, the northern bur, and other provincial as well as personal blemishes, I considered under the metaphor of a bad violin, certainly not worthy of imitation; the expressions of *piano* and *forte*, of quantities *staccato* and *sostenuto*, of accents *alto* and *basso*, of emphasis *arsis* and *thesis*, and of measured *pauses*, are the musical materials of speech, reducible to rules of art: all these are provided for by distinct symbols, and if by their aid as much may be performed, as the candid remarker acknowledges in his last paragraph, the author expects no more.

REMARKS.

REMARKS.

'In p. 80, the dactylic verse is set to triple time, contrary to
'the practice of the antients, who called all rhythm that was
'divided into two equal parts (like our common time) dactylic.

'In the following page, Mr. Steele makes no elisions in the
'verse

"Littora; multum ille et terris jactatus et alto;"

'by which means it has two redundant syllables, and cannot be
'measured by dactyls and spondees. What a verse is

"Monstrum horrendum informe ingens cui lumen ademptum,"

'without elision? surely not dactylic.'

ANSWER.

In page 89, I made my request not to be drawn into any contest with the champions of the antient Greeks and Romans. If it were possible for me to have a conversation with Dionysius of Halicarnassus, Demosthenes, Plato, or even Cicero, I should have no doubt of our general agreement in all these principles of elocution; but as their commentators, from Quintilian down to our days, have confounded accent, quantity, and emphasis, so as to make no account at all of the last, though the most important of the three, I cannot agree to be tried by their laws, though I am very ready to submit to be judged by those of common sense, that is, by the judgement of the ears on our native language.

My apology for the liberty I took with the antient dactyl has been repeatedly made; I shall say no more in its defence, but leave it to time, and to the refurrection of thofe dead languages to approve or condemn it, and will here fet the *monſtrum horrendum* both according to the old rules, and according to mine, in order to ſhew that they both are exactly equal in time, if repeated to the ſwings of the fame pendulum.

Let the diſtance of time between theſis △ and theſis △́ be equal to one ſtep of walking.

```
 |ϒ·       ϒ·| ϒ·    ϒ·|ϒ·    ϒ·| ϒ·   ϒ·|ϒ·   |·|·|ϒ·    ϒ·|
2|Monſt'   hor|rend'  in|form' in|gens cui|lumen a |demptum|
 |△        ∴|△    ∴|△   ∴|△  ..  ∴|△    ∴|
 |ϒ·    |  ϒ|ϒ·  |   ϒ|ϒ· |  ϒ|ϒ·   ϒ|ϒ·  |  ϒ|ϒ·   ϒ·|
3|Monſtrum hor|rendum in|forme in|gens cui|lumen a |demptum|
 |△    ..    ∴|△ ..  ∴|△ ..  ∴|△    ∴|△ ..  ∴|△    ∴|
```

When the conſtruction of a language depends on the terminations of its words; eliſions, by which thoſe terminations are concealed, muſt contribute to render ſuch a language obſcure; but if this practice was the mode, and at all times favoured by the Greeks and Romans, I pretend no right to oppoſe it; I only have ventured to ſhew by theſe examples, that, for our reading, ſuch eliſions are not abſolutely neceſſary. Some of our faſhionable authors in the laſt and about the beginning of this century, were pleaſed to write *of 'em* and *to 'em,* and were very near founding an authority for ſuch eliſions in Engliſh; but ſince the improvement of our ears in muſic and in grammar, they, for the moſt part, ſeem to be diſcountenanced.

Having on the recommendation of one of my friends peruſed Dr. Pemberton's Section of Verſification in his *Obſervations on Epic Poetry*, I find he has been in the general error of other

learned

learned men, in confounding *accent* and *quantity* with EMPHASIS, by not seeing that EMPHASIS was an accident *sui generis*, or sole of its kind, and so indispensably necessary, that the significant expression of language could not exist without it; and indeed so singularly important is this in regard to rhythmus and metres, that, I think, without it they are unintelligible; but that there can be no difficulty in understanding them and all their adjuncts, as applied to language, as soon as EMPHASIS is considered as a distinct property or accident.—And so far is English from wanting that certainty of measure which Dr. Pemberton and other eminent writers attribute so exclusively to the learned languages, it is the only one wherein an English ear can perceive the properties of accent, quantity, and emphasis, to exist most positively and distinctly: for, the properties of enunciation in the dead languages, we must take upon the credit of those who heard them spoken as living languages, whether they have described those properties right or not.

Dr. Pemberton, in page 125 of his essay, gives us the four following lines thus marked:

Ōnce ŏn ă | tīme, ăs ōld | stŏriĕs rĕ | hearse,
Ă frī | ăr wŏuld needs | shĕw hĭs tā | lĕnt ĭn Lā | tin;
Bŭt wăs sōre | lў pŭt tŏ't | ĭn thĕ mīdst | ŏf ă vĕrse,
Bĕcaūse | hĕ coŭld fīnd | nō wōrd | tŏ cŏme pāt | in.

In these lines the Doctor intending to shew (after Dr. Wallis) that we had both dactylic and anapestic measures in our language, has from the notion of dividing the first line into dactyls, accidentally marked the bars, which are emphatic, in the right places; but thinking to prove the other three lines anapestic, he loft all idea of emphasis, and of rhythmical agoghè, and placed the bars quite wrong.

These lines, however, are a very proper example to prove the propriety of our manner of varying the proportions of the members of the dactyl, to the satisfaction of an English ear in our language, being set thus:

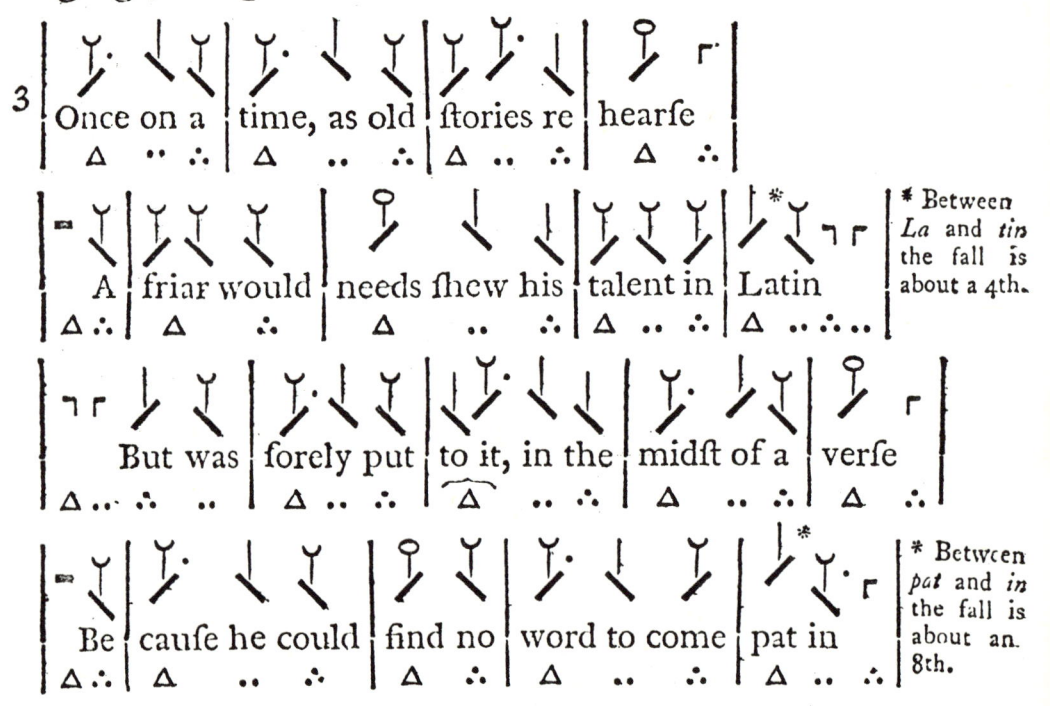

[musical notation]
Once on a | time, as old | stories re | hearse

[musical notation]
A | friar would | needs shew his | talent in | Latin

* Between *La* and *tin* the fall is about a 4th.

[musical notation]
But was | sorely put | to it, in the | midst of a | verse

[musical notation]
Be | cause he could | find no | word to come | pat in

* Between *pat* and *in* the fall is about an 8th.

In this manner of setting these lines, every English ear will readily agree that the *thesis* △ or heavy emphasis is properly placed; very few, if any, will dispute the quantities, and perhaps not many the accentual marks; then if the reader will consider the cadences, and use that latitude which may be allowed under the remark quoted from *Bacchius Senior* (in p. 207), he will find they contain *dactyls*, one *amphibrachys*, *trochees*, *iambics*, a 2d *pæon*, and either the *tribachys* or *molossus*, that is, a foot of three syllables of equal length, the difference being only shorter or

longer;

longer; in the above example, I would say, *friar would* was a *molossus*, and *talent in*, the same. But within the limits of each cadence or bar in the above lines, there is contained no *anapest*. All this variety of feet are, however, under a rhythmus of triple metres, without any mixture of common metre.

It happened while the author was explaining this passage to a friend, a sudden summer torrent of hail and rain fell, and beat into the next room, when we heard the house-keeper exclaim, 'some came down the chimney, some came in at the sash',— which being set exactly in her tone and manner of articulation, furnishes another very good example of emphasis, accent, and quantity, and in which the rhythmical agoghe cannot be mistaken:

and here the word *chiminey* is an *anapest*.

But to return to our examination of Dr. Pemberton's section on Versification; in p. 106, that gentleman says, "these measures "were of such efficacy in those languages (Greek and Latin) "that the adjusting of their periods to some agreeable rhyth- "mus or movement, by an apt succession of long and short "syllables, was considered in oratory as an art of great im- "portance towards the perfection of eloquence. In our lan- "guage this seems to be scarce thought of, though perhaps what
"we

"we commonly call smoothness of style is in part owing to "something analogous, namely such a rangement of the words "whereby the syllables follow one another with a free and easy "cadence." Here the instinctive sense of this ingenious author was ready to lead him right if he had dared to have followed it a little further, but the glimmering of the learned lamp led him astray. P. 107. "But in relation to the antient verse, "we find some of their measures easily read in rhythmus suited "to our ear; so there are others which in reciting must appear "lame and defective." "In speech the simple proportion of "2 to 1 is most natural to be observed between the length of "the longer and shorter syllables. And those measures which "appear harmonious in reading are divisible, according to this "proportion, either into common or triple time, as tunes are "divided in the modern music; the dactylic and anapestic mea- "sures move in common time; the iambic and trochaic, ac- "cording to the triple; the other measures are not divisible in "that manner. And if we enquire how these movements, irre- "gular in reading, could be fitted to music, we shall find one of "these two means necessary for that purpose, either by inter- "posing rests or pauses to supply the measure, where deficient, "or by taking some liberty with the syllables, so as upon occasion "to vary the common proportion between the longer and the "shorter. St. Austin has written a treatise expressly to re- "concile the various measures of the antient verse with the "principles of music; and whenever any verses are composed "of feet consisting of different measures of time, he endeavours

"to

" to fill up the incomplete measures by the assistance of pauses
" only."

123.—" Metre and verse differ from simple rhythmus in this,
" that rhythmus in speech is a very orderly succession of long
" and short syllables, which will pass agreeably over the ear, but
" metre and verse is such rhythmus confined within a short
" compass and successively repeated." 125. " What has caused
" our measures to be so little attended to, I suppose, is the un-
" certainty in the quantity of the greatest part of our syllables.
" This must frustrate all attempts to bring the antient hexa-
" meters into our narrative poetry; for that verse being com-
" posed of a discretionary mixture of two different feet, we
" seldom can be led by the sound of the words into the true
" movement of each verse." P. 126. " Whereas the antient
" accent is represented to be only a variation in the tone of the
" voice, and had no relation to the quantity of the syllable, nor
" of consequence any influence over the movement of their
" verse, any more than the pitch of the notes in a tune affect
" its movement, our accent is constantly attended with an em-
" phasis, which implies greater length in the syllable, and
" thereby regulates our verse."

P. 131. " The *emphasis* or *accent* falling upon the foremost
" of the two syllables in any foot, except the first, which will
" make that foot resemble a trochaic, or two syllables placed
" together in the same foot, which must both of necessity be
" pronounced short, will certainly destroy the harmony of the
" verse."

With

With great respect for this learned author, I must, however, deny the authority of this rule; it is derived from the error which the learned have been too long in, of confounding *accent*, *emphasis*, and *quantity*, altogether, as inseparable accidents of one and the same syllable: but whoever takes the pains to distinguish and divide these accidents as we have done in this essay, will be convinced that △ the *heavy emphasis*, may fall on a *short* syllable as well as on a *long* one, and that the same *emphasis* may be occasionally either *grave* or *acute*; and that both *grave* and *acute* may occasionally be either *long* or *short*.

For example, the learned Doctor having, in page 133, marked the *quantities* of the following line, has placed the mark of *long* over every syllable which he thought should be in thesis, or emphatic, as thus:

Whōse ānnŭăl wōund ĭn Lēbănŏn ăllūr'd.

But if the same line be noted according to the rules proposed in this essay, the *quantities* and *emphasis* will be thus:

$$2\ \Big|\ \text{Whose}\ \Big|\ \text{annual}\ \Big|\ \text{wound in}\ \Big|\ \text{Lebanon}\ \Big|\ \text{al}\ \Big|\ \text{lur'd}\ \Big|$$

And here by distinguishing and distributing *emphasis* and *quantity*, without marking the *accent* at all (which though essential in pointing out the sense of words and periods of sentences, is no more affected to poetry than to prose), we find that WHOSE is *long*, and AN, in ANNUAL, *short*, but that AL, is *long*, both in ANNUAL and ALLUR'D; and LE, in LEBANON, is *short*, and that NON, in LEBANON is under *arsis*, and *unemphatic*.

I have

I have marked the measure here by the common notes of music, as in this instance where the *accent* is omitted, they may give a more familiar idea of the time or *quantity* of these syllables to any person versed in music than the new marks generally used in the foregoing treatise.

The native taste, ear, and discernment, of this author, was such, that if in the matter treated of in this section, he had been guided by his instinctive senses, I think he would have left nothing for me to have said on the subject; but I apprehend his great learning led him astray; nature held out her light to him in vain, he had devoted himself to the authorities of the antients; and although in some points he had the courage to differ in opinion from Aristotle, yet in the doctrine of *accent* and *quantity*, he has, in this section, faithfully followed them through all their errors.

In several examples given in this section by the learned Doctor, and in the several passages which are here quoted, he has shewn the justice of his instinct concerning *emphasis*, and also at the same time the inconsistency of his reasoning, in artificially confounding it with *accent* and *quantity*, from which nature had made it clear and distinct.

The learned Dr. Foster (whose essay on *Accent* and *Quantity* is many years later than Dr. Pemberton's), has certainly rescued the *acute accent* from the confusion it was involved in with the *long quantity*; and having shewn that *accent* being quite distinct, and a different affection from *time* or *quantity*, has proved that a syllable, whether *short* or *long*, may, at the same time, be either *acute* or *grave*; and that the *acute* is by no means necessarily coupled with a *long*, nor does it require the *short* syllable to be lengthened on its account. But notwithstanding his accuracy on this head, he has nevertheless left the *acute* still confounded with the *thesis* or the *emphatic* syllable, which we call the *heavy* △; and, in that respect, is in as great an error as Vossius, Henninius, or his opponent Dr. G. In fact they are all in an error of the same kind, as it is the want of separating these three accidents distinctly from each other, which variously affect every syllable in language; I say it is for want of having separately defined and distinguished the powers and uses of these three accidents, that all our commentators have been in contentious confusion for above fifteen hundred years. In page 192, Dr. Foster gives for an example, the word ALLY, which he said, five years before, was an *oxytone*, having the last syllable *acute*, as *allý*; but was afterwards become *barytone*, with the *acute* on the first syllable, as *álly*: whereas in truth the *accent* has nothing to do with this difference of pronunciation in either case; it is the *thesis* or *heavy poize* only which marks the difference, as *ally* in one case and *ally* ∴△ in the other; and the speaker may make either the first or △∴ the last syllable *acute*, without any alteration in the *emphasis*: for it has been proved in the foregoing essay, that *emphasis*, or the *heavy poize* △, is as independant of the *acute*, as the *acute* is independant of a *long quantity**.

It

---

* In page 10 of the foregoing essay, where I was treating of accent only, I endeavoured to obviate a doubt of the learned author of *Origin and Progress of Language*, why the *grave*, marked on a last syllable, should (by some commentators) be said to denote the *acute*? But to what I have there offered, I would add further, that I suspect, in several cases, the last syllable of a Greek word, though *grave*, might require to be under *thesis* △, or the *emphatic poize*; which

It is plain from the whole tenor of Dr. Foster's essay, that he had no distinct idea of *rhythmus*, nor of its great governing principle, the *emphatic poize* of △ heavy, and ∴ light; and though he and several other writers talk of *thesis* and *arsis*, they never find out the great ruling power of them, and that they are uniformly alternate and periodical; for the periodical returns of thesis △, or the heavy syllable, govern the rhythmus or measure of speech, as forcibly as the beating of time does that of modern music or dancing*.

When I see such respectable men as Doctor Pemberton and Mr. Foster wandering in the mazes of antient learning, I cannot help comparing them to blind men laboriously groping for an object which they are continually near but never find. Had I been half as studious, and a quarter part as learned, as either of those authors, I think I should have gone astray as they did. But instead of endeavouring to discover the mine by following the obscure traces of antient adventurers, I made use of my natural senses, like those animals whose instinctive smell leads them directly to the subterraneous *trufle*; and by confining my enquiry chiefly within the limits of my native language, I gradually discovered that the materials I was in search of, required not to be dug for, they lay upon the surface: Then having found them, it was matter of amusement to me to look into the antient ruins; where I perceived the old materials were, in their original nature, the same as ours when picked clean from the

which affection of the voice has hitherto been mistaken for the *acute accent*: and if I am right in this conjecture, it may be the means of reconciling that apparent inconsistency in the rules and observations of the commentators.
* See Foster's Essay, p. 51, and 59.

learned rubbish, with which the mistaken industry of commentators had mixed and confounded them.

The rapid improvements made, of late years, in the practice of music and other polite arts are proofs, that the present age is not deficient in genius and application necessary for aspiring towards that degree of perfection, in which the universal consent of the learned admits those arts to have been about two thousand years ago.

I therefore most earnestly recommend to the professors and lovers of music and poetry, to exert their faculties in endeavouring to recover a proper musical accompaniment for theatrical declamation; which we are assured was the delight of a people who were the most refined judges in literary elegance, of whom we have any historical knowledge, and of which we have a testimony in their works still existing.

An Italian author (DONI) has left us proofs, that a society of ingenious and learned virtuosi (of whom he was one) took a great deal of pains in Italy, under the auspices of some celebrated patrons, above a century ago, in an endeavour of this kind; in which, though they did not entirely succeed, it is probable the Italian recitative owes much of its present merit to those endeavours; for, when it is performed by their best actors, it comes so near the common melody of the Italian language, as that the musical accompaniment has no other effect on the audience than to give an additional force to the sentiments intended by the words. And it is remarkable, that the most pleasing and most affecting parts of the Italian recitative are those which are spoken exactly with the same accentuation, and with the same

energic

energic expreffion, with which a good actor would have delivered them if he had been fpeaking without any mufical accompaniment; but to which that accompaniment, properly fuited, gives a moft exquifite relief.

On the contrary, when the recitative as formed for, and fitted to, the Italian fpeech, is applied by ignorant imitators to other languages, whofe melodies in their natural accentuation are very different from that of the Italian; fuch an aukward adaption becomes ridiculous and difgufting; and is the reafon why recitative, even in Italian, is difagreeable to the general tafte of thofe who do not underftand that language.

But now, having proved in the foregoing effay, that our language, in common fpeech, has all the variety of melody by accents, and of rhythmus by emphafis, quantity, and metres, which human organs are capable of; it follows, that it muft have a fpecies of fong peculiar to itfelf, though perhaps not fo agreeably chanting as the fong of the Greek and Italian languages. It remains, therefore, for our profeffors in mufic and poetry to make experiments; in the firft place, to mark by an apt notation, the natural melody and meafure of fome celebrated cantata or monologue; and in the next place, to find out what fpecies of accompaniment will be moft fuitable and moft advantageous to that melody and meafure, and to embellifh by proper interjected interludes, the fentiments capable of fuch ornamental relief.

INDEX.

INDEX.

A.

Accents, notes of, pages 7, 8, 9. 13. 24.
——— demonſtrated by example of the ſame word in a noun and a verb, 151.
——— liable to be changed ſometimes, 145.
——— Rules for finding the difference of, 75. 131. 197.
——— Standard of, 75.
——— have nothing to do with rhythmus, metre, or quantity, 215.
Accentual ſlides, diſtinguiſhed by poſition of their ſymbolic marks, 30. 192.
Accentuation, a general term for all the five orders of accidents, 150.
——— of the ſame words in different intentions, 87.
Accidents, five orders of, 24.
——— illuſtrations of, 26. 31, &c.
Accompanyment, for theatrical declamation, 35, 36. 40. 47. 236, 237.
Additions to this eſſay, 194.
Agoghe, or drift of rhythmical emphaſis, 183. 186. 188. 191. 223.
Analyſis of the accidents in the melody and meaſure of ſpeech, 24.
Anſwers to the firſt ſet of obſervations of the author of the Origin of Language, 85.
——— to the ſecond ſet 113.
——— to the third ſet, in the poſtſcript, 183.
Anſwer to a letter from Glaſgow, 200.
——— to extracts from other letters, 204.
——— to remarks on Mr. Steele's treatiſe, 209.
Apology for the neglect of accentuation in modern languages, 171.
Appoggiatura, or inſinuator, 145.
Ariſtides, on reſts and pauſes, 78.
Arſis and *Theſis*, 11, 12. 20. 27. 88. 115. 117. 132. 170. 183. 216, 217. 235.
Articulation of language and of muſic, 65.
Auſtin, Saint, his treatiſe on pauſes, 230.

B.

Bars, 11. 22, 23. 155.
——— not uſed by the Greeks, 127.
Beating of Time derived from the beating of our pulſe, 20.

C.

Cadence, 11, 12. 25. 113. 123.
——— heavy and light, 20. 34. 41. 43. 45. 77. 87. 117. 144. 170. 209.
——— example of, when doubtful in muſic, 218, 219, 220.
——— ſubdiviſion of, 25. 114.
——— the governing power of rhythmus, 87. 154. 235.
——— definition of, 116.
——— not quite the ſame as the Greek metre, 113.
——— difference from the Greek metre, 115. 120.
——— impulſe of, accounted for, 118.
——— often divides a foot, 116. 148.
Characters, or ſymbolic marks of accentuation, 24.
——— of the melody and meaſure of ſpeech in an example, 13.
Cibber, Mrs. excellence of her pronunciation, 48.
Circumflexes, their forms, 6, 7. 13. 24. 85, 86, 87.
——— as inſinuators, or graces, 146.
Compaſs of the ſlides, moſt agreeable, 48, 49.
Curſing and ſwearing, rhythmical expletives, 67.

D.

Dactyl, why ſo called; and apology for the liberty taken with it, 81.

Definition

INDEX.

Definition of the chromatico-diatonic, or ordinary music, 4.
———— of the melody of speech, *ibid.*
———— of rhythmus, 72. 114. 127.
———— of quantity, 72. 116.
———— of rhythmus and metre left in great confusion by all the commentators antient and modern, 201. 209. 214.
Difference of elocution, exemplified on a sentence from Demosthenes, in three different manners, 51, 52, 53.
———— between loudness and emphasis, 68. 88. 165. 183.
———— between cadences and Greek metres, 115. 120.
———— of rhythmus, metres, feet, and quantity, 148.
———— of English and French pronunciation in the same words, 120. 150.
Diphthongs, how made, ix.
———— dissection of, *ibid.*
———— in English, described, xi.
———— definition of, *ibid.*
Diversity of measure in the same speech, 25. 28. 42. 51, 52, 53. 218.
Drift of rhythmical impulse, 183. 191.

E.

Elision of syllables seldom necessary in good poetry, 75. 81. 225, 226.
Emphasis, 11, 12. 24. 28. 30. 49 87. 117. 132. 154. 165. 183. 195. 213. 215, 216. 227. 234.
English Heroics, are hexametres, 27.
———— *Hexametres*, in Greek metres and modern cadences, 163.
Examples, a line from Pope, 13. 26. 38. 129.
———— from others, 26, 27. 31, 32, 33. 76.
———— from Shakespear's Hamlet, 40.
———————————— variation, 45.
———— of Mr. Garrick's manner, 31. 47.
———— of a sentence from Demosthenes, in three manners, 51, 52, 53.
———— of articulation of sound on a single syllable, 66.
———— of four lines from Milton's Paradise Lost, 77.
———————————— the same defended, 167.
———— of four lines from the Æneid, 79, 80.
———— of four lines from the Iliad, 82.
———— of a false emphasis in Virgil, 210.

Examples, of the same in Pope, 212.
———— of a line in Gay, 213.
———— of erroneous accentuation in Dr. Pemberton and Dr. Wallis, 227. 232.
———— of the necessary changes in accentuation, 87. 134. 136.
———— to shew how far accentuation is fixed in English words, 136, 137, &c.
———— of circumflexed graces, 146.
———— of several lines from Milton that want great help from the notes of accentuation, 159, &c.
———— to shew, that English heroics may have more or less than ten syllables in each line, 163. 165.
———— of varying melody by change of the measure, or time, 70.
———— of doubtful cadences in music, 218, 219, 220.
———— on the word impossible, 119, 120. 146.
———— on the words pensioner and pensionaire, 150.
———— to shew how frequently the emphasis falls on the shortest syllables in English, 214.
Experiment to make the accentual slides by a bass viol, 16.
Extracts of letters with remarks on the melody and measure of speech, 202. 208.

F.

Five orders of accidents in speech, 24.
Foster on accent and quantity, quoted with remarks, 3. 201. 211. 233. 235.

G.

Garrick, Mr. 47. 54. 203. 223.
General precept and example, 28.
Graces, 145. 192.
———— circumflexed, 146.
Grave accent on a last syllable in Greek, why said by commentators to denote an acute? 10. 234, in the note.

H.

Heavy poize, note, or syllable, 20. 27.
Heavy and light, emphasis or poize, affections entirely different from loud and soft, 12. 23. 29. 32. 68. 88. 165. 183. 195.

Heroics,

INDEX.

Heroics, in Greek and Latin, are truly octometers, 81.
—— in English, are truly hexameters, 26.

I.

Insinuators, or graces, 145.
Integral monads in cadence, 123.
Intercession in favour of the mother tongue, 154.
Italian recitative, not suited to other languages, and why generally disagreeable to an English ear, 237.

L.

Letter to the author of the Origin of Language, 63.
—— from ditto, 90.
—— to ditto, 92. 181.
—— from ditto, 93. 174.
—— from Mr. ———, of Glasgow, 194.
Lines, from Paradise Lost, that require great assistance by the marks of poize, quantity, and pauses, 159, &c.
Loud, not necessarily heavy, 12. 23. 29. 32. 68. 88. 165. 183.

M.

Manner of poizing the four first lines of Paradise Lost, defended, 167.
Measure of Time, the Greeks had three sorts of quantities, 207.
Melody, common to all languages, 171.
—— of diastematic music, definition, 4.
—— of speech, defined, 4. 18.
—————— delineated, 6.
—————— formed by slides, 14. 17.
Metre, or *Metron*, 25. 72, 73. 77. 79. 84. 113, 114, 115. 120. 128, 129. 131. 135. 170. 187.
—— with the Greeks, always comprehended a whole foot at least; but never divided one, 116. 148.
—— makes the distribution of quantities, 155.
Metrical cadences, 158. 188.
—————— subdivision of cadence, 123.
Mixture of triple and common measure, 25. 28, 29. 40, 41. 73. 121. 201.
Modes of time, 11. 21, 22.

Monosyllables, in general, either heavy or light, 134.
—————— an exception, 166.
—————— advantageous in a language redundant with consonants, 168, in a note.
Monotony, exemplified, 15.
Musical materials of speech, 24. 197. 224.

N.

Necessity of joining the knowledge of music and letters together, xiii.
—————— proved from antient authorities, xiv.
—————— recommended to the universities, xvi.
—————— to the ladies, xvii.
Non-rhythmical quantity, 128.
Notes of accent, 7, 8, 9. 13. 24.
—————— quantity, 7, 8. 13. 24.
—————— emphasis, 20. 22. 24.
—————— loud and soft, 13. 22. 24.
—————— pause or silence, 8. 13. 22. 24.
Noun and verb, distinguished by accent and emphasis, 147. 151.

O.

Observations and queries, by the author of the Origin of Language, 56. 94. 175.

P.

Parallel, between an illiterate genius, and a learned Dunce, 157, 158.
Pauses, their use, 170.
—————— notes of, 8. 13. 22. 24.
Pemberton, Dr. remarks on his section on versification, 226. 228. 232. 233. 235.
Poize, 77. 117. 144. 184. 195.
—————— governs rhythmus, 87. 170. 215.
—————— distinguishes verb from noun, 147. 151.
—————— of polysyllables, fixed, 166.
—————— of monosyllables, *ad libitum*, ibid.
—————————— exceptions, 166.
—————— difference of, between French and English, in the word IMPOSSIBLE, 120.
—————————— and in the words PENSIONER and PENSIONAIRE, 150.
—————— has the same effect on an audience as beating time among musicians, 188. 191. 235.

Poize

INDEX

Poize the most important accident in language, 195. 215.
—— misapplied by Virgil, 211.
—————— by Mr. Pope. 212.
—— variously applied to a line of Mr. Gay, 213.
Postscript, 174.
Project of accompanying the declamation of the stage by a continual bass, 35.
—————— recommended to poets and musicians to find out a proper accompanyment, 236, 237.
Propositions (of the author of the Origin of Language) controverted 2.

Q.

Quantity, 7, 8. 24. 116. 136. 156. 186.
———— what, 72.
———— standard of, 75. 131. 197.
———— distinguished from rhythmus, 114. 148.
———— its proportions, 144. 184.
———— the Greeks owned three sorts, 207.
———— subservient to rhythmus, 170.
———— to metre, 155.
———— occasionally varied, 144.
Qualities, essential in elocution, 48, 49.
Quintilian, accuses Virgil of a false quantity, 210.
———— mistakes *emphasis* for *quantity*, 211.

R.

Recitative in music, why generally disagreeable to English ears, 237.
Remarks, on the giga in the devil's sonata, 125.
———— on Corelli's jigg, 203. 205. 224.
———— on Mr. Steele's Treatise, 208.
———— on a line of Mr. Pope, 212.
———— ———— of Mr. Gay, 213.
———— on Dr. Pemberton's section on versification, 226 228 232, 233. 235.
———— on Mr. Foster, 3. 201. 211. 233. 235.
Rhythmical clauses, 30. 125. 162.
———— pulsation, accounted for, 118.
Rhythmus, 18. 22 to 25. 72. 170. 186.
———— its office, 117.
———— its proper meaning, 114. 177.
———— general precept and example, 28.

Rhythmus instinctive, 67. 78.
———— governed by cadence or emphasis, 87. 154. 170. 215.
———— in prose, 222.
———— common to all languages, 171.
———— distinguished from quantity, 114. 148.
———— agoghe, or drift of, 183. 186. 191.
———— how pointed out by a speaker to his audience, 188 191. 223.
———— standard of, 25.
———— in tactics, 152.
Round quantity, 129.
Rule to keep time to pronunciation by steps, 122.
———— to find out the different accents of syllables, 131.

S.

Scale for making the slides of speech, 6, 16.
Speech, not monotonous, 15. 17.
———— in Hamlet, set, 40.
———— Mr. Garrick's manner, 47 to 49.
Sliding tones, how to make them, xiv. 16.
Soft, not necessarily unemphatic, 12, 23. 29. 32. 68. 88.
Standard of time or quantity, 75 131.
———— for accent, 75.
———— for poize, 197.
Stuttering, conjecture of the cause and cure, 190.
Superabundant quantity, 129.
Swing of the arm, &c. beating of time, 67.
Syllables joined by vowels, may be contracted, 146.

T.

Ten syllables, not the number absolutely necessary for English heroic lines, 158. 163.
Thesis and arsis, 11, 12. 20. 27. 88. 115. 117. 132. 170. 183. 216. 217. 235.
Time, 69. 130 131.
———— rhythmical and non-rhythmical, 128.
———— round and superabundant, 129.
———— not so accurately defined by the Greeks as by the moderns, 147. 206.

Verb

U.

Verb and noun, distinguished by different poize, 147. 151.
Virgil, accused of a false quantity by Quintilian, 210
Vowels, more sounds than marks to represent them, viii.
―― their natural number, seven, *ibid.*
―― their definition, *ibid.*
―― their tones and marks to represent them, x.
―― long and short, xii.
―― seven used by the antient Greeks, *ibid.*
Vowels, modern Greeks use the marks but have lost the distinction of the seven sounds, xiii.
Utmost extent of the slides, 37.

W.

Words of different import, distinguished by accent, quantity, and poize, 188
―― marked with proper accent, quantity, and poize, 136.
―― the same, sometimes either dactyl or spondee, 146.
―― explained, 29.
―― 29. 121.

THE END.